Treasures

A Reading/Language Arts Program

 Macmillan/McGraw-Hill

21684

Contributors

Time Magazine

RFB&D
learning through listening

Students with print disabilities may be eligible to obtain an accessible, audio version of the pupil edition of this textbook. Please call Recording for the Blind & Dyslexic at 1-800-221-4792 for complete information.

A

The McGraw·Hill Companies

 Macmillan/McGraw-Hill

Published by Macmillan/McGraw-Hill, of McGraw-Hill Education, a division of The McGraw-Hill Companies, Inc., Two Penn Plaza, New York, New York 10121.

Printed in the United States of America

1 2 3 4 5 6 7 8 9 006/055 13 12 11 10 09

A Reading/Language Arts Program

Program Authors

Dr. Diane August
Senior Research Scientist, Center for
  Applied Linguistics
Washington, D.C.

Dr. Donald R. Bear
University of Nevada, Reno
Reno, Nevada

Dr. Janice A. Dole
University of Utah
Salt Lake City, Utah

Dr. Jana Echevarria
California State University, Long Beach
Long Beach, California

Dr. Douglas Fisher
San Diego State University
San Diego, California

Dr. David J. Francis
University of Houston
Houston, Texas

Dr. Vicki L. Gibson
Educational Consultant, Gibson Hasbrouck
  and Associates, Massachusetts

Dr. Jan E. Hasbrouck
Educational Consultant – J.H. Consulting
Los Angeles, California

Dr. Scott G. Paris
Center for Research and Practice,
National Institute of Education
Singapore

Dr. Timothy Shanahan
University of Illinois at Chicago
Chicago, Illinois

Dr. Josefina V. Tinajero
University of Texas at El Paso
El Paso, Texas

 Macmillan/McGraw-Hill

Program Authors

Dr. Diane August

Center for Applied Linguistics, Washington, D.C.

- Principal Investigator, Developing Literacy in Second-Language Learners: Report of the National Literacy Panel on Language-Minority Children and Youth
- Member of the New Standards Literacy Project, Grades 4–5

Dr. Donald R. Bear

University of Nevada, Reno

- Author of *Words Their Way* and *Words Their Way with English Learners*
- Director, E.L. Cord Foundation Center for Learning and Literacy

Dr. Janice A. Dole

University of Utah

- Investigator, IES Study on Reading Interventions
- National Academy of Sciences, Committee Member: Teacher Preparation Programs, 2005–2007

Dr. Jana Echevarria

California State University, Long Beach

- Author of *Making Content Comprehensible for English Learners: The SIOP Model*
- Principal Researcher, Center for Research on the Educational Achievement and Teaching of English Language Learners

Dr. Douglas Fisher

San Diego State University

- Co-Director, Center for the Advancement of Reading, California State University
- Author of *Language Arts Workshop: Purposeful Reading and Writing Instruction* and *Reading for Information in Elementary School*

Dr. David J. Francis

University of Houston

- Director of the Center for Research on Educational Achievement and Teaching of English Language Learners (CREATE)
- Director, Texas Institute for Measurement, Evaluation, and Statistics

Dr. Vicki Gibson

Educational Consultant Gibson Hasbrouck and Associates, Massachusetts

- Author of *Differentiated Instruction: Grouping for Success*

Dr. Jan E. Hasbrouck

Educational Consultant JH Consulting, Los Angeles

- Developed Oral Reading Fluency Norms for Grades 1–8
- Author of *The Reading Coach: A How-to Manual for Success*

Dr. Scott G. Paris

Center for Research and Practice, National Institute of Education, Singapore

- Principal Investigator, CIERA, 1997–2004

Dr. Timothy Shanahan

University of Illinois at Chicago

- Member, National Reading Panel
- President, International Reading Association, 2006
- Chair, National Literacy Panel and National Early Literacy Panel

Dr. Josefina V. Tinajero

University of Texas at El Paso

- Past President, NABE and TABE
- Co-Editor of *Teaching All the Children: Strategies for Developing Literacy in an Urban Setting* and *Literacy Assessment of Second Language Learners*

Consulting and Contributing Authors

Dr. Adria F. Klein
Professor Emeritus,
California State University,
San Bernardino

- President, California Reading Association, 1995
- Co-Author of *Interactive Writing* and *Interactive Editing*

Dolores B. Malcolm
St. Louis Public Schools
St. Louis, MO

- Past President, International Reading Association
- Member, IRA Urban Diversity Initiatives Commission
- Member, RIF Advisory Board

Dr. Doris Walker-Dalhouse
Minnesota State University,
Moorhead

- Author of articles on multicultural literature and reading instruction in urban schools
- Co-Chair of the Ethnicity, Race, and Multilingualism Committee, NRC

Dinah Zike
Educational Consultant

- Dinah-Might Activities, Inc. San Antonio, TX

Program Consultants

Kathy R. Bumgardner
Language Arts Instructional
Specialist
Gaston County Schools, NC

Elizabeth Jimenez
CEO, GEMAS Consulting
Pomona, CA

Dr. Sharon F. O'Neal
Associate Professor
College of Education
Texas State University
San Marcos, TX

Program Reviewers

Mable Alfred
Reading/Language Arts Administrator
Chicago Public Schools, IL

Suzie Bean
Teacher, Kindergarten
Mary W. French Academy
Decatur, IL

Linda Burch
Teacher, Kindergarten
Public School 184
Brooklyn, NY

Robert J. Dandorph
Principal
John F. Kennedy Elementary School
North Bergen, NJ

Suzanne Delacruz
Principal, Washington Elementary
Evanston, IL

Carol Dockery
Teacher, Grade 3
Mulberry Elementary
Milford, OH

Karryl Ellis
Teacher, Grade 1
Durfee School, Decatur, IL

Christina Fong
Teacher, Grade 3
William Moore Elementary School
Las Vegas, NV

Lenore Furman
Teacher, Kindergarten
Abington Avenue School
Newark, NJ

Sister Miriam Kaeser
Assistant Superintendent
Archdiocese of Cincinnati
Cincinnati, OH

LaVonne Lee
Principal, Rozet Elementary School
Gillette, WY

SuEllen Mackey
Teacher, Grade 5
Washington Elementary School
Decatur, IL

Jan Mayes
Curriculum Coordinator
Kent School District
Kent, WA

Bonnie Nelson
Teacher, Grade 1
Solano School, Phoenix, AZ

Cyndi Nichols
Teacher, Grade K/1
North Ridge Elementary School
Commack, NY

Sharron Norman
Curriculum Director
Lansing School District
Lansing, MI

Renee Ottinger
Literacy Leader, Grades K–5
Coronado Hills Elementary School
Denver, CO

Michael Pragman
Principal, Woodland Elementary School
Lee's Summit, MO

Carol Rose
Teacher, Grade 2
Churchill Elementary School
Muskegon, MI

Laura R. Schmidt-Watson
Director of Academic Services
Parma City School District, OH

Dianne L. Skoy
Literacy Coordinator, Grades K–5
Minneapolis Public Schools
Minneapolis, MN

Charles Staszewski
ESL Teacher, Grades 3–5
John H. William School, No. 5
Rochester, NY

Patricia Synan
New York City Department
of Education

Stephanie Yearian
Teacher, Grade 2
W. J. Zahnow Elementary
Waterloo, IL

Unit 2   The Big Question

What do you like to do with your friends?

Enduring Understanding and Essential Questions

In this unit, children will read and write about their friends. As they progress through the unit, they will also develop and apply key comprehension skills that good readers use as they read.

Big Idea	Enduring Understanding	Essential Questions
Theme: Friends	Making friends is fun and important.	What do you like to do with your friends?

Comprehension	Enduring Understanding	Essential Questions
Identify Character Week 1 Week 3	Good readers understand the characters of a story and what they do.	Who are the main characters in the story and why are they important?
Compare and Contrast Week 2	Good readers can compare and contrast details from the story.	What details from the story can you use to compare and contrast different events or characters?

Theme: Friends

Unit Theme Opener

Planning the Unit

Teaching the Unit

Literature Selections

Wrapping Up the Unit

Additional Resources

Unit Assessment

Theme: Friends

Unit Theme Opener, page xvi

Big Book

Big Book

ORAL LANGUAGE

- **Oral Vocabulary**
- **Phonemic Awareness**

WORD STUDY

- **Phonics**
- **High-Frequency Words**

READING

- **Listening Comprehension**
- **Fluency**
- **Leveled Readers**

LANGUAGE ARTS

- **Grammar**
- **Writing**

WEEK 1

Theme
Learning About Friends

Phonemic Awareness
Phoneme Isolation
Phoneme Categorization (Initial/Final /s/)
Phoneme Blending

Phonics
Introduce /s/s
(Initial and Final)

High-Frequency Word
like

Comprehension
Strategy: Ask Questions
Skill: Identify Character

Fluency
Build Fluency: Word Automaticity
Echo-Reading, Choral-Reading, Read for Fluency

Approaching *We Like*

On Level *We Like the Playground*

Beyond *Sam Likes School*

ELL *The Playground*

Grammar
Naming Words

Writing
Sentence

WEEK 2

Theme
What Is a Friend?

Phonemic Awareness
Phoneme Isolation (Initial/Final /p/)
Phoneme Identity (Initial and Final /p/)
Phoneme Blending

Phonics
Introduce /p/p
(Initial and Final)

High-Frequency Word
a

Comprehension
Strategy: Ask Questions
Skill: Compare and Contrast

Fluency
Build Fluency: Word Automaticity
Echo-Reading, Choral-Reading, Read for Fluency

Approaching *Animal Friends*

On Level *We Can Share*

Beyond *I Like My Friends*

ELL *We Like It*

Grammar
Naming Words

Writing
Picture Web

Read-Aloud Trade Book

WEEK 3

Theme
Getting Along

Phonemic Awareness
Phoneme Isolation
Phoneme Categorization
Phoneme Blending

Phonics
Review Initial: /s/s, /p/p; Final: /s/s, /p/p

High-Frequency Words
like, *a*

Comprehension
Strategy: Ask Questions
Skill: Identify Character

Fluency
Build Fluency: Word Automaticity
Echo-Reading, Choral-Reading, Read for Fluency

Approaching *We Like Painting*
On Level *Hats*
Beyond *Ice Skating Fun!*
ELL *Hats*

Grammar and Writing
Naming Words, Sentence

Half-Day Kindergarten

Use the chart below to help plan your half-day kindergarten schedule. Choose Small Group and Workstation Activities as your time allows during the day.

ORAL LANGUAGE

- **Phonemic Awareness**
- **Build Background**
- **Oral Vocabulary**

WORD STUDY

- **Phonics:** /s/s, /p/p
- **High-Frequency Words:** *like, a*

READING

- **Share the Big Books:** *What Do You Like?; Friends All Around*
- **Read-Aloud Trade Book:** *Simon and Molly plus Hester*
- **Read-Aloud Anthology**
- **Big Book of Explorations**
- **Fluency Practice**

LANGUAGE ARTS

- **Shared Writing**
- **Interactive Writing**
- **Independent Writing**

INDEPENDENT PRACTICE

- **Activity Book Pages**
- **Practice Book Pages**
- **Handwriting Practice**

Theme: Friends

Literature

Big Book

Big Book

Read-Aloud Trade Book

Pre-decodable Readers

Big Book of Explorations (2)

Approaching Level

On Level

Beyond Level

ELL

Leveled Readers

Read-Aloud Anthology
Includes Plays for Readers Theater

Oral Vocabulary Cards
(30 sets)

Retelling Cards

Teaching Support

Teacher's Edition

Teacher's Resource Book

Home-School Connection

High-Frequency Word Cards

Word-Building Cards

Sound-Spelling WorkBoards

Puppet

Sound-Spelling Cards

Photo Cards

Teaching Chart

Student Practice

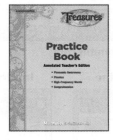

Activity Book

Practice Book

Handwriting
- Ball and Stick
- Slant

Literacy Workstation Flip Charts

Class Management Tools

How-to Guide

Rotation Chart

Weekly Contracts

Differentiated Resources

English Language Learners

ELL Resource and Practice Books

Visual Vocabulary Resources

Response to Intervention

 Tier 2 **Tier 3**

- Phonemic Awareness
- Phonics
- Vocabulary
- Comprehension
- Fluency

Assessment

Unit Assessment

Assess Unit Skills
- Phonemic Awareness
- Phonics
- High-Frequency Words
- Listening Comprehension

Digital Solutions

☑ Prepare/Plan

☑ Teach/Learn

ONLINE www.macmillanmh.com

Teacher's Edition Online

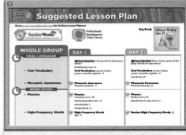

TeacherWorks™ Plus
All-In-One Planner and Resource Center

Available on CD-ROM
• Interactive Teacher's Edition
• Printable Weekly Resources

Implementation Modules

• Support on how to implement the reading program

Balanced Literacy Planner

Balanced Literacy Lesson Plan
▶ Oral Language Development
▶ Word Work
▶ Focus Lesson
  ▶ Shared Reading
  ▶ Read Aloud
▶ Guided Reading
  ▶ Literacy Centers
▶ Writing Workshop

• Create customized weekly balanced literacy planners

ELL Strategies

• Teaching strategies for English Language Learners

Reading Video Library

• Video clips of instructional routines

Leadership Handbook

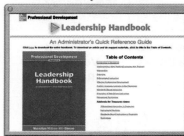
• Professional development for school principals

ONLINE www.macmillanmh.com

Animated Activities

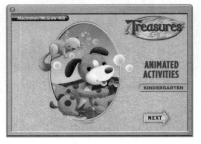

• Animated comprehension activities

Classroom Presentation Toolkit

• Weekly transparencies, graphic organizers, and guided instruction and practice

Additional Professional Development

• **Instructional Routine Handbook**
• **Writing Professional Development Guide**
• **Managing Small Groups**
• **Leadership Handbook:**
  An Administrator's Quick Reference Guide

Also available
Reading Yes!
Video Workshops on CD-ROM

LOG ON ▶ VIEW IT READ IT LEARN IT FIND OUT

☑ **Assess**

Leveled Reader Database

- Search and print Leveled Reader titles

Weekly Activities

- Oral Language
- Research Roadmap
- Research and Inquiry
- Vocabulary and Spelling
- Author and Illustrator

ONLINE   www.macmillanmh.com

Progress Monitoring

- Prescriptions for Reteaching
- Student Profile System

Online and CD-ROM materials are **Interactive White Board Ready!**

 IWB

Unit 2 Resources

Available on CD

 AUDIO CD
- **Listening Library**
- **Sound Pronunciation**

 CD-ROM
- **New Adventures with Buggles and Beezy**

Diagnostic Assessment

Screening, Diagnosis, and Placement

Use your state or district screener to identify children at risk. In addition, see tests in the **Diagnostic Assessment** book for information on determining the proficiency of children according to specific skills. Use the results to place children in the program.

- Diagnostics should be given at the beginning of the school year after you have had time to observe children and they become familiar with classroom routines. Use the diagnostics to determine children in need of intervention or to identify specific prerequisite skill deficiencies that you need to teach during Small Group differentiated instruction time.

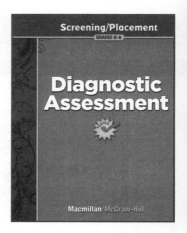

Progress Monitoring Assessment

Meeting Grade-Level Expectations

Use these tests at the end of each unit (every 3 weeks). Multiple questions and next-steps information are provided.

Ongoing Informal Assessments
- Daily Quick Check Observations

Formal Assessments
- **Unit Assessment**

Benchmark Assessment

Give once a year to determine whether children have mastered the grade-level content standards and to document long-term academic growth.

Test Alignment

GRADE K UNIT 2 ASSESSED SKILLS	TerraNova/ CAT 6	SESAT	TPRI	DIBELS*
COMPREHENSION STRATEGIES AND SKILLS				
• Strategies: Ask questions	◆	◆	◆	◆
• Skills: Identify character, Compare and contrast	◆	◆	◆	◆
VOCABULARY/HIGH-FREQUENCY WORDS				
• Color and number words				
• *like, a*	◆	◆	◆	◆
PHONEMIC AWARENESS				
• Phoneme isolation (initial and final /s/, /p/)	◆	◆	◆	◆
• Phoneme blending (/s/, /p/)	◆	◆	◆	◆
PHONICS				
• *s, p*	◆	◆	◆	◆
TEXT FEATURES				
• Use photographs, Use illustrations				
GRAMMAR				
• Nouns				

*Data from DIBELS serve as indicators of overall reading comprehension performance, not specific skills.

KEY

TerraNova/CAT 6	TerraNova, The Second Edition
SESAT	Stanford Early School Achievement Test
TPRI	Texas Primary Reading Inventory
DIBELS	Dynamics Indicators of Basic Early Literacy Skills

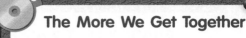

Theme Project: Making Friends

Unit 2 Opener

Introduce the Theme

Sing the theme song. Then guide children to generate questions related to the theme and topic of class-wide interest. For example: *How do you make friends? What do you like to do with your friends?*

The More We Get Together

The more we get together, together, together,

The more we get together, the happier we'll be.

'Cause your friends are my friends, and my friends are your friends.

The more we get together, the happier we'll be.

Song on Listening Library Audio CD

Research and Inquiry
Self-Selected Theme Project

 Step 1

Planning a Project
What do I want to learn about being a friend?

- Use library books to show pictures of what friends do together.
- Ask children to tell how they would get to know a new classmate.
- Have various reference materials and magazines available. Show children how to use a table of contents to locate information.

 Step 2

Doing the Project

- Guide children to use text sources found at the library to gather evidence.

 Step 3

Document and Evaluate Research
How can I share what I have learned?

You might suggest:
- an oral book report
- a skit
- an advertisement using pictures and writing about what it means to be a good friend

Help children decide what they will need for their presentation. Encourage children to speak audibly and clearly.
See the Unit Closer on pages 510–511.

Research Strategy

Informational books are different from story books:

- Informational books are about real people and real events. Use them to find out about the importance of sharing and friendship.

Unit 2
Friends

The Big Question

What do you like to do with your friends?

14A

Teaching Chart 14A

Introduce Theme Project

FRIENDS

Let's look at this photo. It is two girls and a dog. Point to the girls and dog as you describe the picture. *What are the children doing?*

Look at the photo as you discuss the following:

- Ask: *What kinds of activities do you and your friends like to do?*

- Ask: *Have you played with your friends' pets?*

- Ask: *Have you included your pet when you played with friends?*

- *Throughout this unit, we will be learning about friends, what a friend is, and getting along with friends.*

Gifted Talented

Connect to Content

Listening and Speaking

Explain to children that when they listen, they should listen with full attention. They should sit quietly and look at the speaker while he or she is talking. Point out that when children want to share information and ideas in a discussion, they should speak clearly so everyone can hear them. They should respond clearly in complete and coherent sentences.

Connect to Content

Activity: Friendship Tree

Ask: *What nice things can friends do for each other?*

- Have children create a "helping tree" from construction paper.

- Ask children to observe their classmates helping a friend. Then have them make leaf-shaped announcements to show the act of kindness.

- Hold a friendship ceremony once a week, having children hang their leaves on the tree and explain how and why he or she helped the friend. Encourage children to speak audibly and clearly.

Character Building: Thank-You Note

Point out to children that it is good manners to send a thank-you note to someone who does something nice for you. Explain that you, as the sender, are thanking someone for their kindness and why you appreciated it. The receiver, or the person getting the note, will feel good that their act of kindness was appreciated. Have children dictate a thank-you note for a gift. Record sentences on chart paper and read aloud with children.

Minilesson

Asking Questions to Clarify Information

Explain When you interview someone, you ask questions to find out more. You might interview an athlete about his favorite sport or an actress about her favorite movie role. Being able to ask good questions is an important skill.

Discuss Ask: *What questions might you ask if you were interviewing me about my job?* (Do you like being a teacher? How long have you been teaching? What is your favorite subject to teach?)

Apply Have children interview a classmate about what he or she thinks makes a good friend. Remind children to ask questions that begin with who, what, where, why, and when. Then, have children report the results of their interview to their classmates using complete sentences.

Connect to Content

Activity: New Friends Handbook

Ask: *How could we make a new classmate feel welcome?*

- Have children dictate an ending to the sentence *We can* _____.

- Ask them to illustrate their *We can* sentence.

- Help children assemble the sentences and illustrations into a book.

- Invite them to take turns reading their sentences aloud and sharing their illustrations.

Classroom Behavior

Help children

- discuss classroom procedures and rules;

- respect one another and the space of those around them.

Character Building: Trustworthiness

Discuss why it's important to be honest and do what you say you will do. Explain that part of friendship is trusting each other.

Minilesson

Writing an Invitation

Explain Have you ever gotten an invitation in the mail? It may have been to a birthday or holiday party or even to a special event, such as a concert or play. An **invitation** is a written request for someone to attend an event.

Discuss Ask: *What information should an invitation have?* (the date and time of the event, where it is being held, who is hosting the event, etc.)

Apply Have children design an invitation for a classmate, inviting him or her to participate in an activity at a certain time and place. For example: the reading corner for story time at 3 P.M.

 FIND OUT

Research For technology research and presentation strategies, see the Computer Literacy lesson on pages 508–509. For additional research and inquiry, go to **www.macmillanmh.com**.

Week 1 ★ At a Glance

Priority Skills and Concepts

 Comprehension
- **Genre:** Fiction, Expository, Fable
- **Strategy:** Ask Questions
- **Skill:** Identify Character
 • **Skill:** Make Predictions

 High-Frequency Word
- *like*

Oral Vocabulary
- Build Robust Vocabulary: *compete*, *favorite*, *friend*, *hobby*, *partner*

Fluency
- Word Automaticity
- Sound-Spellings

 Phonemic Awareness
- Phoneme Isolation
- Phoneme Blending
- Phoneme Categorization

 Phonics
- *Ss*

Grammar
- Naming Words (Nouns)

Writing
- Sentences

Key

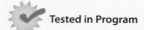 Tested in Program  Review Skill

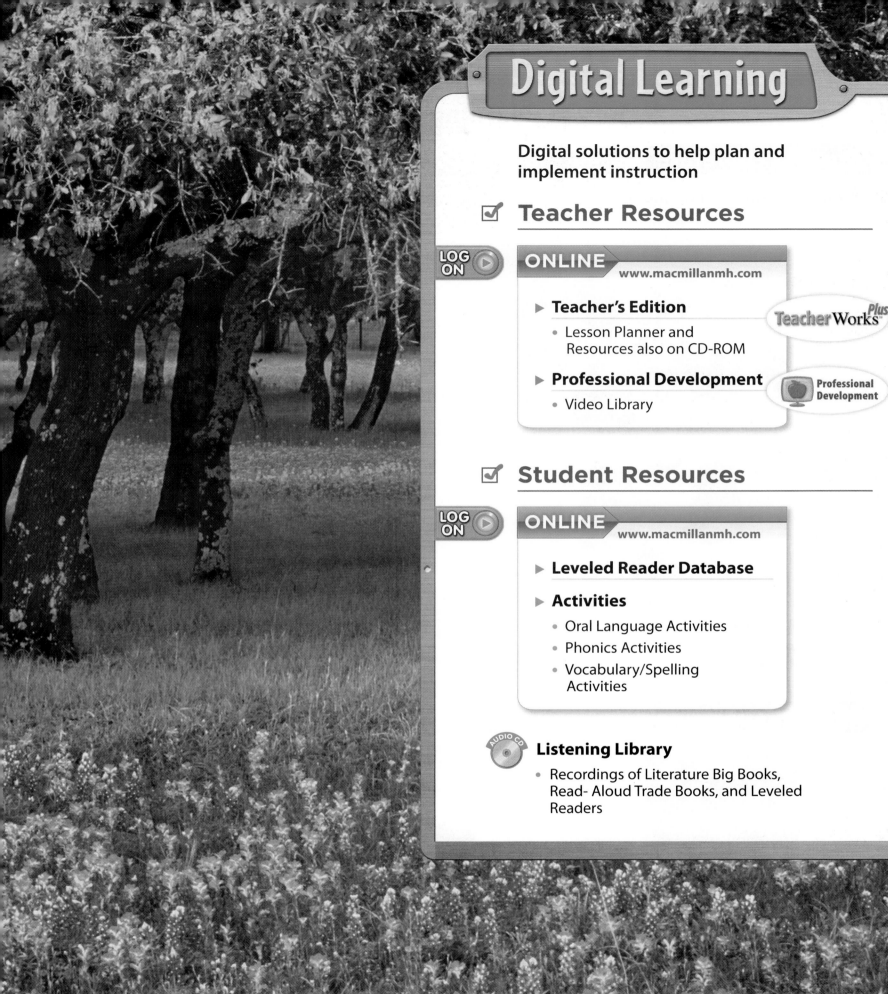

Digital Learning

Digital solutions to help plan and implement instruction

☑ **Teacher Resources**

LOG ON ▶

ONLINE www.macmillanmh.com

▶ **Teacher's Edition**
- Lesson Planner and Resources also on CD-ROM

TeacherWorks^Plus

▶ **Professional Development**
- Video Library

Professional Development

☑ **Student Resources**

LOG ON ▶

ONLINE www.macmillanmh.com

▶ **Leveled Reader Database**

▶ **Activities**
- Oral Language Activities
- Phonics Activities
- Vocabulary/Spelling Activities

AUDIO CD **Listening Library**
- Recordings of Literature Big Books, Read- Aloud Trade Books, and Leveled Readers

Weekly Literature

Theme: Learning About Friends

A mix of fiction and nonfiction

Big Book

Genre Fiction

Big Book of Explorations

Genre Expository

Support Literature

Interactive Read-Aloud Anthology

Genre Fable

Oral Vocabulary Cards
- Listening Comprehension
- Build Robust Vocabulary

Pre-decodable Readers

Resources for Differentiated Instruction

Leveled Readers

GR Levels Rebus-C

Genre	Fiction

- Same Theme
- Same Vocabulary/Phonics
- Same Comprehension Skills

Approaching Level

On Level

Beyond Level

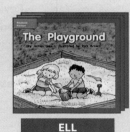
ELL

LOG ON **Leveled Reader Database**
Go to www.macmillanmh.com.

Practice

Activity Book

Practice Book

ELL Practice Book

Response to Intervention

Tier 2

- Phonemic Awareness
- Phonics
- Vocabulary
- Comprehension
- Fluency

Tier 3

Unit Assessment

Assess Unit Skills

- Phonemic Awareness
- Phonics
- High-Frequency Words
- Listening Comprehension

HOME-SCHOOL CONNECTION

- Family letters in English and Spanish
- Take-home stories and activities

Suggested Lesson Plan

Go to **www.macmillanmh.com** for Online Lesson Planner

 **TeacherWorks** *Plus*
All-In-One Planner and Resource Center

Professional Development Video Library

Big Book

 What Do You Like?
Michael Grejniec

WHOLE GROUP

ORAL LANGUAGE

- **Oral Vocabulary**

- **Phonemic Awareness**

WORD STUDY

- **Phonics**

- **High-Frequency Words**

READING

- **Listening Comprehension**

- **Apply Phonics and High-Frequency Words**

- **Fluency**

LANGUAGE ARTS

- **Writing**

- **Grammar**

ASSESSMENT

- **Informal/Formal**

DAY 1

❓**Focus Question** What can you do with your friends?
Build Background, 266
Oral Vocabulary *compete, favorite, friend, hobby, partner,* 266

✦ **Phonemic Awareness**
Phoneme Isolation, 269

✦ **Phonics**
Introduce /s/s, 270
Handwriting: Write *Ss*, 271
Activity Book, 4
Practice Book, 41

✦ **High-Frequency Words**
like, 268

Share the Big Book
What Do You Like?
Strategy: Ask Question, 267
✦ **Skill:** Identify Character, 267

 Big Book

Shared Writing
Lists, 273
Grammar
Naming Words, 272

Quick Check Phonemic Awareness, 269

DAY 2

❓**Focus Question** Do friends always like the same things?
Oral Vocabulary *compete, favorite, friend, hobby, partner,* 274
Color Words, 281

✦ **Phonemic Awareness**
Phoneme Blending, 282

✦ **Phonics**
Review, 282
Blend with /s/s, 283

✦ **Review High-Frequency Words**, 284

Reread the Big Book
What Do You Like?
Strategy: Ask Questions, 276
✦ **Skill:** Identify Character, 276
Retell, 280
Pre-decodable Reader: *I Like*, 284
Activity Book, 5–6
Practice Book, 42
Fluency Echo-Read, 280

What Do You Like?
Big Book

Interactive Writing
Sentences, 285

Quick Check Comprehension, 280

SMALL GROUP Lesson Plan ▶ **Differentiated Instruction 260–261**

Priority Skills ✓

| Phonemic Awareness/Phonics /s/s | High-Frequency Words *like* | Oral Vocabulary Color Words | Comprehension Strategy: Ask Questions Skill: Identify Character |

Half-Day Kindergarten

Teach Core Skills
Focus on tested skill lessons, other lessons, and small group options as your time allows.

DAY 3

❓ Focus Question What games do you like to play outside?

Oral Vocabulary *compete, favorite, friend, hobby, partner*, 286

Oral Vocabulary Cards: "Games Around the World"

✦ **Phonemic Awareness**
Phoneme Isolation, 291

✦ **Phonics**
Review /s/s, 292
Blend Words, 293
Read Words, 293

✦ **High-Frequency Words**
like, 290
Read for Fluency, 290
Activity Book, 7–8
Practice Book, 43–44

Read the Big Book of Explorations
"Friends Follow Rules," 24–25

Text Feature: Photographs, 288

Big Book of Explorations

Independent Writing
Prewrite and Draft Sentences, 295
Grammar
Naming Words, 294

Quick Check High-Frequency Words, 290

DAY 4

❓ Focus Question Some friends like the city and others like the country. Which do you like?

Oral Vocabulary *compete, favorite, friend, hobby, partner*, 296

Color Words, 299

✦ **Phonemic Awareness**
Phoneme Categorization, 300

✦ **Phonics**
Picture Sort, 300
Blend with /s/s, 301
Activity Book, 10
Practice Book, 46

✦ **Review High-Frequency Words**, 302

Interactive Read Aloud
Listening Comprehension, 298

Read Aloud: "The City Mouse and the Country Mouse"

Pre-decodable Reader:
We Like Sam!, 302

Read Aloud

Independent Writing
Revise and Edit Sentences, 303

Quick Check Phonics, 301

DAY 5
Review and Assess

❓ Focus Question What do you and your friends like to read?

Oral Vocabulary *compete, favorite, friend, hobby, partner*, 304

Color Words, 306

✦ **Phonemic Awareness**
Phoneme Categorization, 307

✦ **Phonics**
Read Words, 308
Dictation, 308
Activity Book, 12

✦ **High-Frequency Words**
like, *the*, *me*, *I*, *can*, 306

Read Across Texts
Strategy: Ask Questions, 305
✦ Skill: Identify Character, 305
Activity Book, 11

Fluency Word Automaticity, 306

Independent Writing
Publish and Present Sentences, 309

✦ **Weekly Assessment, 336–337**

Differentiated Instruction

What do I do in small groups?

Teacher-Led Small Groups

Independent Activities

LOG ON ▶

Focus on Skills

IF... children need additional instruction, practice, or extension based on your **Quick Check** observations for the following priority skills

 Phonemic Awareness
Phoneme Isolation, Categorization, Blending

 Phonics
Ss

 High-Frequency Words
can, *I*, *like*, *the*, *we*

✔ **Comprehension**
Strategy: Ask Questions
Skill: Identify Character

THEN...

Approaching	Preteach and
ELL	Reteach Skills
On Level	Practice
Beyond	Enrich and Accelerate Learning

Suggested Small Group Lesson Plan

CD-ROM — TeacherWorks™ *Plus*
All-In-One Planner and Resource Center

	DAY 1	DAY 2

Approaching Level
 Tier 2
 • **Preteach/Reteach**
 Tier 2 Instruction
	• Oral Language, 310
	 • High-Frequency Words, 310 **ELL**
	   High-Frequency Words Review, 310
	 • Phonemic Awareness, 311
	 • Phonics, 311
	   Sound-Spellings Review, 311
		• High-Frequency Words, 316 **ELL**
		 • Pre-decodable Reader, 316
		 • Phonemic Awareness, 317
		 • Phonics, 317

On Level • **Practice**	• High-Frequency Words, 312 • Phonemic Awareness/Phonics, 312 **ELL**	• Pre-decodable Reader, 318

Beyond Level
 • **Extend/Accelerate**
  Gifted and Talented
	• High-Frequency Words/Vocabulary, 313 **ELL**
	   Expand Oral Vocabulary, 313
	 • Phonics, 313
		• Pre-decodable Reader, 318

ELL • **Build English Language Proficiency** • See **ELL** in other levels.	• Oral Language Warm-Up, 314 • Academic Language, 314 • Vocabulary, 315	• Access to Core Content, 319

Small Group

Focus on Leveled Readers

Levels Rebus–C

Approaching

On Level

Beyond

ELL

Manipulatives

Sound-Spelling WorkBoards

Sound-Spelling Cards

Photo Cards

High-Frequency Word Cards

Additional Leveled Readers

LOG ON ▶ **Leveled Reader Database**
www.macmillanmh.com

Search by

- Comprehension Skill
- Content Area
- Genre
- Text Feature
- Guided Reading Level
- Reading Recovery Level
- Lexile Score
- Benchmark Level

Subscription also available

Visual Vocabulary Resources

DAY 3

- High-Frequency Words, 320 **ELL**
- Phonemic Awareness, 320
- Phonics, 321
- Pre-decodable Reader, 321

- Phonics, 322

- Phonics, 322

- Access to Core Content, 323
- Grammar, 323

DAY 4

- Phonemic Awareness, 324
- Phonics, 324 **ELL**
- Leveled Reader Lesson 1, 325

- Leveled Reader Lesson 1, 326 **ELL**

- Leveled Reader Lesson 1, 327
  Analyze, 327

- Leveled Reader, 328–329

DAY 5

- Phonemic Awareness, 330
- Phonics, 330 **ELL**
- Leveled Reader Lesson 2, 331
- High-Frequency Words, 331

- Leveled Reader Lesson 2, 332

- Leveled Reader Lesson 2, 333 **ELL**
- Expand Vocabulary, 333

- Fluency, 334
- High-Frequency Words, 335
- Writing, 335

Managing the Class

What do I do with the rest of my class?

- Activity Book
- Practice Book
- ELL Practice Book
- Leveled Reader Activities
- Literacy Workstations
- Online Activities
- Buggles and Beezy

Classroom Management Tools

Weekly Contract

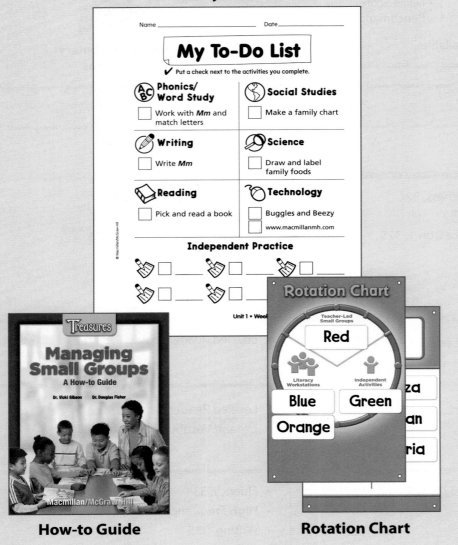

Name _____ Date _____

My To-Do List

✓ Put a check next to the activities you complete.

(ABC) **Phonics/ Word Study**	🌎 **Social Studies**
Work with *Mm* and match letters	Make a family chart
✏️ **Writing**	🔬 **Science**
Write *Mm*	Draw and label family foods
📖 **Reading**	🖱️ **Technology**
Pick and read a book	Buggles and Beezy www.macmillanmh.com

Independent Practice

Unit 1 • Week

How-to Guide

Treasures
Managing Small Groups
A How-to Guide
Dr. Vicki Gibson   Dr. Douglas Fisher
Macmillan/McGraw-Hill

Rotation Chart

Rotation Chart

Teacher-Led Small Groups

Red

Literacy Workstations   Independent Activities

Blue   **Green**

Orange

Rotation Chart

Digital Learning

Phonics Activities

- Match Letters
- Match Letters to Sounds
- Blend Words

Meet the Author/Illustrator

Lisa Jahn-Clough

- Lisa has taught both writing and illustrating for many years at a college in Maine.
- Lisa lives in Portland, Maine, but was born on a small farm in Rhode Island.
- Lisa's father was a zoologist and she even had a pet monkey, named Zepher, when she was young.

Other books by Lisa Jahn-Clough
- Jahn-Clough, Lisa. *Simon and Molly Plus Hester*. Boston, MA: Houghton Mifflin, 2001.
- Jahn-Clough, Lisa. *My Friend and I*. Boston, MA: Houghton Mifflin, 1999.

- Read Other Books by the Author or Illustrator

Practice

Activity Book

Practice Book

ELL Practice Book

Independent Activities

ONLINE INSTRUCTION www.macmillanmh.com

Available on CD

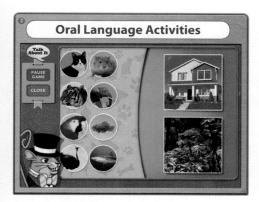

Oral Language Activities

- Focus on Unit Vocabulary and Concepts
- English Language Learner Support

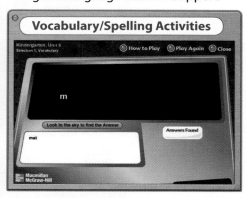

Vocabulary/Spelling Activities

- Differentiated Lists and Activities

Leveled Reader Database

- Leveled Reader Database
- Search titles by level, skill, content area, and more

LISTENING LIBRARY
Recordings of selections
- Literature Big Books
- Read-Aloud Trade Books
- Leveled Readers
- ELL Readers

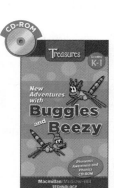

NEW ADVENTURES WITH BUGGLES AND BEEZY
Phonemic awareness and phonics activities

Leveled Reader Activities

Approaching

On Level

Beyond

ELL

See inside cover of all Leveled Readers.

Literacy Workstations

Reading

Phonics/ Word Study

Writing

Science/ Social Studies

See lessons on pages 264–265

Managing the Class

What do I do with the rest of my class?

 Reading

Objectives

- Read and discuss a book with a partner
- Read a book aloud

 Phonics/Word Study

Objectives

- Sort pictures by initial sounds and letter /a/a, /m/m, and /s/s
- Use the letters /a/a, /m/m, and /s/s to make words

Reading — **Book Club** — 20 Minutes

Read about friends. Talk about the main characters.

❶ Sit in a circle. ❷ Read the book together. ❸ Talk about it.

Do More
- Listen to the CD of *What Do You Like?*
- Talk about the main characters in *What Do You Like?*

For more book titles, go to the Meet the Author/ Illustrator page on www.macmillanmh.com

7

© Macmillan/McGraw-Hill

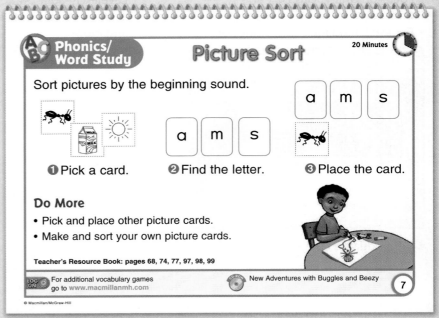

Phonics/ Word Study — **Picture Sort** — 20 Minutes

Sort pictures by the beginning sound.

a m s

❶ Pick a card. ❷ Find the letter. ❸ Place the card.

Do More
- Pick and place other picture cards.
- Make and sort your own picture cards.

Teacher's Resource Book: pages 68, 74, 77, 97, 98, 99

For additional vocabulary games go to www.macmillanmh.com

New Adventures with Buggles and Beezy

7

© Macmillan/McGraw-Hill

Reading — **Book Buddies** — 20 Minutes

Make a book buddy. Read to it.

❶ Make a buddy. ❷ Read to your buddy.

Do More
- Draw a picture of you and your book buddy reading together.
- Retell an important event from the story.

We like to read.

For more book titles, go to the Meet the Author/ Illustrator page on www.macmillanmh.com

8

© Macmillan/McGraw-Hill

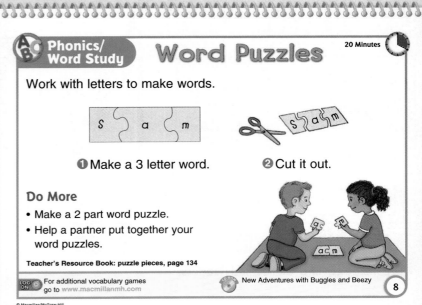

Phonics/ Word Study — **Word Puzzles** — 20 Minutes

Work with letters to make words.

s a m

❶ Make a 3 letter word. ❷ Cut it out.

Do More
- Make a 2 part word puzzle.
- Help a partner put together your word puzzles.

Teacher's Resource Book: puzzle pieces, page 134

For additional vocabulary games go to www.macmillanmh.com

New Adventures with Buggles and Beezy

8

© Macmillan/McGraw-Hill

Literacy Workstations

 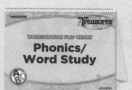  

Reading

Phonics/ Word Study

Writing

Science/ Social Studies

Literacy Workstation Flip Charts

Writing

Objectives

- Write capital and lowercase letters *Aa*, *Mm*, and *Ss*
- Form words that begin with /s/s

Content Literacy

Objectives

- Use the sense of hearing to identify sounds
- Identify different ways that friends play together

Writing — Write Ss — 20 Minutes

Write capital and lowercase Ss.

❶ Dip in sand. ❷ Write Ss. ❸ Say Ss.

Do More
- Write Mm and Aa in sand. Say the letter.
- Write Ss on writing paper.

Marta
SSSSS
SSSSS
SSSSS
SSSSS

7

© Macmillan/McGraw-Hill

Science — Name That Sound — 20 Minutes

Use the sense of hearing to identify sounds.

❶ Choose a friend. ❷ Make a sound. ❸ Listen to a sound.

Do More
- List inside and outside sounds.
- Read a friend's list.

Internet Research and Inquiry Activity
www.macmillanmh.com

8

© Macmillan/McGraw-Hill

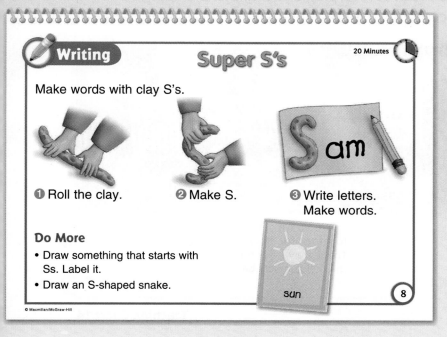

Writing — Super S's — 20 Minutes

Make words with clay S's.

❶ Roll the clay. ❷ Make S. ❸ Write letters. Make words.

Do More
- Draw something that starts with Ss. Label it.
- Draw an S-shaped snake.

sun

8

© Macmillan/McGraw-Hill

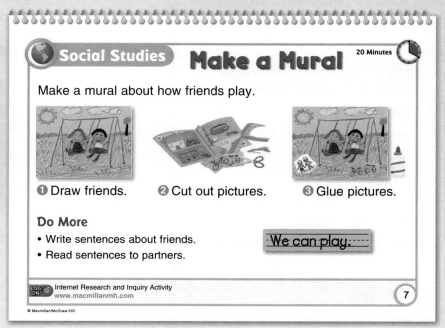

Social Studies — Make a Mural — 20 Minutes

Make a mural about how friends play.

❶ Draw friends. ❷ Cut out pictures. ❸ Glue pictures.

Do More
- Write sentences about friends.
- Read sentences to partners.

We can play.

Internet Research and Inquiry Activity
www.macmillanmh.com

7

© Macmillan/McGraw-Hill

WHOLE GROUP

Oral Language
- Build Background

✔ **Comprehension**
- Read *What Do You Like?*
- Strategy: Ask Questions
- Skill: Identify Character

✔ **High-Frequency Words**
- Introduce *like*

✔ **Phonemic Awareness**
- Phoneme Isolation

✔ **Phonics**
- Introduce /s/s
- Handwriting: Write *Ss*

Grammar
- Naming Words (Nouns)

Writing
- Shared Writing: Lists

SMALL GROUP

- Differentiated Instruction, pages 310–335

Oral Vocabulary

Week 1

compete	favorite	friend
hobby	partner	

Review

celebrate	change	eager
occasion	relative	

Use the **Define/Example/Ask** routine in the **Instructional Routine Handbook** to review the words.

Oral Language

 Build Background: *Friends*

INTRODUCE THE THEME

Tell children that this week they will be talking and reading about **friends**, the people you like to be with, and the things you like to do with them.

Write the following question on the board: *What can you do with your friends?* Use your finger to track the print as you read aloud the message. *The first word in our sentence is* What. *I left a space to show that the next word,* can, *is a separate word. Count the words in the sentence with me.* Prompt children to answer the question.

ACCESS PRIOR KNOWLEDGE

Explain to children that a friend is someone you like very much and enjoy being with. Ask children about the kinds of activities that they like to do with friends. *I like to go to the park with friends. What is your* **favorite** *thing to do with friends? What do you like to do by yourself?*

Think Aloud   Let's look at this picture. It is a boy and some girls playing. They are playing together in a pile of leaves that have fallen from a tree. (**Point to the boy, girls, and leaves as you describe the picture.**) Have you ever played in leaves with friends?

■ Look at the photographs together and sing the song. Discuss how doing favorite things with friends makes you feel happy.

 INNOVATE ON THE SONG

Write new verses by replacing *get* with other things children do together, such as *read, play,* and *sing*. Have children use complete sentences to discuss how friends often like to do the same activity.

The more we get together,
together, together.
The more we get together
the happier we'll be.

Oral Language

Unit 2
Sing About It

Song: *The More We Get Together*
Friends   Week 1   14

Teaching Chart 14

Share the Big Book

Listening Comprehension

PREVIEW Display the cover. *I see two friends. One friend is a boy and one is a girl. It looks like they are sharing an umbrella.* Point to the two friends and umbrella as you talk. *Now let's read about* **friends***.*

Read the title and the name of the author/illustrator as you track the print. *What do you think the boy and girl will do?*

Big Book

GENRE: LITERARY TEXT/FICTION
Tell children *What Do You Like?* is **fiction**, a make-believe story.

STRATEGY Ask Questions

EXPLAIN/MODEL Point out that the title asks a question. *Asking questions is a good way to understand what a story is about.*

Think Aloud The boy and the girl are on the cover. I'll ask myself who the boy and girl are. Are the boy and girl friends? How will I know? As I read, I'll ask myself questions to understand the story.

SKILL Identify Character

EXPLAIN/MODEL Point out that a story often has characters. The characters do the actions in the story.

Think Aloud I see a boy and a girl on the cover. I think the story is about the boy and girl characters. As I read, I'll ask myself about what the characters do and how they feel.

Read the Big Book

SET PURPOSE *As you listen to the story, you can use the words and pictures to find out about the characters.* Use the **Define/Example/Ask** routine to teach the story words on the inside back cover.

Respond to Literature

MAKE CONNECTIONS Ask children to tell you about their **favorite** character of the story. *Did you find things that the boy or the girl likes that you like, too?* Have children describe the characters from the story and compare them with the children in their community.

Objectives

- Discuss the theme
- Recognize words separated by spaces in a sentence
- Use oral vocabulary words *friend* and *favorite*
- Ask questions; identify and describe characters
- Make connections to larger community

Materials

- Teaching Chart 14
- Big Book: *What Do You Like?*

ELL

Use the **Interactive Question-Response Guide** for *What Do You Like?*, **ELL Resource Book** pages 32–39, to guide children through a reading of the book. As you read *What Do You Like?*, make meanings clear by pointing to pictures, demonstrating word meanings, paraphrasing text, and asking children questions.

Digital Learning

Story on **Listening Library Audio CD**

Objectives

- Read the high-frequency word *like*
- Review the high-frequency words *can, I, the, we*
- Identify the word *like* in text and speech

Materials

- High-Frequency Word Cards: *can, I, like, the, we*
- Teaching Chart 15

ELL

Display the High-Frequency Word Cards *can, I, like, the, we* and use them in sentences about **Teaching Chart 15**. For example, point to the sun and say: *I like the sun.* Then have a group of children say: *We like the sun.* Repeat with other nouns pictured on the Teaching Chart.

High-Frequency Words

 like

INTRODUCE Display the **High-Frequency Word Card** for **like**. Use the **Read/Spell/Write** routine to teach the word.

- **Read** Point to and say the word *like. I like books.*

- **Spell** *The word* like *is spelled* l-i-k-e. *What's the first sound in* like? *That's right. The first sound in* like *is /l/. That's why the first letter is* l. *After the* l, *I see* i, k, *and* e. *Let's read and spell* like *together.*

- **Write** *Now let's write the word* like *on our papers. Let's spell aloud the word as we write it:* like, l-i-k-e.

SPIRAL REVIEW

REVIEW *I, we, can, the* Display each card and have children read the word. Repeat several times.

I	we
can	the

READ THE RHYME AND CHIME Have children point to *I, like,* and *the*. Repeat the rhyme for fluency. Add *like* to the class Word Wall for children to refer to later.

Teaching Chart 15

For Tier 2 instruction, see page 310.

TIME TO MOVE!

Have children dance, clap, march, and move to the "I Like the Sun" Rhyme and Chime. Then have children create their own verses with movement words and act them out.

Phonemic Awareness

 ## Phoneme Isolation

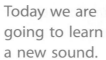

Model

Display the **Photo Card** for *sun*.

Repeat with the Photo Card for *soap*.

Today we are going to learn a new sound. Listen for the sound at the beginning of *sun*: /sss/, *sun*. *Sun* has /s/ at the beginning. Say the sound with me: /sss/. We'll hiss like a snake when we hear /s/ at the beginning of a word.

Read the Rhyme and Chime "I Like the Sun" again. Have children hiss like a snake every time they hear /s/.

I like the sun.

I like the sea.

I like sailboats.

I like me!

 Review /m/, /a/
Display the Photo Card for *map*. Repeat for *apple*.

This is a *map*. The beginning sound in *map* is /m/. Listen: /mmmap/. **(Stretch the beginning sound.)** What is the sound?

Guided Practice/Practice
Display Photo Cards.

Children identify initial sounds. Guide practice with the first card, using the same routine.

Continue orally with the words *sun, sap, at, mad, tail, set, silly, ant, mitt, soup, top, sing.*

Say each picture name with me. Tell me the sound you hear at the beginning of the word.

Quick Check

Can children identify initial sound /s/?

During **Small Group Instruction**

If No → **Approaching Level** Provide additional practice, page 311.

If Yes → **On Level** Children are ready to read words with *Ss*, page 312.

Beyond Level Children are ready to read words with *Ss*, page 313.

Objectives

- Listen for initial /s/
- Review initial /m/ and /a/
- Isolate the initial sounds /s/, /m/, /a/ in one-syllable spoken words

Materials

- Photo Cards: *anchor, ant, apple, man, map, moon, mouse, soap, sock, sun*

ELL

Pronunciation Display and have children name Photo Cards from this and prior lessons to reinforce phonemic awareness and word meanings. Point to a card and ask: *What do you see?* (the sun) *What is the sound at the beginning of the word* sun? (/s/) Repeat with other cards.

Objectives

- Match the letter *s* to /s/ the sound
- Handwriting: Write uppercase and lowercase *Ss*

Materials

- Sound-Spelling Card: *Sun*
- Teaching Chart 15
- Word-Building Cards
- Handwriting
- Handwriting Teacher's Edition
- Activity Book, p. 4
- Practice Book, p. 41

ELL

Variations in Languages
For children who may have difficulty pronouncing /s/, us the Approaching Level Phonics lessons for additional pronunciation and decoding practice.

Sound Pronunciation

See **Sound Pronunciation CD** for a model of the /s/ sound. Play this for children needing additional models.

Phonics

✔ Introduce /s/s

Model

Display the *Sun* Sound-Spelling Card.

This is the *Sun* card. The sound is /s/. The /s/ sound is spelled with the letter *s*. Say it with me: /s/. This is the sound at the beginning of the word *sun*. Listen: /sss/…*un, sun.* What is the name of this letter? What is the sound?

Read the "I Like the Sun" Rhyme and Chime. Reread the title. Point out that the word *Sun* in the title begins with the letter *s*. Model placing a self-stick note beneath the *S* in *Sun*.

Teaching Chart 15

Guided Practice/Practice

Read the rest of the rhyme. Stop after each line. Children place self-stick notes below words that begin with *s*. Guide practice with *sun* in line 1. Repeat the routine with *m*.

Let's put a sticky note below the word in the line that begins with the letter *s*. The word *sun* begins with the letter *s*.

Corrective Feedback

If children have difficulty with words with /s/, review the word *sun*: *I hear the /s/ sound at the beginning of* sun: /sss/…un, sun. *Let's say it together:* /sss/…un, sun. *What is the sound? Say it again.* Repeat with *sad, set, sip,* and *soon.*

Build Fluency: Sound-Spellings

 Display the following **Word-Building Cards**: *a, m, s*. Have children chorally say each sound. Repeat and vary the pace.

Handwriting: Write *Ss*

MODEL Model holding up your writing hand. Say the handwriting cues below as you write the capital and lowercase forms of *Ss* on the board. Trace the letters on the board and in the air as you say /s/.

Circle back, sweep around, and back again.

Circle back, sweep around, and back again.

PRACTICE Ask children to hold up their writing hand.

- Say the cues together as children trace with their index finger the letters you wrote on the board.

- Have children write *S* and *s* in the air as they say /s/.

- Distribute handwriting practice pages. Observe children's pencil grip and paper position, and correct as necessary. Have children say /s/ every time they write the letter *s*.

For Tier 2 instruction, see page 311.

Daily Handwriting

Check that children form letters starting at the top and moving to the bottom. See **Handwriting Teacher's Edition** for ball-and-stick and slant models.

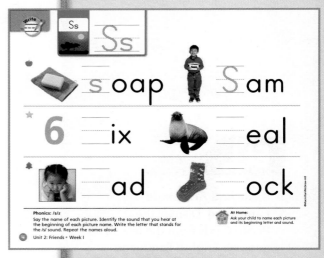

Activity Book, page 4
Practice Book, page 41

Objective

- Recognize naming words (nouns)

Materials

- Photo Cards: *astronaut, girl, man, nurse*
- Big Book: *What Do You Like?*

Grammar

Naming Words (Nouns)

MODEL Use the **Big Book** *What Do You Like?* to introduce naming words. *Words that name people are nouns.*

Point to the story characters as you say these words: *boy, girl, mother.* Explain that all these words name people.

- Use *boy, girl*, and *mother* to start a list. Add your own name and children's names. Explain that your names are words that name people, too.

PRACTICE Show **Photo Cards** for *astronaut, girl, man*, and *nurse*.

- Help children identify who is in each picture. Model saying sentences about each of the people in the pictures, such as:

> *The* astronaut *flew in a rocket ship.*
>
> *The* girl *played ball.*

- After each sentence, ask children which word names who did the action in the sentence. Then have children make up their own sentences using the Photo Cards. Guide them to speak in complete sentences and to tell the naming word in each sentence.

Writing

Shared Writing: Lists

BRAINSTORM

Remind children that the boy and girl in the **Big Book** *What Do You Like?* like all kinds of things. *Some things **friends** like are the same and some are different. What are some of these things?*

WRITE

- Make two lists—one for the girl and one for the boy. Read each list heading aloud as you track the print. Have children repeat. Point out how the words are written one under the other. *A list helps us to remember information and ideas.*

- Model by rereading pages 4–7 of *What Do You Like?* *The girl and boy both like a rainbow, so I will write* rainbow *on both lists.*

- Write children's ideas on the lists. Read the completed lists together, tracking the print.

- Help children to identify the words in the list that are naming words or nouns. Have them use each word in a complete sentence.

- Save the lists to refer to in other activities this week.

Girl Likes

| rainbow |
| cat |
| apple |
| mother |

Boy Likes

| rainbow |
| cat |
| apple |
| mother |

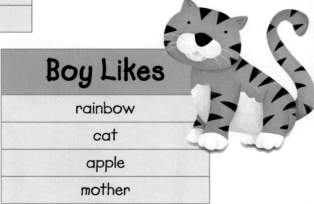

Write About It

Have children draw a picture of something they like. Help them label their picture.

Objective

- Dictate information for lists to compare people

Materials

- Big Book: *What Do You Like?*

5-Day Writing

Sentences	
DAY 1	Shared: Lists
DAY 2	Interactive: Sentences
DAY 3	Independent: Prewrite and Draft Sentences
DAY 4	Independent: Revise and Edit Sentences
DAY 5	Independent: Publish and Present

ELL

Prewriting Planning
Provide the Big Book for children to point to and name things they like. List responses on the board. Then have children work on their journal entries. Help children name and label their pictures.

Transitions That Teach

While children are packing up, have them say what toy is their **favorite** and why.

Oral Language
- Build Robust Vocabulary

Comprehension ✓
- Reread *What Do You Like?*
- Strategy: Ask Questions
- Skill: Identify Character
- Fluency: Echo-Read

Vocabulary
- Color Words
- Story Word: *rainbow*

Phonemic Awareness ✓
- Phoneme Blending

Phonics ✓
- Review /s/s, /m/m, /a/a
- Blend with /s/s
- Pre-decodable Reader: *I Like*

Writing
- Interactive Writing: Sentences

SMALL GROUP

- Differentiated Instruction, pages 310–335

Oral Vocabulary

Week 1

compete	favorite	friend
hobby	partner	

Review

celebrate	change	eager
occasion	relative	

Use the **Define/Example/Ask** routine in the **Instructional Routine Handbook** to review the words.

Oral Language

 Talk About It ## Build Robust Vocabulary

INTRODUCE WORDS Tell children they are going to talk about the characters' favorite things in the **Big Book** *What Do You Like? Something that is your favorite is the one you like the best. My favorite thing to do with a friend is to take a long walk. Friends can like the same things and also like different things. What is a friend? Friends are people you like and enjoy spending time with them.* Read pages 6–9 aloud.

Vocabulary Routine

Use the routine below to discuss the meaning of each word.

Define: If you like something best, it's your **favorite**. Say the word with me.
Example: My favorite fruits are oranges, but my brother's favorite fruits are grapes.
Ask: What is your favorite story?

Define: A **friend** is someone you like and who likes you, too. Say the word with me.
Example: On the weekend I like to play with my friends.
Ask: What do friends like to do together?

CREATE A DIAGRAM

Use yarn to create a Venn diagram. Place index cards for the headings inside the diagram. Read the chart together as you track the print. *The friends both like cats. I will put the word* cats *under* Both Like. *I will put* pet cat *under* Girl Likes *and* tiger *under* Boy Likes. *Where should I put the word* apples?

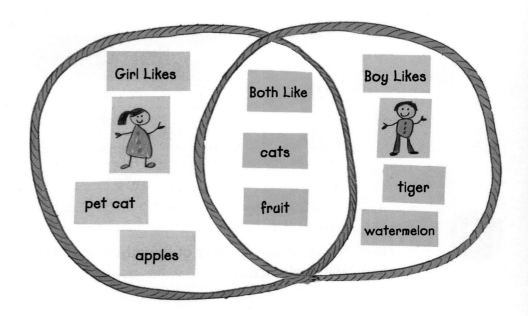

Listen for Rhyme

IDENTIFY RHYME

Tell children that words rhyme when they have the same ending sounds. *The word* hill *rhymes with* Jill. Tell children *hill* and *Jill* end with the sounds /il/, /iiilll/. Guide children to generate new words that rhyme with *hill*. After singing the song, have children identify the words that rhyme.

SING ABOUT FRIENDS

Let's sing a fun song about friends, or the people we like to do things with. Have children name activities that friends like to do together, such as run, jump, or play games. *Today we will sing about two friends, blackbirds, who like to fly away together.* Play the fingerplay "Two Little Blackbirds" using the **Listening Library Audio CD**. Then teach children the words and actions. Sing the song several times together.

Two Little Blackbirds

Two little blackbirds sitting on a hill.

Two hands closed with thumbs up.

One named Jack, one named Jill.

Bounce one hand, then the other.

Fly away, Jack. Fly away, Jill.

Right hand is open, raised above head, then same with left.

Come back, Jack. Come back, Jill.

Right hand and left back to original position.

ELL ENGLISH LANGUAGE LEARNERS

Beginning	Intermediate	Advanced
Confirm Understanding Review oral vocabulary from previous lessons using the **Big Book** *What Do You Like?* For example, say: *Show me the rainbow* and have children find the rainbow in the book. Ask: *Do you like the rainbow?*	**Enhance Understanding** Display the page with the rainbow and ask: *What can you tell me about this rainbow?* (The rainbow has many colors.) Guide children to use complete sentences when answering.	**Share Information** Pair children and have partners talk about what they like and don't like.

Objectives

- Ask and respond to questions
- Identify character
- Retell a story
- Develop fluency

Materials

- Big Book: *What Do You Like?*
- Activity Book, pp. 5–6
- Practice Book, p. 42

Big Book

Digital Learning

Story on **Listening Library Audio CD**

ELL

Gesture and Talk Use gestures and other strategies, such as asking questions, to help make the text comprehensible.

pp. 4–5, 6–7
rainbow: Tell children to touch and say *rainbow.* Point to the colors and say each color word with children.

Reread the Big Book
Listening Comprehension

CONCEPTS ABOUT PRINT Display the cover and read the title aloud with children as you track the print. Have them tell what they remember about the story.

 STRATEGY Ask Questions

Remind children that asking questions helps them understand the story. *We ask ourselves questions to figure out things in the story. As you become a better reader, you will begin to ask questions about what has happened to the characters in the story and what will happen next. Let's read, ask, and answer questions about* What Do You Like?

 SKILL Identify Character

Remind children that yesterday they asked questions to help understand the story. *Did finding out about the characters help?*

Think Aloud The cover shows me the two characters—a boy and a girl—holding an umbrella. I wonder if they are **friends**. I will read the book to find out if they are.

Read the **Big Book** and use the prompts on the inside covers.

pages 4–5

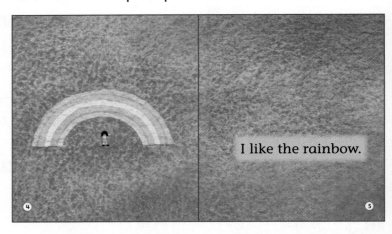

I like the rainbow.

pages 6–7

ASK QUESTIONS
- *I ask myself why both children like the rainbow. Why might they both?*

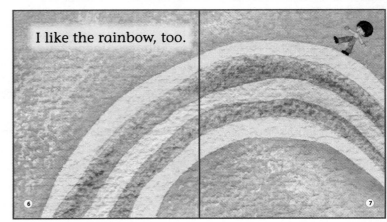

I like the rainbow, too.

Develop Comprehension

pages 8–9

ASK QUESTIONS
Think Aloud The girl says: *I like to play*. What does the girl like to play? Looking at the illustration, I see the girl jumping rope. The girl must like to play and jump rope.

I like to play.

pages 10–11

IDENTIFY CHARACTER
■ *What does the boy like to do when he plays?* (The boy likes to throw a boomerang. It looks like a boomerang is a toy.)

I like to play, too.

pages 12–13

SPIRAL REVIEW

MAKE PREDICTIONS
■ *Do you think that the boy will also like a cat? Why?* (Possible answer: Yes. The boy likes the same things that the girl likes.)

I like my cat.

pages 14–15

ASK QUESTIONS
Think Aloud What have I learned about the boy and girl so far? The girl likes jump ropes and cats. The boy likes boomerangs and tigers.

I like my cat, too.

Comprehension

Use Illustrations
- *(pages 8–9)* This picture shows me that the girl likes to jump rope.

Ask Questions
- *(pages 16–19)* I see that the boy and the girl both like fruit. I will ask myself what kind of fruit they each like. I see that the girl likes apples and the boy likes watermelon.

Story Words
(page 5) rainbow   *(page 28)* mother

About the Author/Illustrator: Michael Grejniec
Michael Grejniec, who is from Poland, has written and illustrated many books for children. He always keeps a pencil in his pocket so that he can draw the things that he sees.

**Big Book
Inside Back Cover**

ELL

pp. 10–11
play: Point to the illustration. Then gesture playing with a boomerang and throwing it in the air. Ask children to gesture as they follow your modeling, saying the word *play*.

pp. 12–13
cat: Point to the illustration of the cat and make a meowing sound. Have children repeat and say *cat*.

pp. 14–15
cat (tiger): Point to the tiger's stripes and say *cat. Is this a big cat or a little cat?*

Text Evidence

Identify Character

Explain Remind children that when they answer a question about a selection, they need to find evidence in the text to support their answer.

Discuss Have children reread pp. 16–19. Guide children to identify the characters and describe the reason(s) why they might be friends. Ask: *What tells us that they are friends?*

ELL

pp. 16–17
fruit: Point to the apples and gesture eating an apple. *What fruit do you like to eat?*

pp. 18–19
fruit: Point to the watermelon. Tell children to touch the picture of the watermelon, gesture eating watermelon with two hands, and say: *Watermelon is a fruit.*

pp. 20–21
music: Gesture playing the piano and then point to your ear as you say *music.* Have children repeat *music.*

pp. 22–23
music: Gesture playing the flute and then point to your ear as you say *music.* Have children repeat *music.*

Develop Comprehension

pages 16–17

HIGH-FREQUENCY WORDS
- *Can you find the words I and* like *on this page? Point to them. Say the words with me: I, like.*

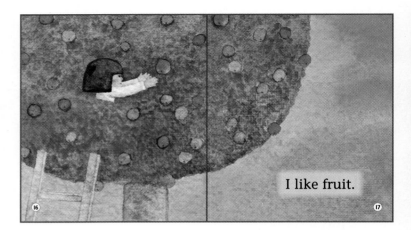

pages 18–19

pages 20–21

IDENTIFY CHARACTER
- *What kind of musical instrument does the girl like to play?* (the piano)

ILLUSTRATOR'S CRAFT
- *Why do you think the illustrator shows birds coming out of the piano?*

pages 22–23

ASK QUESTIONS
- *What kind of musical instrument does the boy like to play?* (He likes to play the flute.)

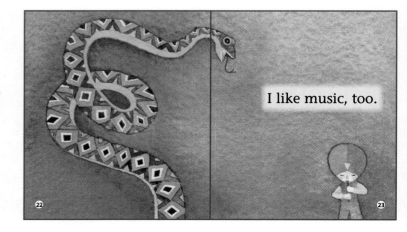

pages 24–25

CONCEPTS ABOUT PRINT

- *Now let's count the number of words in this sentence.* (4)

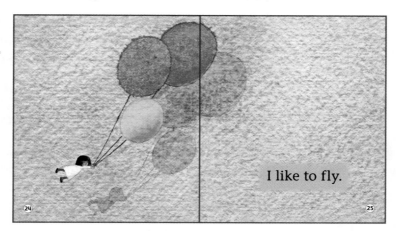

I like to fly.

pages 26–27

ASK QUESTIONS

Think Aloud I wondered how the girl was flying. I saw that the balloons were lifting her up. I was surprised to see that the boy was flying in a plane.

I like to fly, too.

pages 28–29

IDENTIFY CHARACTER

- *How do the children show that they love their mother?* (Each brings her a flower.)

I love my mother.
I love my mother, too.

pages 30–31

AUTHOR'S PURPOSE

- *Why do you think the author wrote questions at the end?* (Possible answer: He is asking the reader to think and talk more about what happened in the book.)

What do you like?
What do you love?

Activity Book, pages 5–6
Practice Book, page 42

Respond to Literature

TALK ABOUT IT Guide children to talk about the characters and to point out words and describe illustrations in the story. Have them refer to the book as they answer the questions.

- *What things does the girl like? What does the boy like?* LOCATE

- *What are some of the things that both the girl and the boy like?*
  CONNECT

- *Is this story true (real) or fantasy (make-believe)? How do you know?*
  (The story is fantasy or make-believe because the boy does things that a boy cannot do in real life. He rides a tiger and flies an airplane.) COMBINE

Retell

GUIDED RETELLING
Tell children that they will now use the illustrations to retell a main event from *What Do You Like?* Guide them to recall the text from memory and to use complete sentences.

- Display pages 4–7. *What does the girl like? What does the boy like?*

- Display pages 16–19. *What kind of fruit does the girl like? What kind of fruit does the boy like?*

- Display page 28. *Who do the boy and the girl both love? What does this tell us about them?*

- Discuss the story: *How are the boy and the girl like each other? How are they different from each other?*

- Have partners act out the differences and similarities between what the boy and the girl like.

Fluency: Echo-Read

MODEL Use a gentle tone of voice as you read what the children say about their mother on pages 28 and 29. *Listen to how I read this part of the story.* Then reread the lines and have children echo-read as you track the print.

Retelling Rubric

4 Excellent

Retells the selection without prompting, in sequence, and using supporting details. Clearly describes the setting, main characters, and complete plot.

3 Good

Retells the selection with little guidance, in sequence, and using some details. Generally describes the setting, main characters, and plot.

2 Fair

Retells the selection with some guidance, mostly in sequence, and using limited details. Partially describes the setting, main characters, and plot.

1 Unsatisfactory

Retells the selection only when prompted, out of sequence, and using limited details. Does not describe the main characters or plot.

Quick Check

Can children identify and describe characters to understand a story?
Can children begin to retell a story?

Vocabulary

Color Words

Chant the following jingle:

> *Roses are red,*
>
> *Violets are blue.*
>
> *You are my **friend**,*
>
> *And I like you!*

■ Repeat the first line and tell children the word *red* tells a color name. Ask children to name **favorite** things that are red. Repeat with the second line.

■ Display the pocket chart with squares of colored paper. Name each color with children. Point to each color at random and ask children to name it.

NAME COLOR WORDS Have children play the game "I Spy," taking turns saying, *I spy something [color word]*, while other children figure out the object. Repeat using pictures of objects of different colors.

Story Word: *rainbow*

Display page 4 of *What Do You Like?* and point out the picture of a rainbow. *What colors do you see? Have you ever seen a rainbow in the sky after it rained?*

Explain that a *rainbow* is made up of tiny drops of water in the air that the sun shines through.

COMPOUND WORDS Tell children that the word *rainbow* has two parts: *rain* and *bow. The word* rainbow *is a compound word because it is made up of the shorter words* rain *and* bow. Draw a picture of some raindrops and a bow (as in a bow and arrow) to help children understand where the word *rainbow* comes from.

TIME TO MOVE!

Have children follow simple two-step directions that contain color words, such as: *If you are wearing something blue, please stand up. If you are wearing something red, touch your head.* Ask all children wearing red to stand together.

Objectives

- Use color words
- Learn the story word *rainbow*
- Recognize compound words

Materials

- pocket chart
- squares of colored paper (red, yellow, blue, green, orange, and purple)
- pictures of colored objects
- Big Book: *What Do You Like?*
- Activity Book, p. 6

Digital Learning

LOG ON ► For children who need additional language support and oral vocabulary development, use the activities found at **www.macmillanmh.com**.

ELL

Use Labels Ask about children's clothing to reinforce the names of colors. For example, say: *Stand up if you are wearing a red shirt. Raise your hand if you have blue pants.*

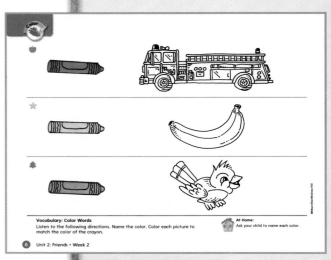

Vocabulary: Color Words
Listen to the following directions. Name the color. Color each picture to match the color of the crayon.

At Home: Ask your child to name each color.

Unit 2: Friends • Week 2

Activity Book, page 6

Objectives

- Orally blend sounds in words with /s/ and /a/
- Identify the common sounds that letters represent
- Blend sounds in words with /s/s
- Blend sounds in words with short /a/a, /m/m

Materials

- Puppet
- Word-Building Cards
- pocket chart

Phonemic Awareness

Phoneme Blending

Model

Use the **Puppet** to model how to blend the word *Sam*.

Repeat the same routine with *sap* and *sit*.

Happy is going to say the sounds in a word. Listen to Happy as he says each sound: /s/ /a/ /m/. Happy can blend these sounds together: /sssaaammm/, *Sam*. Say the sounds with Happy: /s/ /a/ /m/, /sssaaammm/. Now say the word with Happy: *Sam*.

Guided Practice/Practice

Have the Puppet say the sounds. Children blend them to form words. Guide practice with the first word, using the same routine.

Happy is going to say the sounds in a word. Listen carefully to Happy as he says each sound. You repeat the sounds, and then blend them.

/s/ /a/ /d/   /m/ /a/ /n/   /k/ /a/ /t/

/m/ /a/ /t/   /k/ /a/ /n/   /s/ /a/ /t/

Phonics

Review /s/s, /m/m, /a/a

	S

Model

Hold up **Word-Building Card** *s*.

Repeat the routine for the letters *m* and *a*.

This is the letter *s*. The letter *s* stands for /sss/. What is the letter? What does this letter stand for?

Say the word. Write the letter. Repeat with *map* and *ant*.

Listen as I say the word: *sun*. The letter *s* stands for the /sss/ sound. I'll write *s*.

Guided Practice/Practice

Children write the letter that stands for the beginning sound. Do the first word with children.

Listen as I say a word. Write the letter that stands for the beginning sound.

seal	ant	mix	sip	sun	at
ax	soup	man	apple	mop	see

Build Fluency: Sound-Spellings

 Display the following **Word-Building Cards**: *a, m, s*. Have children chorally say each sound. Repeat and vary the pace.

✔ Blend with /s/s

Model

Place Word-Building Card *S* in the pocket chart.	This letter is capital *S*. The letter *s* stands for the /s/ sound. Say /s/.
Place Word-Building Card *a* next to *S*. Move your hand from left to right.	This is the letter *a*. The letter *a* stands for the /a/ sound. Listen as I blend the two sounds together: /sssaaa/. Now you blend the sounds with me: /sssaaa/.
Place Word-Building Card *m* next to *Sa*. Move your hand from left to right.	This is the letter *m*. This stands for the /m/ sound. Listen as I blend the three sounds together: /sssaaammm/. What is the word? (/sssaaammm/, *Sam*)

Repeat the routine with the word *am*.

Guided Practice/Practice

Children blend sounds to form words. Guide practice using the routine.	Sam am

For Tier 2 instruction, see page 317.

For Tier 2 instruction, see page 317.

ELL

Reinforce Meaning Review the following words: *mom, map, soap, sun, am*, and *apple*. Model saying each word and ask children to repeat. Have them explain what each word means by pointing to pictures or real objects, acting out, or paraphrasing.

Objectives

- Read the high-frequency words *we, the, can, I*
- Make predictions based upon cover, title, and illustrations
- Demonstrate proper book handling
- Reread for fluency

Materials

- Pre-decodable Reader: *I Like*
- High-Frequency Word Cards: *can, I, the, we*
- pocket chart

Pre-decodable Reader

Read *I Like*

Pre-Decodable Reader

I Like
by Lila Torres • illustrated by Miriam Sagasti

Sight Word Practice

I Like

 SPIRAL REVIEW **REVIEW HIGH-FREQUENCY WORDS** Display **High-Frequency Word Cards** for **I**, **can**, **we**, and **the** in the pocket chart. Review the words using the **Read/Spell/Write** routine.

MODEL CONCEPTS ABOUT PRINT Demonstrate book handling. Guide children to follow along with their books. *I hold the book so that the cover is on the front and the words are not upside down. I open the book by turning the cover. Then I turn each page as I read it.*

PREDICT Read the title. Look at the illustration. Ask children what they think the girl on the cover might like at the beach.

FIRST READ Point out the rebus and discuss what it stands for. Have children point to each word, saying the sight words quickly. Have children chorally read the story the first time through.

DEVELOP COMPREHENSION Ask the following:

- *Look at pages 3 and 4. What do the girl and boy like to play with?* (sand, sailboat)

 PARTNERS **SECOND READ** Have partners reread the book together. Circulate, listen in, and provide corrective feedback.

I like the 〰 .
beach
2

I like the 〰 .
sand
3

I like the ⛵ .
sailboat
4

I like the ☀ .
sun
5

I like the ☂ .
umbrella
6

I like the 🥪 .
sandwich
7

I like Saturday.
8

Pre-decodable Reader

Writing

Interactive Writing: Sentences

REVIEW

- Display and read aloud the lists that children created for the Shared Writing activity.

WRITE

- Tell children that today you are going to write sentences together about **favorite** things the boy and girl like.

- Collaborate with them to write the sentence frames on chart paper one word at a time.

> The boy likes _____.
> The girl likes _____.

- Have children suggest words to complete each sentence, using the lists of things the boy and girl like. Write the names of the objects in the frames to complete the sentences.

- Have children help by writing all of the letters they know.

- Read the completed sentences together as you track the print.

- To extend the lesson, have children select an illustration from *What Do You Like?*, such as the birds flying out of the piano, and dictate a class story about it. Guide children to check that the sentences make sense and are in chronological order.

Write About It

Have children draw a picture of a fruit they like to eat. Guide them to use the high-frequency words *we* and *the* in writing or to dictate a caption for their pictures. *We like the _____.*

Objectives

- **Write complete simple sentences**
- **Use letter knowledge to write letters in a word**

Materials

- Shared Writing lists from Day 1

5-Day Writing

	Sentences
DAY 1	Shared: Lists
DAY 2	Interactive: Sentences
DAY 3	Independent: Prewrite and Draft Sentences
DAY 4	Independent: Revise and Edit Sentences
DAY 5	Independent: Publish and Present

ELL

Use New Language Help children write a story about what the class likes to do. Have them dictate the story for you to write down. Guide them to add details: *When do we like to sing? What do we sing?*

Transitions That Teach

While lining up, have children tell ways to be a good **friend**.

Oral Language
- Build Robust Vocabulary
- Oral Vocabulary Cards: "Games Around the World"

✓ **Comprehension**
- Read "Friends Follow Rules"
- Text Feature: Use Photographs

✓ **High-Frequency Words**
- Review *like*

✓ **Phonemic Awareness**
- Phoneme Isolation

✓ **Phonics**
- Review /s/s
- Blend with /s/s
- Read Words

Grammar
- Naming Words (Nouns)

Writing
- Independent Writing: Prewrite and Draft Sentences

SMALL GROUP

- Differentiated Instruction, pages 310–335

Additional Vocabulary

To provide 15–20 minutes of additional vocabulary instruction, see Oral Vocabulary Cards 5-Day Plan. The pre- and posttests for this week can be found in the **Teacher's Resource Book**, pages 216–217.

Oral Language

Build Robust Vocabulary

BUILD BACKGROUND

Introduce the story "Games Around the World" using **Oral Vocabulary Card 1** and read the title aloud. *What is your favorite game? Do you play games with your friends?* Ask children to tell what they think is happening in the picture.

■ Read the selection on the cards. You may wish to check children's understanding using the Relate to Personal Experience, Compare and Contrast, and Compose Sentences prompts. Pause at each oral vocabulary word and read the definition.

Oral Vocabulary Cards

Vocabulary Routine

Use the routine below to discuss the meaning of each word.

<u>Define:</u> A **partner** is someone who works together with you. Say the word with me.
<u>Example:</u> You may need a partner to hold down a ribbon while you tie a bow.
<u>Ask:</u> What games do you play with a partner? What games do you play alone?

<u>Define:</u> A **hobby** is an activity you enjoy doing in your free time. Say the word with me.
<u>Example:</u> Building model boats is a popular hobby.
<u>Ask:</u> Which is a hobby: doing homework or making paper dolls?

<u>Define:</u> When you **compete**, you try to do something better than other people. Say the word with me.
<u>Example:</u> Runners compete to see who will win the race.
<u>Ask:</u> What game or sport do you like to compete in?

■ Use the routine on Cards 1 and 3 to review the words **favorite** and **friend**.

■ Review last week's words: *celebrate, change, eager, occasion, relative.*

Listen for Rhyme

IDENTIFY RHYME

Tell children that they will sing another song about friends. Play the rhyme and have children join in. Explain that the word *fun* rhymes with *run* because *fun* and *run* both end in *-un*. Then guide children to name which two of the following words rhyme: *see, be, friend*. (*see, be*)

Be a Friend

If you want to be a friend,
Be a friend.
If you want to see a smile,
Be a smile.
If you want to have fun
With each and every one,
Be a friend, be a friend,
Be a friend.

Objectives

- Discuss the theme
- Recognize rhyme
- Use oral vocabulary words *compete, favorite, friend, hobby,* and *partner*
- Listen and respond to a nonfiction selection

Materials

- Oral Vocabulary Cards: "Games Around the World"

Digital Learning

Song on **Listening Library Audio CD**

Objectives

- Retell important facts
- Use photographs to find information
- Identify the topic and details in expository text
- Discuss rules for school and home

Materials

- Big Book of Explorations, Vol. 1: "Friends Follow Rules," pp. 23–25
- drawing paper

Content Vocabulary

fair acting in a way that is right for everyone
rule a statement that tells people how to act

Inside and Outside Voices

Point out the importance of using an inside voice in places such as the school library, where being quiet is important. Point out that an outside voice is used in places such as the playground. Ask children to give examples of other places where they might use an inside voice or an outside voice.

Social Studies Informational Text

Genre

Big Book of Explorations

INFORMATIONAL TEXT: EXPOSITORY Tell children that this selection is **expository** text, a text that explains or gives information. Some expository text gives information using words and photographs. Tell children that sometimes photographs can give more information than words can.

READ "FRIENDS FOLLOW RULES"

- **Preview and Predict** Display the first page and read the title as you track the print. To build background, point to your classroom rules chart, and remind children what it contains. *What is a rule that we follow in school?* Show children the photographs in the selection. *What do you think this selection will be about?*

- **Content Vocabulary** Introduce and discuss the vocabulary words.

- **Text Feature: Photographs** *Photographs tell a reader that the book is about real people, places, or things.* Point to the children playing soccer. *This photograph shows real children doing something together. What are these children doing?*

CONTENT FOCUS

As you read page 23, ask children to tell what they think it means to "play fair." Ask children what might happen if someone doesn't follow the rules when playing with friends.

Point to the top picture on page 24 and ask children what it shows. *Why is it important to follow the rule about taking turns?* Ask children to describe ways that they take turns at home, at school, and when playing with friends.

Read aloud the bottom of page 24 and point to the photograph. *Where are these children?* (at school) *What rule are these children following?* (share) *Why are these friends sharing a book?* (They both want to read it.) Discuss what children learned from these two pages. *Why is it important to follow rules?*

page 23   **pages 24–25**

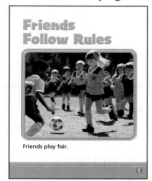

Retell and Respond

- *What is the topic, or main idea, of this selection?*

- *Tell one important rule that you learned.*

- *Explain why it is important to follow rules at school. Why is it important for friends to follow rules?*

- *What rule tells us how to treat others?*

Connect to Content

Social Studies: Class Rules Book

- Review the rules that friends follow to get along and stay safe.

- Have children draw pictures of themselves following a rule that they read in the selection.

- Help children label their pictures.

- Collect children's pictures and bind them into a class book titled "We Follow Rules."

ELL

Beginning

Introduce Rules Model classroom rules, such as *Sit down* or *Please be quiet*. Say the words as you act them out. Have children repeat the words as they repeat the actions.

Intermediate

Discuss Rules Talk about the rules that friends follow. Ask questions about each rule on pages 23 and 24. *When do friends play fair? How do friends take turns? How do friends share?*

Advanced

Understand Rules Have children discuss why friends need to follow rules. *Why is it important to play fair? What happens if friends do not take turns? How do you feel if your friend does not share?*

Objective

- Read the high-frequency word *like*

Materials

- High-Frequency Word Cards: *can, I, like, the, we*
- Photo Cards: *berries, blue, soup*
- index card with: period mark
- pocket chart
- High-Frequency Word Cards; Teacher's Resource Book, pp. 103–110
- Activity Book, pp. 7–8
- Practice Book, pp. 43–44

Activity Book, pages 7–8
Practice Book, pages 43–44

High-Frequency Words

 *like*

REVIEW Display the **High-Frequency Word Card** for **like**. Review the word using the **Read/Spell/Write** routine.

Repeat the routine for **I**, **can**, **we**, and **the**.

PRACTICE Build sentences in the pocket chart using High-Frequency Word Cards and **Photo Cards**. Read each sentence aloud, then have children chorally read it as you track the print with your finger. Use the sentence below and the following: *We like blue. I like the berries.*

| I | like | the | | . |

APPLY Distribute copies of High-Frequency Word Cards *we* and *like*. Have children take turns saying a sentence using the words.

READ FOR FLUENCY Have children use the Take-Home Book to review high-frequency words and practice fluency.

Quick Check

Can children read the word *like*?

During **Small Group Instruction**

If No → **Approaching Level** Provide additional practice, page 320.

If Yes → **On Level** Children may read the Take-Home Book.

Beyond Level Children may read the Take-Home Book.

TIME TO MOVE!

Say: *We like to jump.* Ask five children to take one jump. Say: *We like to hop.* Ask five children to hop twice. Say: *We like to take giant steps.* Ask five children to take three giant steps. Continue until all children have had a turn.

Phonemic Awareness

Phoneme Isolation

Objective

- Identify initial and final /s/ in words

Materials

- Sound Box
- WorkBoard Sound Boxes; Teacher's Resource Book, p. 136
- markers

Model

Use the **Sound Box**.

Place a marker in the first box as you say the initial /s/ sound in *sun*.

Listen for the beginning sound in *sun*. *Sun* has /sss/ at the beginning. Say the sound. (/s/) I'll put a marker in the first box to show that I hear the /s/ sound at the beginning of *sun*.

Place a marker in the last box as you say the final /s/ sound in *bus*. Repeat the routine with the words *seal* and *yes*.

Now listen as I say a new word: *bus*. (Clearly enunciate and emphasize the ending sound.) I can hear the /s/ sound at the end of the word *bus*. I'll put a marker in the last box to show that I heard the /s/ sound at the end of *bus*.

Guided Practice/Practice

Distribute Sound Boxes and markers. Children use the Sound Boxes to show where they hear /s/. Guide practice with the first word.

Say each word with me. If you hear /s/ at the beginning, place a marker in the first box. If you hear /s/ at the end, place a marker in the last box.

| side | yes | sale | sack | less | soap |
| sock | sun | gas | pass | set | suit |

For Tier 2 instruction, see page 320.

Objectives

- Match the letter *s* to the /s/ sound
- Identify /s/s in words and sentences

Materials

- Word-Building Cards
- pocket chart

Phonics

 ## Review /s/s

S

Model

Display **Word-Building Cards**.

This is the letter *s*. The letter *s* stands for the /s/ sound you hear at the beginning of *sun*. I will say a word: *sat*. The word *sat* has /s/ at the beginning. Watch as I write the word: *s-a-t*. The word *sat* begins with the letter *s* because *sat* has the /s/ sound at the beginning.

Guided Practice/Practice

Children point to the letter *s* if /s/ is the initial sound in a word. Guide practice with the first two words. Repeat for final *s*.

Now I am going to say a word. Point to the letter *s* if you hear the /s/ sound at the beginning of the word.

sock	gas	bus	sad	sun
yes	soap	soup	miss	sat

Build Fluency: Sound-Spellings

 Display the following Word-Building Cards: *a, m, s*. Have children chorally say each sound. Repeat and vary the pace.

Blend with /s/s

Model

Place **Word-Building Card** *S* in the pocket chart.

This letter is capital *S*. It stands for /s/. Say /s/.

Place Word-Building Card *a* next to *S*. Move your hand from left to right.

This letter is *a*. It stands for /a/. Listen as I blend the two sounds together: /sssaaa/. Now you say it. (/sssaaa/)

Place Word-Building Card *m* next to *Sa*. Move your hand from left to right.

Repeat with *am*.

The letter is *m*. It stands for /m/. Listen as I blend the three sounds together: /sssaaammm/. Now you say it. (/sssaaammm/)

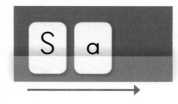

Guided Practice/Practice

Children blend with /s/.   Sam   am

Read Words

Apply

Write the words and sentences. Guide practice with *am*, using the blending routine.

Read the sentences with children.

> am   Sam
> I like Sam.
> We like Sam.

Corrective Feedback

Blending: Sound Error Model the sound that children missed, then have them repeat the sound. For example, for the word *Sam*, say: *My turn.* Tap under the letter *S* in the word *Sam* and say: *Sound? What's the sound?* Then return to the beginning of the word. Say: *Let's start over.* Blend the word with children again.

For Tier 2 instruction, see page 321.

Objective

- Understand and use naming words (nouns)

Materials

- Big Book: *What Do You Like?*
- Photo Cards: *alligator, bear, camel, deer, fox, koala*

ELL

Basic and Academic Language Display the Photo Cards from the lesson and pair English Language Learners with fluent English speakers. Have partners make up sentences about the animals pictured on the cards. Write their sentences, read them with the children, and say: *Tell me the word in your sentence that names the animal. This word is a naming word or noun.*

Grammar

Naming Words (Nouns)

MODEL Remind children that naming words tell the names of people, animals, places, and things. Use the **Big Book** *What Do You Like?* to review naming words. Point to the illustrations as you say these words: *cat, tiger, birds, snake.* Explain that all these words name animals.

- Use *cat, tiger, birds*, and *snake* to start a list. Have children tell other animal names. Add their ideas to the list. Point out that these words name animals, too.

- Say sentences using the animal names from the list. Have children repeat the sentence. Help them identify the naming word. Use these sentences and others: *The* cat *walks. The* tiger *leaps.*

PRACTICE Show **Photo Cards** for *alligator, bear, camel, deer, fox,* and *koala*. Help children identify each picture name. Model saying sentences about each of the animals in the pictures, such as:

- *The* alligator *is quiet.*

- *I see a* bear.

After each sentence, ask children which word names the animal.

Then have children make up their own sentences using the animals shown on the Photo Cards. Guide children to use complete sentences.

Writing

Independent Writing: Sentences

Display the sentences that children created for the Interactive Writing activity.

BRAINSTORM
Tell children that today they will write their own sentences about things that they like. Ask children to work in pairs to think of and then tell the class some of their **favorite** things.

PREWRITE
On the board or drawing paper, write the sentence frame *I like* _____. Then write a word in the frame to complete the sentence.

- Share your sentence with children and track the print as you read it.

- Ask children to pick a favorite thing and draw a picture of it.

DRAFT
- Have children write the sentence frame *I like* _____. under their pictures and help them complete the sentence by writing the name of an object.

I like apples.

Write About It

Ask children to draw a picture of an activity they like to do indoors. Help them to write a caption for their drawing.

Objectives
- Plan and draft writing
- Use letter knowledge to write letters in a word
- Draw a picture

Materials
- Interactive Writing sentences from Day 2

5-Day Writing

Sentences	
DAY 1	Shared: Lists
DAY 2	Interactive: Sentences
DAY 3	Independent: Prewrite and Draft Sentences
DAY 4	Independent: Revise and Edit Sentences
DAY 5	Independent: Publish and Present

Transitions That Teach

While packing up to go home, have children name games in which players **compete**.

DAY 4
At a Glance

WHOLE GROUP

Oral Language
- Build Robust Vocabulary

Comprehension
- Read Aloud: "The City Mouse and the Country Mouse"

Vocabulary
- Color Words
- Story Word: *rainbow*

Phonemic Awareness
- Phoneme Categorization

Phonics
- Picture Sort: /s/s, /m/m, /a/a
- Blend with /s/s
- Pre-decodable Reader: *We Like Sam!*

Writing
- Independent Writing: Revise and Edit Sentences

SMALL GROUP

- Differentiated Instruction, pages 310–335

Oral Language

Talk About It **Build Robust Vocabulary**

OPPOSITES

Talk about what opposites are. *Opposites are things that are completely different from one another.* Hot *is the opposite of* cold.

- Show children something that is big (your chair) and something that is small (a child's chair). Have children share ideas with a **partner** of their **favorite** small and big toys.

CREATE A CHART Draw a chart like the one shown or use **Teaching Chart G3**. Write the heading and read the word aloud.

Think Aloud We said that a chair is big, so I will write *big*. The opposite of *big* is *small*, so I will write *small*. A big city can be noisy, so I will write *noisy*. What is the opposite of *noisy*?

Have children suggest other opposites to add to the chart. Guide them to use words and concepts that will be introduced in "The City Mouse and the Country Mouse." Say opposite pairs and have children repeat several times.

Opposites	
big	small
noisy	quiet
city	country
cold	hot
summer	winter

ELL ENGLISH LANGUAGE LEARNERS

Beginning	**Intermediate**	**Advanced**
Confirm Understanding Ask either/or questions such as *Is an elephant big or small?* (big) Elaborate: *Yes, an elephant is big. Is it cold in winter or in summer?* (winter) Elaborate: *Yes, it is cold in winter.* Use gestures to facilitate understanding.	**Questions and Answers** Ask questions about opposites, such as: *Is cold* the opposite *of hot? What is* the opposite *of noisy? What is the* opposite *of city?* Tell children to play a game in which they ask partners questions about opposites.	**Share Information** Ask children personal questions: *What do you wear when it's* hot? *What do you wear when it's* cold? *Do you have a pet? What size is it?*

Listen for Rhyme

IDENTIFY RHYME

Remind children that words rhyme when they have the same ending sounds. *The word* hill *rhymes with* Jill. Tell children *hill* and *Jill* end with the sounds /iiilll/, *ill*. Have children orally generate rhymes in response to the spoken words *hill* and *Jill*.

RHYME ABOUT FRIENDS

Tell children that they will say "Two Little Blackbirds," the rhyme they learned about two friends, the little blackbirds. *The two friends like to sit together and then fly away together. They like to spend time with each other.* Play the recording and have children join in. Guide children to use the hand movements to show what is happening in the rhyme. Then have children discuss what friends can do together to have fun.

Two Little Blackbirds

Two little blackbirds sitting on a hill.

Two hands closed with thumbs up.

One named Jack, one named Jill.

Bounce one hand, then the other.

Fly away, Jack. Fly away, Jill.

Right hand is open, raised above head, then same with left.

Come back, Jack. Come back, Jill.

Right hand and left back to original position.

Objectives

- Discuss the theme
- Develop oral language by discussing opposites
- Complete a chart
- Use oral vocabulary words *compete, favorite, friend, hobby,* and *partner*
- Orally generate rhymes

Materials

- Graphic Organizer; Teaching Chart G3

Oral Vocabulary

Have children use each word in a sentence about this week's stories.

compete	favorite	friend
hobby	partner	

Review Work with children to review last week's words. Provide a sentence starter for children to repeat and complete, such as: *I _____ with my family.*

celebrate	change	eager
occasion	relative	

Digital Learning

Rhyme on **Listening Library Audio CD**

Objectives

- Listen and respond to a story
- Retell a main event from a story read aloud
- Discuss the big idea of a fable

Materials

- Read-Aloud Anthology: "The City Mouse and the Country Mouse," pp. 33–36
- Story Patterns; Teacher's Resource Book, pp. 171–198

ELL

Develop Vocabulary Tell children that a *feast* is a big meal with specials foods. *Do you have feasts in your house?* Explain that a *pantry* is a place to keep food. Say that a mouse might keep food in its *pantry*. Have children echo the word *cheese*. Say that a mouse might like to eat *cheese*.

Readers Theater

BUILDING LISTENING AND SPEAKING SKILLS
Distribute copies of "Who Helped the Lion?" Read-Aloud Anthology pages 160–162. Have children practice performing the play throughout the unit. Assign parts and have children present the play or perform it as a dramatic reading at the end of the unit.

Interactive Read Aloud

Listening Comprehension

Read Aloud

GENRE: LITERARY TEXT/FICTION

Tell children that today we are going to read fiction. *One type of fiction is a* **fable**. *A fable is a tale that has been told and retold aloud for many, many years.* Remind children of other fables they have read ("The Little Red Hen," "The Clever Turtle"). *What were the lessons we learned?*

CULTURAL PERSPECTIVES

Tell children that "The City Mouse and the Country Mouse" was told by a storyteller named Aesop, who told stories many years ago.

READ "THE CITY MOUSE AND THE COUNTRY MOUSE"

- **MODEL ASKING QUESTIONS** Use the Think Alouds provided at point of use in the fable for the strategy.

- **MODEL FLUENT READING** Have children listen as you read aloud the fable with fluent expression. Stop occasionally so that children can predict what will happen next and ask any questions they have about the story elements.

- **EXPAND VOCABULARY** See page 33 of the **Read-Aloud Anthology** to teach new words.

Respond to Literature

TALK ABOUT IT Ask children to retell a main event from the fable.

- *Who were the characters? Where did the story take place?*

- *Why did the two characters view the story events differently?*

- *Can the country mouse and the city mouse be* **friends** *even though they don't like each other's homes? Why or why not?*

- Provide another version of the fable. Guide children to compare the two versions. Guide them to retell the main events.

Write About It

Have children draw their favorite character. Have children dictate or write a caption.

Vocabulary

Color Words

REVIEW COLORS

Display the pocket chart with the squares of colored paper. Ask a child to point to each square and say the color word.

Give each child a square of colored paper. *When I say a color word, if you have that color, hold it up.*

Read the following story:

> *One morning Alice put on her* blue *coat and waited for the school bus. Soon the* yellow *school bus pulled up. Alice waved to Jack, who was wearing his* purple *and* green *jacket. Jack said, "I brought a* red *apple to eat at snack time today." Alice replied, "I brought an* orange *orange!" They laughed.*

Give pairs a picture of an object of a single color. Have them identify the name of the color and place it under the correct color square in the pocket chart.

Story Word: *rainbow*

Display pages 4–5 of the **Big Book** *What Do You Like?* Ask children what colors they see in the rainbow.

Have them describe the colors in other rainbows they have seen.

REVIEW COMPOUND WORDS Ask children to identify the two smaller words that make up the word *rainbow*.

TIME TO MOVE!

Tell children who are wearing blue shoes to walk to the sink. Count how many children are wearing blue shoes. Continue with different colors. Have children take turns giving simple directions using color words.

Objectives

- Identify and use color words
- Review story word *rainbow*
- Review compound words

Materials

- pocket chart
- squares of colored paper (red, yellow, blue, green, orange, and purple)
- pictures of colored objects (red, yellow, blue, green, orange, and purple)
- Big Book: *What Do You Like?*

ELL

Reinforce Vocabulary
Point to items of clothing you and the children are wearing. Name the items and their color. For example: *blue shirt*. Then ask the child wearing the shirt: *What color is your shirt?*

Objectives

- Categorize words with initial /s/, /m/, /a/ sounds
- Identify the letter that stands for initial sounds in words
- Use letter-sound relationships to read words

Materials

- Puppet
- Word-Building Cards
- pocket chart
- Photo Cards: *ant, astronaut, man, map, mouse, saw, seal, sock*
- Activity Book, p. 10
- Practice Book, p. 46

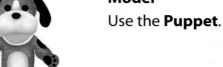

Phonemic Awareness

Phoneme Categorization

Model

Use the **Puppet**.

Happy will say three words. Two words begin with /s/, and one does not: *soup, moon, silly.* (Emphasize and extend the beginning sounds.) *Soup* and *silly* begin with /s/. The word *moon* doesn't belong. It does not begin with /s/.

Repeat with *soap, tear,* and *sock*.

Guided Practice/Practice

Children categorize words with /s/. Guide practice with the first row, using the routine.

Which word does not belong?

soft, mix, seed	mop, sand, same
sit, sock, mother	you, mat, me
met, sack, sip	son, take, sew

Phonics

Picture Sort

S

Model

Place **Word-Building Card** *s* in the pocket chart.

This is the letter *s*. The sound for this letter is /s/.

Follow the routine for *m* and *a*.

This is the letter *m*. The sound for this letter is /m/.

Hold up the **Photo Card** for *map*.

Here is the picture of a map. *Map* begins with /m/. (Emphasize the initial sound as you repeat the word.) I will place *map* under the letter *m*.

Repeat with *saw*.

Guided Practice/Practice

Children sort the Photo Cards. Guide practice with the first card, using the routine.

Build Fluency: Sound-Spellings

 SPIRAL REVIEW Display the following **Word-Building Cards**: *a, m, s*. Have children chorally say each sound. Repeat and vary the pace.

Blend with /s/s

Model

Place Word-Building Card *S* in the pocket chart.

This letter is capital *S*. It stands for the /s/ sound. Say /s/.

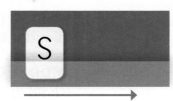

Place Word-Building Card *a* next to *S*. Move your hand from left to right.

This letter is *a*. It stands for /a/. Listen as I blend the two sounds together: /sssaaa/. Now blend the sounds with me. (/sssaaa/)

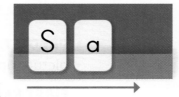

Place Word-Building Card *m* next to *Sa*. Move your hand from left to right.

Repeat the routine with *am*.

This letter is *m*. It stands for /m/. Listen as I blend the three sounds together: /sssaaammm/. What is the word? (/sssaaammm/, *Sam*)

Guided Practice/Practice

Children blend sounds to form words. Guide practice as needed.

Sam   am

Corrective Feedback

Blending: Sound Error Model the sound that children missed, then have them repeat the sound. For example, for the word *Sam*, say: *My turn.* Tap under the letter *S* in the word *Sam* and say: *Sound? What's the sound?* Then return to the beginning of the word. Say: *Let's start over.* Blend the word with children again.

For Tier 2 instruction, see page 324.

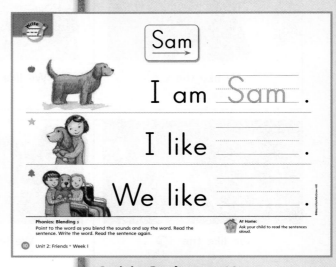

Activity Book, page 10
Practice Book, page 46

Objectives

- Read decodable words with /s/s
- Read the high-frequency word *like*
- Review the high-frequency words *we* and *I*

Materials

- Pre-decodable Reader: *We Like Sam!*
- High-Frequency Word Cards: *I, like, we*
- pocket chart

Pre-decodable Reader

Read *We Like Sam!*

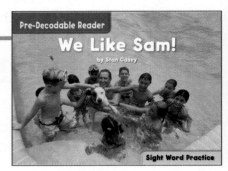

We Like Sam!

 REVIEW Display **High-Frequency Word Cards** for **we**, **I**, and **like** in the pocket chart. Say each word. Have children repeat. Spell each word aloud with children.

MODEL CONCEPTS ABOUT PRINT *I hold the book so that the cover is on the front and the words are not upside down. I open the book by turning the cover. I turn each page as I read it.*

PREDICT Ask children to try to figure out who Sam is, based on the picture on the front cover. Ask them to tell why they think that.

FIRST READ Have children point to each word and say the high-frequency words quickly. If children have difficulty with a word, help them to use picture clues, initial sounds, and word meaning.

DEVELOP COMPREHENSION Ask the following questions, guiding children to respond in complete sentences:

- *What are some of the things the children like?*

- *Who does everyone like?* (Sam)

 SECOND READ Children reread the book to a partner for fluency.

We like the ☀.
sun
2

We like the 〰.
sand
3

We like the ⛵ .
sailboat
4

We like the 🧼.
soap
5

We like the ⚽ .
soccer ball
6

We like the 🥪.
sandwich
7

We like Sam!
8

Pre-decodable Reader

Writing

Independent Writing: Sentences

REVISE AND EDIT

Distribute children's draft sentences. Have them review their pictures and reread the labels, checking for the following:

■ Does my sentence tell what I like?

■ Are the words in the right order?

■ Did I draw a picture of my **favorite** things?

■ Did I write my name at the top of my paper?

■ Did I leave spaces between the words?

Circulate and help children as they review and revise their sentences and check for punctuation. Have children share their sentences with partners. Guide children to revise based on partner and teacher feedback. Suggest that they add details as appropriate. In the sample shown below, Mia may add the color of the apples to her writing: *I like red apples.*

Write About It

Have children draw a picture of something they like. Have children dictate or write a caption about why they like it.

Objectives

- Revise and edit sentences
- Use letter knowledge to write letters in a word

Materials

- children's sentences from Day 3
- Writer's Checklist; Teacher's Resource Book, p. 205

5-Day Writing

Sentences	
DAY 1	Shared: Lists
DAY 2	Interactive: Sentences
DAY 3	Independent: Prewrite and Draft Sentences
DAY 4	Independent: Revise and Edit Sentences
DAY 5	Independent: Publish and Present

ELL

Use New Language Help children elaborate on a description of something they like. Write it down and read it together.

Transitions That Teach

While children line up, have them tell about a **hobby** that they like to do when they have time.

DAY 5
At a Glance

WHOLE GROUP

Oral Language
- Build Robust Vocabulary

✔ **Comprehension**
- Strategy: Ask Questions
- Skill: Identify Character
- Read Across Texts

✔ **Vocabulary**
- Review High-Frequency Words
- Build Fluency
- Color Words

✔ **Phonemic Awareness**
- Phoneme Categorization

✔ **Phonics**
- Read Words
- Dictation

Writing
- Independent Writing: Publish and Present

SMALL GROUP

- Differentiated Instruction, pages 310–335

Review and Assess
Oral Language
Build Robust Vocabulary

REVIEW WORDS

Review this week's oral vocabulary words with children. Explain that all of the words will be used to discuss playing catch. Talk about what it means to play catch. *Playing catch is a game where two people throw a ball to each other. They can use a baseball and wear a baseball glove.*

Use the following questions to check children's understanding:

- What is your **favorite** type of ball to use when playing catch?

- Where might a **friend** like to play catch with you? Why?

- Would someone like to have a **partner** to play catch with or play alone? Why?

- Do you think that collecting baseball gloves and playing catch with them is a good **hobby**? Why or why not?

- Do people like to **compete** while playing catch? Why or why not?

REVIEW SONGS AND RHYMES ABOUT FRIENDS

Say the rhyme "Two Little Blackbirds" and have children join in. Then sing the song "Be a Friend" with children. Have them discuss what it means to be a friend. Then have children generate rhymes in response to each of the following spoken words: *hill, fun, see.*

Review and Assess
Comprehension

STRATEGY Ask Questions

REFLECT ON THE STRATEGY Remind children that they have learned how to ask questions about the stories they have read. *Sometimes we ask questions about the characters to learn more about the story.* Have children ask questions they still have about the story.

> **Think Aloud** I can use the answers to some of these questions to compare two of our **favorite** stories we read this week.

SKILL Identify Character

Have children discuss the characters in the fiction selection *What Do You Like?* and "The City Mouse and the Country Mouse."

- *In* What Do You Like? *did the characters always like the same things?*

- *Did the **friends** in "The City Mouse and the Country Mouse" like the same things?*

- *In* What Do You Like? *the boy rides a tiger and flies an airplane. If the boy asked one of the mice to join him, which mouse might decide to go—the City Mouse or the Country Mouse? Why?*

- *How are the characters similar to your favorite characters from other books, films (movies), or television?*

Reading Across Texts

Discuss that the purpose for listening to various texts is sometimes to become involved in real or imagined events. Explain that good readers sometimes think about how one story is like—or not like—another story.

Create a chart like the one shown to compare the fiction text *What Do You Like?* and the expository text "Games Around the World." You can add information about "The City Mouse and the Country Mouse" as well. Have children draw pictures or write sentences to compare the characters in the selections.

What Do You Like?	Games Around the World
drawings	photographs
make-believe story	real story: expository
two friends	many different friends

Objectives

- Review the strategy and skill
- Compare and contrast genres, stories, and characters
- Listen and share information
- Discuss purpose for listening to various texts

Materials

- Big Book: *What Do You Like?*
- Oral Vocabulary Cards: "Games Around the World"
- Read-Aloud Anthology: "The City Mouse and the Country Mouse," pp. 33–36
- Activity Book, p. 11

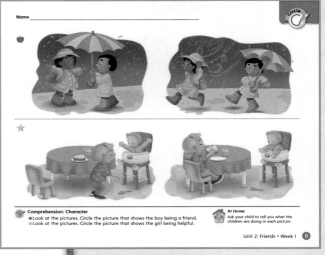

Activity Book, page 11

Objectives

- Review the high-frequency words *like, the, we, I, can*
- Review color words
- Build fluency
- Use oral vocabulary words *compete, favorite, friend, hobby,* and *partner*

Materials

- High-Frequency Word Cards: *can, I, like, the, we*
- High-Frequency Word Cards; Teacher's Resource book, pp. 103–110
- pocket chart
- squares of colored paper (red, yellow, blue, green, orange, and purple)
- classroom pictures of objects of various colors

Fluency

Connected Text Have children reread this week's **Pre-decodable Readers** with a partner. Circulate, listen in, and note those children who need additional instruction and practice reading this week's decodable and sight words.

Review and Assess
Vocabulary

 ## High-Frequency Words

Distribute one of the following **High-Frequency Word Cards** to children: **like**, **the**, **we**, **I**, and **can**. Say: *When you hear the word that is on your card, stand and hold up your Word Card.*

- *Do you* like *bananas?*
- The *puppy is cute.*
- We *read every day.*
- I *get up early each morning.*
- Can *you find my **favorite** blue sweater?*

Build Fluency: Word Automaticity

Rapid Naming Display the High-Frequency Word Cards *like, the, we, I,* and *can.* Point quickly to each card, at random, and have children read the word as fast as they can.

like	the	we	I	can

Color Words

Display the pocket chart with squares of colored paper and say each color word with children. Repeat several times. Under each paper square have children sort pictures by color.

- Ask children to look for something *yellow* and *purple* in the classroom.

TIME TO MOVE!

Ask each child to do a movement for the following phrase: *I can _____.* (Example: *I can clap, bow, and tap.*)

Review and Assess
Phonemic Awareness

 ## Phoneme Categorization

Guided Practice

Display the **Photo Cards** for *seal, ant*, and *soap*.

I will say the three picture names. Two picture names begin with the same sound, and one does not. Listen to the picture names: *seal, ant, soap*. (Emphasize the initial sound.) *Seal* and *soap* begin with the same sound, /s/. *Ant* does not begin with the /s/ sound. It does not belong.

Practice

Children identify the picture name that does not begin with the same sound.

Use these sets of cards: *mouse, man, astronaut; six, ant, sock; saw, map, moon*.

I will show you three cards. Tell me which picture name does not begin with the same sound.

Teacher's Notes

Isolating medial sounds is difficult for most children early in the year. Children can generally isolate initial sounds first, then ending sounds, and finally medial sounds. Therefore, do not expect mastery of this skill. These lessons are designed to get children ready to blend CVC words in upcoming lessons.

Objectives

- Review sound-spellings for /s/s, /m/m, /a/a
- Read simple one-syllable words

Materials

- Word-Building Cards
- pocket chart
- 4 index cards: with *I, am, Sam,* period mark
- 4 index cards with: *We, like, Sam,* period mark
- Sound Boxes
- markers
- WorkBoard Sound Boxes; Teacher's Resource Book, p. 136
- Activity Book, p. 12

Activity Book, page 12

Review and Assess
Phonics

Build Fluency: Sound-Spellings

Rapid Naming Display the following **Word-Building Cards**: *a, m, s.* Have children chorally say each sound. Repeat and vary the pace.

 ## Read Words

Apply

Distribute the first set of cards. Have children stand in sequence.	Let's read the sentence together. *I am Sam.*
Repeat, using the other set of index cards.	Let's read the sentence together. *We like Sam.*

 ## Dictation

Dictate the following sounds for children to write.	Listen as I say a sound. Repeat the sound, then write the letter that stands for the sound. /s/ /m/ /a/
Have children write the letters. Then dictate words for children to spell. Model for children how to use the **Sound Boxes** to segment the word. Have them repeat.	Now let's write some words. I will say a word. I want you to repeat the word, then think about how many sounds are in the word. Use your Sound Boxes to count the sounds. Then write one letter for each sound you hear. am Sam
Write the letters and words on the board for children to self-correct.	

Review and Assess
Writing

Independent Writing: Sentences

PUBLISH

Explain to children that you will gather their sentences to make a class book of **favorites**.

■ Brainstorm ideas for a title, such as "What We Like."

■ Have a few children work on a cover for the book. Write the title on the cover.

■ Make holes along the edges of the cover and the book pages.

■ Bind the pages together with yarn.

PRESENT

Have children take turns reading their sentences to the class and telling what the pictures show.

LISTENING, SPEAKING, AND VIEWING

■ Remind children to speak clearly and to be good listeners by facing the speaker when a classmate is presenting their writing.

■ Praise children for their hard work and place the finished book in the Reading Workstation. Children may wish to add a copy of their work to their Writing Portfolios.

Objectives

- **Publish and present a piece of writing**
- **Speak audibly and clearly when presenting**
- **Listen attentively by facing presenters**

Materials

- **children's writing from Day 4**

5-Day Writing	
Sentences	
DAY 1	Shared: Lists
DAY 2	Interactive: Sentences
DAY 3	Independent: Prewrite and Draft Sentences
DAY 4	Independent: Revise and Edit Sentences
DAY 5	Independent: Publish and Present

Transitions That Teach

While getting ready to leave, have children tell about things that are easier to do when they have **partners**.

Write About It
Tell children to draw a picture of their favorite place. Have them label their drawing.

Approaching Level

Oral Language

Objective Preteach oral vocabulary
Materials • none

THEME WORDS: *friend, favorite*

■ Explain what **friend** and **favorite** mean. *A friend is someone you like very much and enjoy being with. I have many friends at school. If something is your favorite, you like it the most. Spending time with friends is my favorite thing to do.*

■ Ask: *Who are some of your friends? What is your favorite thing to do with friends? What is your favorite thing to do with your family?*

■ Have children use the following sentence frames to generate oral sentences using the words: *I like to have friends because _____.* and *One of my favorite things is _____.*

High-Frequency Words

Objective Preteach high-frequency words
Materials • **High-Frequency Word Cards:** *can, I, like, the, we*

PRETEACH WORD: *like*

■ Display the **High-Frequency Word Card** for **like**.

■ **Read** Point to and say the word *like. This is the word* like. *When you like something, you enjoy it or you are pleased with it. I like having friends.*

■ **Spell** *The word* like *is spelled* l-i-k-e. Have children read and spell *like*.

■ **Write** Finally, have children write the word *like*.

■ Have children work with a partner to make up sentences using the word *like*. Ask them to talk about why they like their friends.

HIGH-FREQUENCY WORDS REVIEW

Display the High-Frequency Word Cards for **I**, **can**, **we**, and **the**, one card at a time, as children chorally read and spell the word. Mix and repeat. Note words children need to review.

Tier **2**

Approaching Level

Phonemic Awareness

Objective Identify initial sound /s/
Materials
- **Photo Cards:** *sandwich, saw, seal, sing, soap, sock, soil, sun*
- **Sound-Spelling Card:** *Sun*

PHONEME ISOLATION

Model

- Display the **Photo Card** for *sun. This is the sun. Listen for the beginning sound in* sun: */sssuuunnn/. Sun begins with /s/. Repeat for seal.*

- Display the *Sun* **Sound-Spelling Card.** Point to the articulation picture. *See how the mouth is partly open. When I say /s/, I place my tongue slightly behind my teeth. I force air over my tongue, past my teeth, and out of my mouth.*

Guided Practice/Practice

- Display the Photo Cards. Have children take turns selecting a picture, naming it, and saying the initial sound of the picture name: *This is a _____. _____ begins with /s/.*

Phonics

Objective Recognize words that begin with /s/s
Materials
- **Sound-Spelling Card:** *Sun* • **Word-Building Cards**
- **Photo Cards:** *sandwich, saw, seal, sing, soap, sock, soil, soup, sun*

PRETEACH: RECOGNIZE /s/s

Model

- Display the Photo Cards for *saw* and *seal* and the *Sun* Sound-Spelling Card. *The name of this letter is* s. S *stands for the /s/ sound that you hear at the beginning of* sun. *I will place the* s *on the picture of the saw. Listen: /sss/, saw.* Repeat with *seal.*

Guided Practice/Practice

- Display the Photo Cards on a table. Point to the soap. *This is soap. What sound do you hear at the beginning of* soap? *What letter stands for /s/? Let's place an* s *on the soap because* soap *begins with /s/.* Repeat with remaining Photo Cards for /s/s.

- For additional practice, point out objects in the classroom with names that begin with /s/.

SOUND-SPELLINGS REVIEW

Display **Word-Building Cards** for *s, a, m,* one at a time. Have children chorally say the sound. Repeat and vary the pace.

Tier
2

Corrective Feedback

Mnemonic Display the *Sun* Sound-Spelling Card. Say: *This is the Sun Sound-Spelling Card. The sound is /s/. The /s/ sound is spelled with the letter* s. *Say /s/ with me: /sss/. This is the sound at the beginning of* sun. *What is the letter? What is the sound? What word begins with /s/?* Sun *is the word we can use to remember the sound for* s, /s/.

On Level

High-Frequency Words

Objective Review high-frequency words *can, like, the,* and *we*

Materials • **High-Frequency Word Cards:** *can, like, the, we*

REVIEW: *can, like, the, we*

- Display the **High-Frequency Word Card** for **like**.

- **Read** Point to and say the word *like. This is the word* like. *When you like something, you enjoy it or are pleased with it. I like going to the beach.*

- **Spell** *The word* like *is spelled* l-i-k-e. Have children read and spell *like*.

- **Write** Finally, have children write the word *like*.

- Repeat with **the**, **we**, and **can**.

Phonemic Awareness/Phonics

Objective Review initial /s/*s*

Materials • **Puppet** • **Word-Building Cards** • **Sound-Spelling WorkBoards**

PHONEME BLENDING

Model

- *Happy is going to say the sounds in a word. Listen: /a/ /m/. Now listen as Happy blends the sounds together: /a/ /m/, /aaammm/, am. The word is am. What's the word? Repeat with Sam: /s/ /a/ /m/, /sssaaammm/, Sam.*

Practice

- *Happy will say the sounds of other words. Listen to Happy as he says each sound. Then blend the sounds to say a word.* Guide practice with the first word: /s/ /a/ /g/, /a/ /d/, /s/ /a/ /t/, /m/ /a/ /p/, /s/ /a/ /d/, /m/ /a/ /t/, /m/ /a/ /d/, /s/ /a/ /p/.

PHONICS

Model

- Display **Word-Building Card** *s. The name of this letter is* s. S *stands for the /s/ sound we hear at the beginning of* sun. *What is the sound? I'll hold up the* s *card because* sun *begins with /s/.*

Guided Practice/Practice

- Say: *sand, mop, ant, sip, sock, sink, milk, apple, soup.* Children hold up the letter *s* and say /s/ for words that begin with /s/.

- Have children write *s* several times on their **WorkBoards** as they say /s/. Have children use small Word-Building Cards to build *Sam* with you. Have them blend the word: /sssaaammm/, Sam.

Sound-Spelling WorkBoard

Beyond Level

High-Frequency Words/Vocabulary

Objectives Review high-frequency words; introduce *was* and *said*

ACCELERATE

- Write *was* and *said* on the board.

- **Read** Point to and say the word *was*. *This is the word* was. *I was happy yesterday. The puppy was funny.*

- **Spell** *The word* was *is spelled* w-a-s. Have children read and spell *was*.

- **Write** Finally, have children write the word *was*.

- Repeat the routine with *said*.

- Have children work with a partner to make up oral sentences using the words *was* and *said*.

EXPAND ORAL VOCABULARY

- **Synonyms** Review the meaning of the oral vocabulary word *friends* with children. Then explain that a *synonym* is a word that means the same thing as another word.

- Say: *A* synonym *for the word* friend *is* pal. *A* pal *is someone you like very much and enjoy spending time with. Think about the classroom* pals *you have made.*

- Have children take turns using the new word *pal* in a sentence. Then tell children that they will work with a partner to talk about things they enjoy doing with their pals.

Phonics

Objectives Review /s/s and introduce initial blends; blend and read words
Materials • **Word-Building Cards** • **Sound-Spelling WorkBoards**

ENRICH

- Display **Word-Building Card** *s*. Tell children that /s/ is spelled with the letter *s*. Sun *and* saw *begin with /s/. Let's say the sound together: /sss/.*

- Display Word-Building Cards *a, i, b, c, ck, d, f, g, h, j, k, l, m, n, p, qu, r, s, t, v, w, x, y, z*. Use the routine above with each letter. Have children repeat as they write each on their **WorkBoards**.

- Write the following words on the board: *am, Sam, ham, bit, fit, quit, map, sap, tap, rip*. Model blending as needed to read words.

ELL ENGLISH LANGUAGE LEARNERS

Oral Language Warm-Up

Content Objective Learn theme vocabulary
Language Objective Repeat and sing the song to demonstrate understanding
Materials • **Visual Vocabulary Resources** • **Listening Library Audio CD**

BUILD BACKGROUND KNOWLEDGE

All Language Levels

- Introduce the unit theme "Friends" using the song "Be a Friend." Display a picture of friends, such as a picture from *What Do You Like?* or one of the **Visual Vocabulary Resources**. Teach the word *friend* as you point to each friend in the picture. Have children repeat the word three times.

- Play "Be a Friend" on the **Listening Library Audio CD**. Act out each line as you sing the song.

- Then teach children the song, one line at a time. Emphasize the key words that tell about friends and what they do, such as *smile, fun, be a friend.*

- Play the song several times until children begin to correctly repeat the song and act it out with a friend.

- Ask children to tell about what they do with their friends. Build on their responses to model speaking in complete sentences. For example: *You play with your friend. You sing with your friend.*

Academic Language

Language Objective Use academic language in classroom conversations

All Language Levels

- This week's academic words are **boldfaced** throughout the lesson. Define the word in context and provide a clear example from the selection. Then ask children to generate an example or a word with a similar meaning.

Academic Language Used in Whole Group Instruction

Oral Vocabulary Words	Vocabulary and Grammar Concepts	Strategy and Skill Words
compete favorite friend hobby partner	color words naming words	identify character ask questions noun

Cognates

Help children identify similarities and differences in pronunciation and spelling between English words and Spanish cognates:

Cognates

compete	*competir*
favorite	*favorito*

ELL ENGLISH LANGUAGE LEARNERS

Vocabulary

Language Objective Demonstrate understanding and use of key words by describing friends and what they do

Materials • **Visual Vocabulary Resources**

PRETEACH KEY VOCABULARY

Visual Vocabulary Resources

All Language Levels

Use the **Visual Vocabulary Resources** to preteach the weekly oral vocabulary words *compete, favorite, friend, hobby,* and *partner.* Focus on one or two words per day. Use the following routine that appears in detail on the cards.

- ■ Define the word in English and provide the example given.

- ■ Define the word in Spanish, if appropriate, and indicate if the word is a cognate.

- ■ Display the picture and explain how it illustrates or demonstrates the word. Engage children in structured partner-talk about the image, using the key word.

- ■ Ask children to chorally say the word three times.

- ■ Point out any known sound-spellings or focus on a key aspect of phonemic awareness related to the word.

PRETEACH FUNCTION WORDS AND PHRASES

All Language Levels

Use the Visual Vocabulary Resources to preteach the function words *quietly* and *firmly.* Focus on one word per day. Use the detailed routine on the cards.

- ■ Define the word in English and, if appropriate, in Spanish. Point out if the word is a cognate.

- ■ Refer to the picture and engage children in talk about the word. For example, children will partner-talk using sentence frames or they will listen to sentences and replace a word or phrase with the new function word.

- ■ Ask children to chorally repeat the word three times.

TEACH BASIC WORDS

Beginning/Intermediate

Use the Visual Vocabulary Resources to teach the basic words *sports, music, poems, pets, artwork,* and *trips.* Teach these "things friends may like" words using the routine provided on the card.

Approaching Level

High-Frequency Words

Objective Reteach high-frequency words
Materials
- **High-Frequency Word Cards:** *can, I, like, the, we*
- **Sound-Spelling WorkBoards**

RETEACH WORD: *like*

Tier **2**

- Distribute a **WorkBoard** to each child. Then display the **High-Frequency Word Card** for **like**.

- Use the **Read/Spell/Write** routine to reteach the word. Point to and say the word. *This is the word* like. Like *means "to enjoy" or "to be fond of." I enjoy being in school with you. I like you.* Like *is spelled* l-i-k-e. Have children read and spell *like*. Then have them write the word on their WorkBoards.

- Have children work with a partner to make up sentences using the word *like*. Ask them to talk about things they like to do with friends.

HIGH-FREQUENCY WORDS REVIEW

Display the High-Frequency Word Cards **I**, **can**, **we**, and **the,** one card at a time, as children chorally read and spell the word. Mix and repeat. Note words children need to review.

Pre-decodable Reader

Objective Teach Pre-decodable Reader *We Like Sam!*
Materials
- **Pre-decodable Reader:** *We Like Sam!*

TEACH *We Like Sam!*

- Display the cover of the book and read the title. Help children identify the cover. *Let's read the title together.* Point to the high-frequency words *We Like* and read them with children. Have children sound out *Sam* as you run your finger under it. *Look at the picture. Who do you think Sam is? What do you think this book is about?*

- Page through the book. Point out and name each rebus. Ask children to find the words *we, like,* and *the*.

- Read the book chorally with children. Have them point to each word as they read it. Provide corrective feedback as needed.

- Ask children to use *we, like,* and *the* to talk about the book. *We like the book. We like the kids. We like Sam!*

- After reading, ask children to recall things they read about.

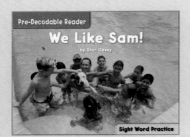

Pre-decodable Reader

Puppet

Approaching Level

Phonemic Awareness

Objective Blend sounds in words with /s/ and /a/

Materials • **Puppet**

PHONEME BLENDING

Tier 2

Model

■ *Listen as Happy says the sounds in a word. First he'll say each sound: /a/ /m/. Then he will blend the two sounds together to say the word: /a/ /m/, /aaammm/, am. The word is am. What is the word? Repeat with Sam: /s/ /a/ /m/, /sssaaammm/, Sam.*

Guided Practice/Practice

■ *Happy will say the sounds in another word: /s/ /a/ /d/. Now you say the sounds with Happy: /s/ /a/ /d/. Let's blend the sounds with Happy: /s/ /a/ /d/, /sssaaad/, sad. What's the word?*

■ Repeat with the following words. Guide practice with the first word using the same routine.

/s/ /a/ /t/	/m/ /a/ /n/	/s/ /a/ /p/	/k/ /a/ /n/
/s/ /a/ /g/	/m/ /a/ /t/	/m/ /a/ /d/	/s/ /a/ /l/

Phonics

Objective Reinforce letter-sound correspondence for /s/s

Materials • **Sound-Spelling Card:** *Sun* • **Sound-Spelling WorkBoards**
• **Word-Building Cards**

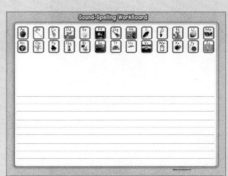

Sound-Spelling WorkBoard

RETEACH Ss

Model

■ Display the *Sun* **Sound-Spelling Card**. *The letter* s *stands for the /s/ sound as in* sun. *What is this letter? What sound does it stand for?* Repeat, using the word *soap.*

■ Trace *s* on a **Word-Building Card**. *I will say a sentence. We will trace* s *when we hear /s/.* Say: *Sam sat and sipped soup.*

Guided Practice/Practice

■ Distribute a **WorkBoard** to each child. Say: *man, sun, mouth, sound, sand, saw, moon, ant, soup, seal.* Children write *s* on their WorkBoard when they hear a word with /s/.

CUMULATIVE REVIEW

Display Word-Building Cards *s, a, m,* one at a time. Point to the letters in a random order. Have children chorally say the sound. Repeat and vary the pace.

Corrective Feedback

If children cannot discern the initial /s/, review the word *sun.* Have children stop at the first sound and repeat /s/, /s/, /s/ before saying *sun.*

Pre-decodable Reader

Pre-decodable Reader

On Level

Pre-decodable Reader

Objective   Reread *I Like* to develop fluency
Materials   • **Pre-decodable Reader:** *I Like*

REREAD FOR FLUENCY

- Ask children to look back at the illustrations in *I Like*. Have children use their own words to retell what the book was about.

- Have children reread a page or two of *I Like*. Work with children to read with accuracy and expression. Model reading a page. Point out how you use your voice to say the words with expression: *When I read, "I like the beach," I say* like *a little stronger than the other words. I want to show how family members feel about the beach. When I read, "I like the sand," I also say the word* like *a little stronger. I want to show how the girl feels.* Have children reread a page, speaking audibly and clearly.

- Provide time to listen as children read their page(s). Comment on their accuracy and expression and provide corrective feedback by modeling proper fluency.

Beyond Level

Pre-decodable Reader

Objective   Reread *I Like* to reinforce fluency
Materials   • **Pre-decodable Readers:** *I Like, We Like Sam!*

REREAD FOR FLUENCY

- Have children reread several pages of *I Like*. Model reading a page. Listen as children read. Comment on their accuracy and expression. Provide corrective feedback by modeling fluency.

INNOVATE

- Have children brainstorm what the family members might say about a day at the park. Have them choose a character, draw the character in the park, and write a caption. Provide time for children to share their pictures with the group and tell what family members like at the park.

- Use the above routine for **Pre-decodable Reader** *We Like Sam!* on Day 4. Have children add to book by drawing pictures and writing captions for additional activities Sam can do with friends.

ELL ENGLISH LANGUAGE LEARNERS

Access to Core Content

Content Objective Develop listening comprehension
Language Objective Discuss text using key words and sentence frames
Materials • **ELL Resource Book**, pp. 32–39

PRETEACH BIG BOOK/TRADE BOOK

All Language Levels

Use the Interactive Question-Response Guide on **ELL Resource Book** pages 32–39 to introduce children to *What Do You Like?* Preteach half of the selection on Day 1 and half on Day 2.

- Use the prompts provided in the guide to develop meaning and vocabulary. Use the partner-talk and whole-class responses to engage children and increase student talk.

- When completed, revisit the selection and prompt children to talk about the illustrations. Provide sentence starters as needed and build on children's responses to develop language.

ELL Resource Book

Big Book

Beginning	Intermediate	Advanced
Use Visuals During the Interactive Reading, select several pictures. Describe them and have children summarize what you said.	**Summarize** During the Interactive Reading, select a few lines of text. After you read them and explain them, have children summarize the text.	**Expand** During the Interactive Reading, select a larger portion of text. After you read it and explain it, have children summarize the text.

Approaching Level

High-Frequency Words

Objective Recognize high-frequency words *can, like, the, we*

Materials
- **High-Frequency Word Cards:** *can, like, the, we*
- **Word-Building Cards**

RETEACH WORDS: *can, like, the, we*

- Display the **High-Frequency Word Card** for **like**. Say the word and have children repeat it. Point to each letter and have children name it.

- Distribute **Word-Building Cards** for *l, i, k,* and *e*. Model putting the letters together to form the word *like*. Then have children form *like*.

- Repeat the above routines with the words **the**, **we**, and **can**.

- Ask a question with *like*: *What do you like to eat?* Have children use *like* to answer the question. Continue with the other words.

HIGH-FREQUENCY WORDS REVIEW

Display the High-Frequency Word Cards for *I, can, we,* and *the,* one card at a time, as children chorally read and spell the word. Mix and repeat. Note words children need to review.

Phonemic Awareness

Objective Identify initial and final /s/s

Materials
- **Photo Cards:** *bus, horse, house, mouse, saw, seal, soap, sock, soup, sun*
- **Sound Boxes** • markers
- **WorkBoard Sound Boxes; Teacher's Resource Book,** p. 136

PHONEME ISOLATION

Tier 2

Model
- Use the **Sound Boxes**. Display the **Photo Card** for *sun*. *Listen for the beginning sound in* sun: /sssuuunnn/. Sun *begins with* /s/. *I'll place a marker in the first box to show that I hear* s *at the beginning of* sun.

- Display the Photo Card for *bus*. *Listen for the end sound in* bus: /buuusss/, bus. Bus *ends with* /s/. *I'll place a marker in the last box to show that I hear* /s/ *at the end of* bus.

Guided Practice/Practice
- Distribute Sound Boxes and markers. Display the Photo Cards. Children take turns selecting a picture and naming it. Have them listen for /s/ and place the marker in the first or last box as they say: *This is a _____. I hear /s/ at the _____ of _____.*

Approaching Level

Phonics

Objectives Review blending initial /s/s; build fluency
Materials • **Word-Building Cards** • pocket chart

REVIEW SKILLS: *Ss*

Tier 2

Model

- Place **Word-Building Card** *S* in the pocket chart. *The name of this letter is* s. *The letter* s *stands for the /s/ sound. Say /s/. What is the letter? What is the sound?*

- Place *a* next to *s*. *The name of this letter is* a. *The letter* a *stands for the /a/ sound. Say /a/. What is the letter? What is the sound?*

- Repeat with *m*.

- Move your hand from left to right below the letters. *Listen as I blend the sounds together: /sssaaammm/,* Sam. *What's the word? Let's blend the word together: /sssaaammm/,* Sam.

Guided Practice/Practice

- Give children small Word-Building Cards *a, m, s*. Have them place *a* and *m* in a row and say the sound for the letters: /a/ /m/. Have them blend the sounds to say a word: /aaammm/, *am*. Repeat with the word *Sam*.

Build Fluency

- Have children blend *am* and *Sam* as quickly as they can.

Pre-decodable Reader

Objective Preteach Pre-decodable Reader *We Like Sam!*
Materials • **Pre-decodable Reader:** *We Like Sam!*

PRETEACH *We Like Sam!*

- Display the cover of the book and read the title. *Let's read the title together.* Point to the high-frequency words *We Like* and read them with children. Have children sound out *Sam* as you run your finger under it. *Look at the picture. Who do you think Sam is? What do you think this book is about?*

- Page through the book. Point out and name each rebus. Ask children to find the words *we, like,* and *the*.

- Read the book chorally with children. Have them point to each word as they read it. Provide corrective feedback as needed.

- Ask children to use *we, like*, and *the* to talk about the book. *We like the book. We like the kids. We like Sam!*

- After reading, ask children to recall things they read about.

Pre-decodable Reader

What Sam Likes

Have children draw a picture of something that Sam the dog might like.

On Level

Phonics

Objective   Review initial /s/s

Materials   • **Word-Building Cards**   • **Sound-Spelling WorkBoards**

REVIEW /s/s

Model

■ Display **Word-Building Card** s. *The name of this letter is* s. *S stands for the /s/ sound we hear at the beginning of* sun. *What is the sound? I'll hold up the* s *card because* sun *begins with /s/.*

Guided Practice/Practice

■ Say: *sand, mop, ant, sip, sock, sink, milk, apple, soup.* Children hold up their small Word-Building Cards and say /s/ for words that begin with /s/. Guide practice with the first two words.

■ Have children write *s* several times on their **WorkBoards** as they say /s/.

■ Have children use small Word-Building Cards to build *Sam* with you. Have them blend the word they build: /s/ /a/ /m/, /sssaaammm/, Sam.

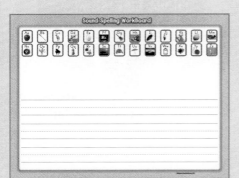

Sound-Spelling WorkBoard

Beyond Level

Phonics

Objectives   Review /s/s and introduce initial blends; blend and read words

Materials   • **Word-Building Cards**   • **Sound-Spelling WorkBoards**

ACCELERATE

■ Write *flip, grin,* and *swap* on the board. Draw a line under *fl, gr,* and *sw* in each word. Point to *fl* in *flip.* Say: *The letter* f *stands for /f/ as in* fire. *The letter* l *stands for /l/ as in* lemon. *I can blend these sounds together. Listen: /f/ /l/, /ffflll/. The blended sound is /fl/.* Then blend: /f/ /l/ /i/ /p/, /fffllliiip/, flip. Repeat with *grin* and *swap.*

■ Write the following on the board: *flag, flip, floss, grab, green, grip, skip, spin, skim, clip, clap, clot, swim.* Model blending as needed.

ELL ENGLISH LANGUAGE LEARNERS

Access to Core Content

Content Objective Develop listening comprehension
Language Objective Discuss text using key words and sentence frames
Materials • **ELL Resource Book,** pp. 40–41

PRETEACH BIG BOOK OF EXPLORATIONS

All Language Levels

Use the Interactive Question-Response Guide on **ELL Resource Book** pages 40–41 to preview the **Big Book of Explorations** selection "Friends Follow Rules." Preteach half of the selection on Day 3 and half on Day 4.

Big Book of Explorations

Grammar

Content Objective Identify nouns
Language Objective Speak in complete sentences, using sentence frames
Materials • **Listening Library Audio CD** • **Photo Cards**

NAMING WORDS (NOUNS)

All Language Levels

- Review naming words. Tell children that nouns are naming words. Sometimes nouns name people or animals. Point to people in the classroom and name them using different nouns (teacher, child, boy, girl). Have children repeat.

> **Two Little Blackbirds**
> *Two little blackbirds sitting on a hill.*
> Two hands closed with thumbs up.
> *One named Jack, one named Jill.*
> Bounce one hand, then the other.
> *Fly away, Jack. Fly away, Jill.*
> Right hand is open, raised above head, then same with left.
> *Come back, Jack. Come back, Jill.*
> Right hand and left back to original position

- Play "Two Little Blackbirds" from the **Listening Library Audio CD**. Tell children to listen for naming words.

- Point out the naming words *blackbirds, hill, Jack,* and *Jill.* Explain that Jack and Jill are names of the birds. Ask children to name friends they know. Display the **Photo Card** for *bird.*

PEER DISCUSSION STARTERS

All Language Levels

- Distribute Photo Cards of things friends like that were discussed this week, such as *sun, dog, apple,* and *balloon.*

- Pair children and have them complete the sentence frame *I like* _____. Ask them to expand by providing as many details as they can. For example: *It is* _____. Circulate, listen in, and take note of each child's language use and proficiency.

Puppet

Approaching Level

Phonemic Awareness

Objective Categorize words using initial sounds
Materials • **Puppet**

PHONEME CATEGORIZATION

Tier 2

Model

■ Hold up the **Puppet**. *Listen as Happy says three words:* sad, sit, mat. *Two words begin with /s/. One does not. Listen again:* /sssad/, /sssit/, /mmmat/. Sad *and* sit *begin with /s/:* /sssaaad/, sad; /sssiiit/, sit. Mat *does not begin with /s/.* Mat *does not belong.* Mat *begins with /m/:* /mmmat/. *Repeat for* soup, mop, *and* seal.

Guided Practice/Practice

■ *Listen to the beginning sounds as Happy says three more words. Have Happy say* sun, six, ant. *Which word doesn't belong?* Repeat with *moon, saw, sock; Sal, Dan, Sis;* and *sip, sit, map.*

Phonics

Objective Blend with /s/s, /a/a, and /m/m
Materials • **Word-Building Cards** • pocket chart

REVIEW SKILLS

Tier 2

Model

■ Place **Word-Building Cards** *a* and *m* in the pocket chart. *The name of this letter is* a. *The letter* a *stands for the /a/ sound. Say /a/. The name of this letter is* m. *The letter* m *stands for the /m/ sound. Say /m/. Move your hand from left to right below the letters. Now listen as I blend the word:* /aaammm/, am. *Blend the word with me:* /aaammm/, am.

■ Add Word-Building Card *S* in front of *am* in the pocket chart. *The name of this letter is* s. *The letter* s *stands for the /s/ sound. Say /s/. Move your hand from left to right below the letters. Now listen as I blend the word:* /sssaaammm/, Sam. *Blend the word with children.*

Guided Practice/Practice

■ Place Word-Building Cards *S, a, m* on the floor. Have children take turns walking by the cards from left to right and saying the sound each letter stands for. Have children blend the sounds and say the word: /sssaaammm/, *Sam.*

Corrective Feedback

Blending Error Say: *My turn.* Model blending. Then lead children in blending the sounds. Say: *Do it with me.* Then say: *Your turn. Blend.* Have children chorally blend. Return to the beginning of the word. Say: *Let's start over.* Blend the word again with children.

ELL

Extra Practice Provide additional practice in pronouncing and blending sounds that do not transfer directly to the native language of some children, such as the short vowel /a/.

Approaching Level

Leveled Reader Lesson 1

Objective Read *We Like* to apply skills and strategies

Materials • **Leveled Reader:** *We Like*

BEFORE READING

- **Preview** Read the title and the names of the author and illustrator. *What are the kids on the cover doing?* Turn to the title page and point out that it also has the title and the names of the author and illustrator. *What do you think the book is about?*

- **Model Concepts About Print** Demonstrate book handling for children. Guide them as they follow along with their books. *This is the top of the page. This is the bottom of the page. When I read the words on the page, I start at the left and read from left to right. Follow my finger as I read.* Read aloud a page as you follow the text with your finger.

- **Review High-Frequency Words** Point to the words **we** and **like** in the title and read them aloud. Guide children as they name the letters in *we* and *like*. Have children find *we* and *like* in the book. Ask them to point to and read the words.

- **Page Through the Book** Name things in the pictures that are unfamiliar to children and identify the rebus pictures.

- **Set a Purpose for Reading** *Let's find out what the children like.*

DURING READING

- Remind children to use the rebuses and illustrations to gain information and to look for the high-frequency words *we* and *like*. Show children how to self-correct if a word doesn't sound correct. *The rebus shows two sand castles. There are two sand castles in the illustrations, too. "We like sand castles." That is correct.*

- Monitor children's reading and provide help as needed.

AFTER READING

- Ask children to identify words they had trouble reading and to share strategies they used to help them. Reinforce good behaviors. For example: *Ann, I noticed that you pointed to the word* like *each time you read it.*

- Have children retell the story and share personal responses. *Did the story remind you of things that you like?*

- Have children turn to a partner and ask each other questions about the story. Tell children to respond in complete sentences.

Leveled Reader

Digital Learning

Use the **Leveled Reader Audio CD** for fluency building *after* children read the book with your support during Small Group time.

Leveled Reader

ELL

Retell Use the Interactive Question-Response Guide Technique to help English Language Learners understand *We Like the Playground*. As you read, make meaning clear by pointing to pictures, demonstrating word meaning, paraphrasing text, and asking children questions.

We Play

Have children draw a picture to show how they play with a friend. Help them write a caption for their picture.

We play ball.

On Level

Leveled Reader Lesson 1

Objective   Read *We Like the Playground* to apply skills and strategies
Materials   • **Leveled Reader:** *We Like the Playground*

BEFORE READING

- **Preview** Read the title and the name of the author and illustrator: *Who is on the cover? What are the girl and boy doing?* Page through the illustrations in the book with children. Name unfamiliar items and identify the rebuses.

- **Model Concepts About Print** Demonstrate book handling. *This is the top of the page. This is the bottom of the page. First, I read the words on the left page. Then, I read the words on the right page.*

- **Review High-Frequency Words** Write **we**, **like**, and **the** on chart paper. Have children find each word in the book and point to the word as they read it aloud.

- **Set a Purpose for Reading** *Let's find out what the children like.*

DURING READING

- Have children turn to page 2 and begin by whisper-reading the first two pages.

- Remind children to look for the new high-frequency word and to use the rebus pictures and illustrations.

- Monitor children's reading and provide help. Stop during the reading and ask open-ended questions to facilitate discussion, such as: *What can you do on a playground? Why is a playground fun?* Build on children's responses to develop deeper understanding of the text.

AFTER READING

- Ask children to point out words they had trouble reading and to share strategies they used to figure them out. Reinforce good behaviors. For example: *Jarrett, I noticed that you used your finger to match the rebus picture with what is in the illustration.*

- **Retell** Ask children to retell the story. Help them make a personal connection. *What things do you like to do on the playground?*

- Have children turn to a partner and ask each other questions about the story. Tell children to respond in complete sentences.

Beyond Level

Leveled Reader Lesson 1

Objective Read *Sam Likes School* to apply skills and strategies
Materials • **Leveled Reader:** *Sam Likes School*

BEFORE READING

- **Preview** Read the title and the names of the author and illustrator. *Where are the children on the cover? What are they doing?* Turn to the title page and point out that it also has the title and the names of the author and illustrator. *Who is the boy in the picture? What do you think he will do in the book?* Page through the book with children and pause to name unfamiliar items.

- **Introduce Story Words** Point to the word *bus* on page 2. Read the sentence. Have children use the picture to explain what a bus is. Repeat with *classroom* on page 3 and *swings* on page 4.

- **Set a Purpose for Reading** *Let's find out why Sam likes school.*

DURING READING

- Remind children that when they come to an unfamiliar word, they can look for familiar chunks in the word, break the word into syllables and sound out each part, or think about what the word might mean. If the word does not sound right or make sense in the sentence, children can self-correct.

- Monitor children's reading and provide help as needed.

AFTER READING

- Ask children to point out words they had trouble reading and to share the strategies they used to figure them out.

- Ask children to retell a main event from the story and to share personal responses. *Can you tell us a story about what you like to do at school?*

- **Analyze** *Compare and contrast how Sam feels at the beginning and the end of the story. How do you think he will feel about school tomorrow?*

- Have children work in pairs to list a few ways that they would make friends at a new school. For example, they might ask if they can join in a game.

- **Model** Have pairs use their ideas to create a skit that shows other ways to make new friends. Demonstrate one idea with a student volunteer. Have the pairs practice their skits before performing them for the class.

- Have children work in pairs to ask each other questions about the story. Have children respond in complete sentences.

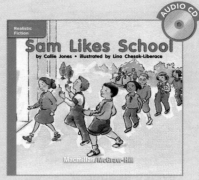

Leveled Reader

New Ending

Encourage children to change the sequence of events in this story to create a different ending.

ON YOUR OWN

We Like to Play

Ask children to draw and write about an activity they like to do with a friend.

We climb trees.

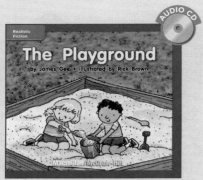

Leveled Reader

Vocabulary

Preteach Vocabulary Use the routine in the **Visual Vocabulary Resources**, pages 307–308, to preteach the ELL Vocabulary listed on the inside front cover of the Leveled Reader.

ELL ENGLISH LANGUAGE LEARNERS

Leveled Reader

Content Objective Read to apply skills and strategies
Language Objective Retell information using complete sentences
Materials • **Leveled Reader:** *The Playground*

BEFORE READING

All Language Levels

- **Preview** Read the title *The Playground.* Ask: *What's the title? Say it again.* Repeat with the author's name. Point to the cover illustration and say: *I see two friends playing.* Point to two friends as you name them. *They are playing in a sand box. Now turn to a partner and name other things you see in this picture.*

- **Page Through the Book** Use simple language to tell about the picture on each page. Immediately follow up with questions, such as: *Is this a swing? Is this a slide or a sand castle?*

- **Review Skills** Use the inside front cover to review the phonics skill and high-frequency words.

- **Set a Purpose** Say: *Let's read to find out about what children like at the playground.*

DURING READING

All Language Levels

- Have children whisper-read each page, or use the differentiated suggestions below. Circulate, listen in, and provide corrective feedback, such as modeling how to correctly pronounce a word.

- **Retell** Stop after every two pages and ask children to state what they have learned so far. Reinforce language by restating children's comments when they have difficulty using story-specific words. Provide differentiated sentence frames to support children's responses and engage children in partner-talk where appropriate.

Beginning	Intermediate	Advanced
Echo-Read Have children echo-read after you.	**Choral-Read** Have children choral-read with you.	**Choral-Read** Have children choral-read.
Check Comprehension Point to pictures and ask questions such as: *Do you see the slide? Point to the slide in the playground.*	**Check Comprehension** Ask questions/prompts such as: *What does this picture show? What are the friends doing?*	**Check Comprehension** Ask: *What did you learn about a playground? Read sentences that tell what friends like to do at the playground. What do you like to do at a playground?*

ELL ENGLISH LANGUAGE LEARNERS

AFTER READING

All Language Levels

Book Talk Children will work with peers of varying language abilities to discuss their books for this week. Display the four **Leveled Readers** read this week: *Sam Likes School* (Beyond Level), *We Like the Playground* (On Level), *We Like* (Approaching Level), and *The Playground* (English Language Learners).

Ask the questions and provide the prompts below. Call on children who read each book to answer the questions or respond to the prompt. If appropriate, ask children to find the pages in the book that illustrate their answers.

- Who was your book about?
- Name the things the people in your book like.
- What did you learn about friends?
- How are your friends like the friend in the book you read? How are they different?
- What did you like best in the book? Tell why you like it.

Develop Listening and Speaking Skills Tell children to remember the following:

- Share information in cooperative learning interactions. Remind children to work with their partners to retell the story and complete any activities. Ask: *What happened next in the story?*

- Employ self-corrective techniques and monitor their own and other children's language production. Children should ask themselves: *What parts of this passage were confusing to me? Can my classmates help me clarify a word or sentence that I don't understand?*

- Use high-frequency English words to describe people, places, and objects.

- Narrate, describe, and explain with specificity and detail. Ask: *Where did the story take place? Can you describe the setting? What else did you notice?*

- Express opinions, ideas, and feelings on a variety of social and academic topics. Ask: *What do you think about the characters in the story?*

Puppet

ELL

Letter-Sound Relationships Provide additional practice in pronouncing the sounds /s/, /m/, /a/ and naming the letters *s, m, a,* as children point to them.

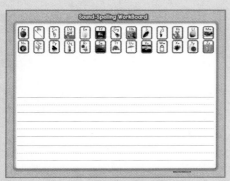

Sound-Spelling WorkBoard

Approaching Level

Phonemic Awareness

Objective   Categorize words using initial sounds

Materials   • **Puppet**   • pocket chart
    • **Photo Cards:** *fish, man, map, moon, sandwich, saw, seal, soap, sock, soup, sun*

 PHONEME CATEGORIZATION

Tier 2

Model
- Display the **Photo Cards** for *sandwich, fish, sun.* Hold up the **Puppet**. *Happy is going to say the names for these cards. Two begin with /s/. One does not. Listen:* sandwich, fish, sun. Sandwich *and* sun *begin with the /s/ sound: /sss/.* Fish *does not begin with /s/.* Fish *does not belong.*

Guided Practice/Practice
- Display the Photo Cards for *saw, man, seal* in a pocket chart. Have children name each photo with you. Repeat the names, emphasizing the initial sound. Ask children which word does not belong. Repeat with the cards for *map, soap, sock* and *soup, sun, moon.*

Phonics

Objective   Identify /s/s, /m/m, /a/a and build fluency

Materials   • **Photo Cards:** *alligator, ambulance, anchor, ant, apple, astronaut, man, map, moon, mop, mouse, saw, seal, soap, sock, soup, sun*
    • **Word-Building Cards**   • pocket chart
    • **Sound-Spelling WorkBoards**

 BUILD FLUENCY: LETTER-SOUND CORRESPONDENCE

Tier 2

Model
- Place **Word-Building Cards** *a, m,* and *s* in the pocket chart. Place the Photo Cards facedown. Pick the first card, name the picture, and say the beginning sound. Then place it in the pocket chart under the corresponding letter.

Guided Practice/Practice
- Have each child choose a Photo Card, say the name of the picture and beginning sound, and place it in the pocket chart. Guide practice with the first card.

Build Fluency
- Display the Word-Building Cards for *a, m,* and *s.* Have children name the letters as quickly as they can. Then ask them to write the letters *a, m,* and *s* on their **WorkBoards** several times as they say /a/, /m/, and /s/.

Approaching Level

Leveled Reader Lesson 2

Objective Reread *We Like* to reinforce fluency and identify characters
Materials • **Leveled Reader:** *We Like*

FOCUS ON FLUENCY

- Tell children that you will read one page of the book and they should read that page right after you. They should follow along in their books and try to read at the same speed and with the same expression that you use.

SKILL IDENTIFY CHARACTER

- *What do the boys on the cover like? What do other children in the book like? Do you like any of the same things? Why are those things fun?*

REREAD BOOKS

- Distribute copies of previously read **Leveled Readers**. Tell children that rereading the books will help them develop their skills.

- Circulate and listen in as children read. Stop them periodically and ask them how they are figuring out words or checking their understanding. Tell children to read other previously read Leveled Readers during independent reading time.

High-Frequency Words

Objective Review high-frequency words *like*, *the*, and *we*
Materials • **High-Frequency Word Cards:** *like*, *the*, *we*

BUILD WORD AUTOMATICITY: *like, the, we*

- Distribute copies of the **High-Frequency Word Card** for **like**. Say the word and have children repeat it. Have children name the letters in the word. Repeat with the words **the** and **we**.

- **Build Fluency** Use the High-Frequency Word Cards to review previously taught words. Repeat, guiding children to read more rapidly.

Leveled Reader

Meet Grade-Level Expectations

As an alternative to this day's lesson, guide children through a reading of the On Level Leveled Reader. See page 326. Because both books contain the same vocabulary, phonics, and comprehension skills, the scaffolding you provided will help most children gain access to this more challenging text.

Corrective Feedback

Throughout the lessons, provide feedback based on children's responses. If the answer is correct, ask another question. If the answer is tentative, restate key information to assist the child. If the answer is wrong, provide corrective feedback such as hints or clues, refer to a visual such as a **Sound-Spelling Card** or story illustration, or probe with questions to help the child clarify any misunderstanding.

Leveled Reader

ON YOUR OWN

Sam Likes the Playground

Have children draw a picture of a character named Sam. Ask them to show what Sam likes to do on the playground. Help children write a sentence about their picture.

On Level

Leveled Reader Lesson 2

Objective   Reread to apply skills and strategies to retell a story

Materials   • **Leveled Reader:** *We Like the Playground*

BEFORE READING

- Ask children to look through *We Like the Playground* and recall what the book is about. Reinforce vocabulary by repeating children's sentences using more sophisticated language and complete sentences. For example: *Yes, the girl and boy enjoy playing in the sandbox together. They enjoy digging in the sand.*

DURING READING

- Have children join you in a choral-reading of the story. Model reading with expression. *When I read page 2, I want to show that the girl and boy like the sandbox, so I emphasize the word* like *by saying it a little stronger. I do the same on page 3 to show that the children like the merry-go-round.* Ask children to use the same kind of expression when they read and to speak audibly and clearly.

- Assign each child a page. Have children practice by whisper-reading. *Follow along as other children read, and be ready to come in when it is your turn. Remember, use lots of expression.*

AFTER READING

- Have children retell the selection in their own words using complete sentences.

- *Who are the different children on each page? What questions did you ask yourself about the children as you read? What do the children like to do?*

Beyond Level

Leveled Reader Lesson 2

Objective Reread to apply skills and strategies to retell a story
Materials • **Leveled Reader:** *Sam Likes School*

BEFORE READING

- Ask children to look back at *Sam Likes School* and recall key events in the book. Ask: *What did you learn about Sam? What does Sam like? Who helps him when he is sad? What does the boy do to help Sam?*

DURING READING

- Assign each child a page of the book to read aloud. Have children practice by whisper-reading. *Follow along as each child reads, and be ready to come in when it is your turn. Remember, use lots of expression.*

AFTER READING

- Explain that if we ask questions about the characters as we read, we can understand a story better. Model: *When I began to read the story, I asked myself:* Why is Sam sad? *I found the answer as I read and looked at the pictures. Sam is sad because he is alone. He wants some friends. What questions did you ask yourself as you read? How did you find the answers?* Have children give examples.

Expand Vocabulary

Objective Learn and apply the meaning of the new words *bus*, *classroom*, and *swings* and brainstorm names of things found in schools
Materials • **Leveled Reader:** *Sam Likes School*

ENRICH: *bus, classroom, swings*

Gifted & Talented

- Write the words *bus*, *classroom*, and *swings* on cards. Display *bus* and read aloud the sentence on page 2: *Sam went to school on the bus.* Have children point to Sam sitting on the bus in the **Leveled Reader**. *Where is Sam sitting on the bus? Who is on the bus with Sam?*

- Ask children to use the picture to tell what a bus is.

- Ask children to use *bus* in sentences. Repeat with *classroom* and *swings*.

- Point out that a bus, a classroom, and swings are all things that can be found at a school. Have children brainstorm other words that name things that can be found at school. Record responses in a web labeled "We Like School!"

ON YOUR OWN

Write a Story

Have children write and illustrate a story about Sam and his friends.

Leveled Reader

ELL

Partners When children write and illustrate a story about Sam and his friends, pair English Language Learners with children who are more proficient.

ELL ENGLISH LANGUAGE LEARNERS

Fluency

Content Objectives Reread Pre-decodable Readers to develop fluency; develop speaking skills

Language Objective Tell a partner what a selection is about

Materials • **Pre-decodable Readers:** *I Like; We Like Sam!*

REREAD FOR FLUENCY

Beginning

■ Review the high-frequency words **like**, **we**, and **the** using the **Read/Spell/Write** routine.

Intermediate/Advanced

■ Use each word in a sentence that illustrates its use, such as: *I like the teddy bear.* Act out hugging a teddy bear. *We like the teddy bear.* Have the whole group act out hugging a teddy bear.

All Language Levels

■ Guide children through a choral-reading of *I Like* and *We Like Sam!* Read the title *We Like Sam!* Point out how you read the words with expression and that you say the word *like* a little stronger than you say the other words. Model reading the title again and have children chorally repeat.

DEVELOP SPEAKING/LISTENING SKILLS

All Language Levels

■ Have children reread *I Like* and *We Like Sam!* to a partner. Remind them to listen carefully and follow along in their book as their partner is reading. Work with children to read with accuracy and appropriate expression.

■ Ask children to tell their partner about the pictures on each page. Then have the other partner describe the pictures. Circulate, listen in, and provide additional language as needed.

Beginning	Intermediate	Advanced
Confirm Understanding Point to the pictures for partners to identify. Ask: *What do you see?* Restate the correct answer in a complete sentence.	**Share Preferences** Ask partners to tell you which is their favorite picture in the book. Prompt them to explain why it is their favorite picture.	**Compare and Contrast** Have partners compare two different pictures and describe them. Prompt them to explain how they are alike and different.

ENGLISH LANGUAGE LEARNERS

High-Frequency Words

Content Objective Spell high-frequency words correctly

Language Objective Write in complete sentences, using sentence frames

Materials • **Sound-Spelling WorkBoards** • **Sound-Spelling Cards** • **Photo Cards**

Beginning/Intermediate

- Write the high-frequency word **like** on the board. Have children copy the word on their **WorkBoards**. Then help them say, then write, a sentence for the word. Provide the sentence starter *I like* _____.

Advanced

- Children should first orally state their sentence. Correct as needed. Then they can draw a picture to complete the sentence. For children who are ready, help them spell words using their growing knowledge of English sound-spelling relationships. Model how to segment the word children are trying to spell and attach a spelling to each sound. Use the **Sound-Spelling Cards** to reinforce the spellings for each English sound.

Writing

All Language Levels

- Dictate the following sound and ask children to write the letter: /s/. Have them write the letter five times as they say /s/. Demonstrate correct letter formation, as needed.

- Then display a set of **Photo Cards**. Select at least five cards whose picture names begin with /s/ (sun, sea, soap, seal, sock) and three whose picture names begin with /m/ (man, mop, moon).

- Say the name of each card, stretching the initial sound to emphasize it. You may also need to reinforce the meaning of each picture as well as model correct mouth formation when forming the sound. Use the articulation pictures and prompts on the back of the small Sound-Spelling Cards for support. Tell children that if the picture name begins with /s/, you want them to write the letter *s* on their WorkBoards.

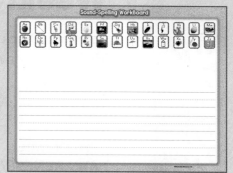

Sound-Spelling WorkBoard

Phonemic Awareness/ Phonics

For English Language Learners who need more practice with this week's phonemic awareness and phonics skills, see the Approaching Level lessons. Focus on minimal contrasts, articulation, and those sounds that do not transfer from the child's first language to English. For a complete listing of transfer sounds, see pages T10–T31.

End-of-Week Assessment

Weekly Assessment

Use your Quick Check observations and the assessment opportunities identified below to evaluate children's progress in key skill areas.

Skills	Quick Check Observations	Pencil and Paper Assessment
PHONEMIC AWARENESS/ PHONICS /s/s **s**	269	Activity Book, pp. 4, 10, 12 Practice Book, pp. 41, 46
HIGH-FREQUENCY WORDS *like* **like**	290	Activity Book, pp. 7–8 Practice Book, pp. 43–44
COMPREHENSION Identify Character	280	Activity Book, pp. 5–6, 11 Practice Book, p. 42

Quick Check Rubric

Skills	1	2	3
PHONEMIC AWARENESS/ PHONICS	Does not connect the /s/ sound with the letter *Ss* and has difficulty blending the CVC word *Sam*.	Usually connects the /s/ sound with the letter *Ss* and blends the CVC word *Sam* with only occasional support.	Consistently connects the /s/ sound with the letter *Ss* and blends the CVC word *Sam*.
HIGH-FREQUENCY WORDS	Does not identify the high-frequency words.	Usually recognizes the high-frequency words with accuracy, but not speed.	Consistently recognizes the high-frequency words with speed and accuracy.
COMPREHENSION	Does not identify characters using pictures and text.	Usually identifies characters using pictures and text.	Consistently identifies characters using pictures and text.

DIBELS LINK

PROGRESS MONITORING

Use your DIBELS results to inform instruction.

IF...
Initial Sound Fluency (**ISF**)   0–7

THEN...
Evaluation for Intervention

TPRI LINK

PROGRESS MONITORING

Use your TPRI scores to inform instruction.

IF...
Phonemic Awareness   Still Developing
Graphophonemic Knowledge   Still Developing
Listening Comprehension   Still Developing

THEN...
Evaluation for Intervention

Diagnose		Prescribe
Review the assessment answers with children. Have them correct their errors. Then provide additional instruction as needed.		
PHONEMIC AWARENESS/ PHONICS /s/s	**IF...** **Quick Check Rubric:** Children consistently score 1 or **Pencil and Paper Assessment:** Children get 0–2 items correct	**THEN...** Reteach Phonemic Awareness and Phonics Skills using the **Phonics** and **Phonemic Awareness Intervention Teacher's Editions**. *SPIRAL REVIEW* Use the Build Fluency lesson in upcoming weeks to provide children practice reading words with /s/s.
HIGH-FREQUENCY WORDS *like*	**Quick Check Rubric:** Children consistently score 1 or **Pencil and Paper Assessment:** Children get 0–2 items correct	Reteach High-Frequency Words using the **Phonics Intervention Teacher's Edition**. *SPIRAL REVIEW* Use the High-Frequency Words lesson in upcoming weeks to provide children practice reading the word *like*.
COMPREHENSION Skill: Identify Character	**Quick Check Rubric:** Children consistently score 1 or **Pencil and Paper Assessment:** Children get 0–2 items correct	Reteach Comprehension Skill using the **Comprehension Intervention Teacher's Edition**.

Response to Intervention

To place children in Tier 2 or Tier 3 Intervention use the *Diagnostic Assessment*.

- Phonemic Awareness
- Phonics
- Vocabulary
- Comprehension
- Fluency

Week 2 ★ At a Glance

Priority Skills and Concepts

 Comprehension
- **Genre:** Expository, Fable
- **Strategy:** Ask Questions
- **Skill:** Compare and Contrast

 Skill: Identify Character

 High-Frequency Words
- *a*

Oral Vocabulary
- Build Robust Vocabulary:
assist, *game*, *honest*, *pleasant*, *world*

Fluency
- Word Automaticity
- Sound-Spellings

 Phonemic Awareness
- Phoneme Isolation
- Phoneme Blending
- Phoneme Identity

 Phonics
- *Pp*

Grammar
- Naming Words (Nouns)

Writing
- Picture Web

Key   Tested in Program  Review Skill

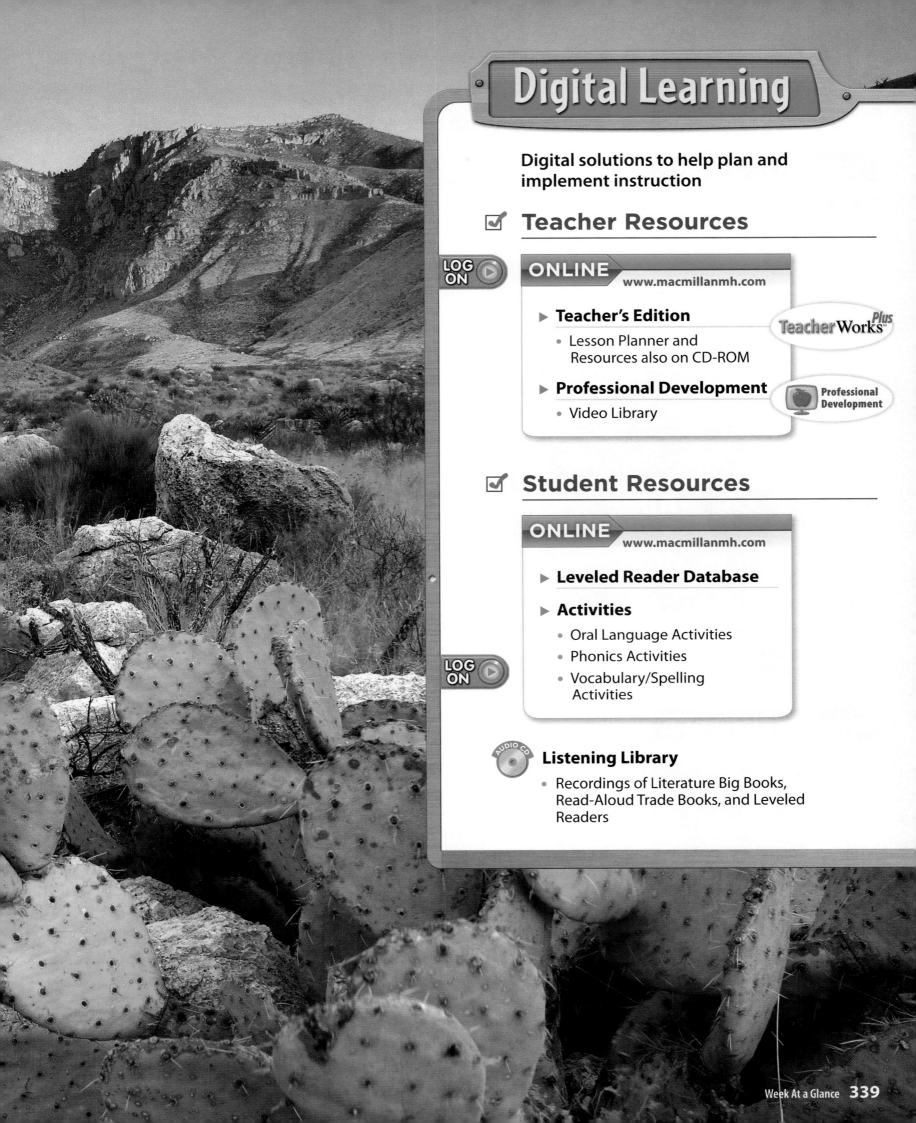

Digital Learning

Digital solutions to help plan and implement instruction

☑ Teacher Resources

LOG ON ▶

ONLINE www.macmillanmh.com

▶ **Teacher's Edition**
- Lesson Planner and Resources also on CD-ROM

TeacherWorks Plus

▶ **Professional Development**
- Video Library

Professional Development

☑ Student Resources

ONLINE www.macmillanmh.com

▶ **Leveled Reader Database**

▶ **Activities**
- Oral Language Activities
- Phonics Activities
- Vocabulary/Spelling Activities

LOG ON ▶

AUDIO CD **Listening Library**
- Recordings of Literature Big Books, Read-Aloud Trade Books, and Leveled Readers

Weekly Literature

Theme: What Is a Friend?

A mix of fiction and nonfiction

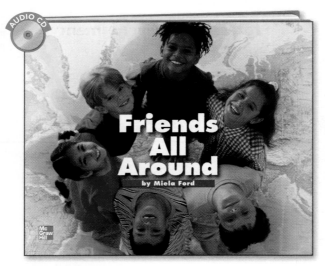

Big Book

Genre Expository

Big Book of Explorations

Genre Expository

Support Literature

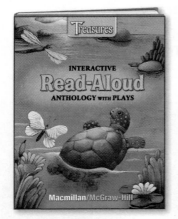

Interactive Read-Aloud Anthology

Genre Fable

Oral Vocabulary Cards
- Listening Comprehension
- Build Robust Vocabulary

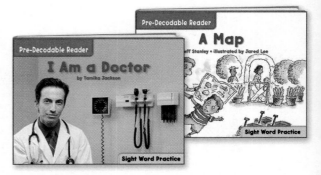

Pre-decodable Readers

Resources for Differentiated Instruction

Leveled Readers: Science

GR Levels Rebus-C

Genre	Expository

- Same Theme
- Same Vocabulary/Phonics
- Same Comprehension Skills

Approaching Level

On Level

Beyond Level

ELL

Leveled Reader Database
Go to www.macmillanmh.com.

Practice

Activity Book

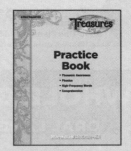

Practice Book

ELL Practice Book

Response to Intervention

Tier 2

- Phonemic Awareness
- Phonics
- Vocabulary
- Comprehension
- Fluency

Tier 3

Unit Assessment

Assess Unit Skills

- Phonemic Awareness
- Phonics
- High-Frequency Words
- Listening Comprehension

HOME-SCHOOL CONNECTION

- Family letters in English and Spanish
- Take-home stories and activities

Go to **www.macmillanmh.com** for Online Lesson Planner

TeacherWorks Plus
All-In-One Planner and Resource Center

Professional Development
Video Library

Big Book

Friends All Around
by Misín Ford

WHOLE GROUP

ORAL LANGUAGE

- **Oral Vocabulary**

- **Phonemic Awareness**

WORD STUDY

- **Phonics**

- **High-Frequency Words**

READING

- **Listening Comprehension**

- **Apply Phonics and High-Frequency Words**

- **Fluency**

LANGUAGE ARTS

- **Writing**

- **Grammar**

ASSESSMENT

- **Informal/Formal**

DAY 1

? Focus Question Who can be a friend?
Build Background, 350
Oral Vocabulary *assist, game, honest, pleasant, world*, 350

Phonemic Awareness
Phoneme Isolation, 353

Phonics
Introduce /p/*p*, 354
Handwriting: Write *Pp*, 355
Activity Book, 14
Practice Book, 47
High-Frequency Words
a, 352

Share the Big Book
Friends All Around
Strategy: Ask Questions, 351
Skill: Compare and Contrast, 351

Big Book

Shared Writing
A List, 357
Grammar
Naming Words (Nouns), 356

Quick Check Phonemic Awareness, 353

DAY 2

? Focus Question Can a brother be a friend?
Can a cousin be a friend?
Oral Vocabulary *assist, game, honest, pleasant, world*, 358
Number Words, 365

Phonemic Awareness
Phoneme Blending, 366

Phonics
Review /p/*p*, /m/*m*, /a/*a*, 366
Blend with /p/*p*, 367

Review High-Frequency Words, 368

Reread the Big Book
Friends All Around
Strategy: Ask Questions, 360
Skill: Compare and Contrast, 360
Retell, 364
Pre-decodable Reader: *I Am a Doctor*, 368
Activity Book, 15–16
Practice Book, 48
Fluency Echo-Read, 364

Big Book

Interactive Writing
A Word Web, 369

Quick Check Comprehension, 364

SMALL GROUP Lesson Plan ▷ **Differentiated Instruction 344–345**

Priority Skills

Phonemic Awareness/Phonics	High-Frequency Words	Oral Vocabulary	Comprehension
/p/p	a	Number Words	**Strategy:** Ask Questions **Skill:** Compare and Contrast

Half-Day Kindergarten

Teach Core Skills
Focus on tested skill lessons, other lessons, and small group options as your time allows.

DAY 3

❓Focus Question What do you do when you meet a new friend?

Oral Vocabulary *assist, game, honest, pleasant, world,* 370

Oral Vocabulary Cards: "Brer Turtle Helps Out"

✔ **Phonemic Awareness**
Phoneme Isolation, 375

✔ **Phonics**
Review /p/p, /s/s, 376
Blend with, 377
Read Words, 377

✔ **High-Frequency Words**
a, 374
Activity Book, 17–18
Practice Book, 49–50
Read for Fluency, 374

Read the Big Book of Explorations
"Helping Hands" and "The Fight," 26–28

Text Feature:
Use Illustrations, 372

Big Book of Explorations

Independent Writing
Prewrite and Draft Picture Webs, 379
Grammar
Naming Words (Nouns), 378

`Quick Check` **High-Frequency Words,** 374

DAY 4

❓Focus Question What do you like best about having a friend?

Oral Vocabulary *assist, game, honest, pleasant, world,* 380

Number Words, 383

✔ **Phonemic Awareness**
Phoneme Blending, 384

✔ **Phonics**
Picture Sort: /s/s, /a/a, /p/p, 384
Blend with /p/p, 385
Activity Book, 20
Practice Book, 52

✔ **Review High-Frequency Words,** 386

Interactive Read Aloud
Listening Comprehension, 382

Read Aloud: "The Lion and the Mouse"

Pre-decodable Reader:
A Map, 386

Read Aloud

Independent Writing
Revise and Edit a Picture Web, 387

`Quick Check` **Phonics,** 385

DAY 5
Review and Assess

❓Focus Question Why is it important to have a friend?

Oral Vocabulary *assist, game, honest, pleasant, world,* 388

Number Words, 390

✔ **Phonemic Awareness**
Phoneme Identity, 391

✔ **Phonics**
Read Words, 392
Dictation, 392
Activity Book, 22

✔ **High-Frequency Words**
a, can, like, we, the, 390

Read Across Texts
Strategy: Ask Questions, 389
✔ **Skill:** Compare and Contrast, 389
Activity Book, 21

Fluency Word Automaticity, 390

Independent Writing
Publish and Present a Picture Web, 393

✔ **Weekly Assessment,** 420–421

Differentiated Instruction

What do I do in small groups?

Teacher-Led Small Groups

Independent Activities

IF... children need additional instruction, practice, or extension based on your **Quick Check** observations for the following priority skills

 Phonemic Awareness
Phoneme Isolation, Blending, Identity

 Phonics
Pp

 High-Frequency Words
a, like, the, we

 Comprehension
Strategy: Ask Questions
Skill: Compare and Contrast

THEN...

Approaching	Preteach and
ELL	Reteach Skills
On Level	Practice
Beyond	Enrich and Accelerate Learning

LOG ON ▶ ## Suggested Small Group Lesson Plan

CD-ROM TeacherWorks Plus
All-In-One Planner and Resource Center

	DAY 1	DAY 2
Approaching Level **•Preteach/Reteach** Tier 2 **Tier 2 Instruction**	• Oral Language, 394 • High-Frequency Words, 394 **ELL** High-Frequency Words Review, 394 • Phonemic Awareness, 395 • Phonics, 395 **ELL** Sound-Spellings Review, 395	• High-Frequency Words, 400 **ELL** • Pre-decodable Reader, 400 • Phonemic Awareness, 401 • Phonics, 401
On Level **•Practice**	• High-Frequency Words, 396 • Phonemic Awareness/Phonics, 396 **ELL**	• Pre-decodable Reader, 402
Beyond Level **•Extend/Accelerate** Gifted Talented **Gifted and Talented**	• High-Frequency Words/Vocabulary, 397 **ELL** Expand Oral Vocabulary, 397 • Phonics, 397	• Pre-decodable Reader, 402
ELL **•Build English Language Proficiency** **•See ELL in other levels.**	• Oral Language Warm-Up, 398 • Academic Language, 398 • Vocabulary, 399	• Access to Core Content, 403

Focus on Leveled Readers

Levels Rebus–C

Approaching

On Level

Beyond

ELL

Manipulatives

Sound-Spelling WorkBoards

Sound-Spelling Cards

Photo Cards

High-Frequency Word Cards

Additional Leveled Readers

LOG ON ▶ **Leveled Reader Database**
www.macmillanmh.com

Search by
- Comprehension Skill
- Content Area
- Genre
- Text Feature
- Guided Reading Level
- Reading Recovery Level
- Lexile Score
- Benchmark Level

Subscription also available

Visual Vocabulary Resources

DAY 3

- High-Frequency Words, 404 **ELL**
- Phonemic Awareness, 404
- Phonics, 405
- Pre-decodable Reader, 405

- Phonics, 406

- Phonics, 406

- Access to Core Content, 407
- Grammar, 407

DAY 4

- Phonemic Awareness, 408
- Phonics, 408 **ELL**
- Leveled Reader Lesson 1, 409

- Leveled Reader Lesson 1, 410 **ELL**

- Leveled Reader Lesson 1, 411
  Evaluate, 411

- Leveled Reader, 412–413

DAY 5

- Phonemic Awareness, 414
- Phonics, 414 **ELL**
- Leveled Reader Lesson 2, 415
- High-Frequency Words, 415

- Leveled Reader Lesson 2, 416

- Leveled Reader Lesson 2, 417 **ELL**
- Expand Vocabulary, 417

- Fluency, 418
- High-Frequency Words, 419
- Writing, 419

Managing the Class

What do I do with the rest of my class?

- Activity Book
- Practice Book
- ELL Practice Book
- Leveled Reader Activities
- Literacy Workstations
- Online Activities
- Buggles and Beezy

Classroom Management Tools

Weekly Contract

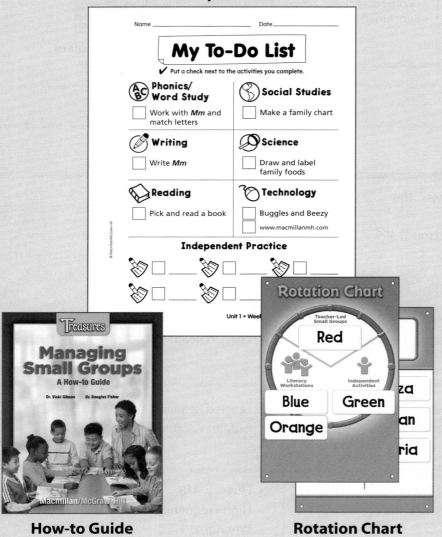

How-to Guide

Rotation Chart

Digital Learning

Phonics Activities

- Match Letters
- Match Letters to Sounds
- Blend Words

Meet the Author/Illustrator

Lisa Jahn-Clough

- Lisa has taught both writing and illustrating for many years at a college in Maine.
- Lisa lives in Portland, Maine, but was born on a small farm in Rhode Island.
- Lisa's father was a zoologist and she even had a pet monkey, named Zepher, when she was young.

Other books by Lisa Jahn-Clough
- Jahn-Clough, Lisa. *Simon and Molly Plus Hester*. Boston, MA: Houghton Mifflin, 2001.
- Jahn-Clough, Lisa. *My Friend and I*. Boston, MA: Houghton Mifflin, 1999.

- Read Other Books by the Author or Illustrator

Practice

Activity Book

Practice Book

ELL Practice Book

Independent Activities

ONLINE INSTRUCTION www.macmillanmh.com

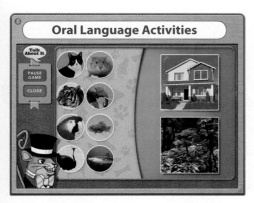

Oral Language Activities

- Focus on Unit Vocabulary and Concepts
- English Language Learner Support

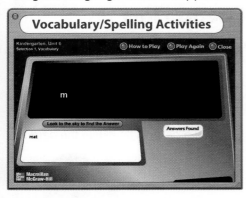

Vocabulary/Spelling Activities

- Differentiated Lists and Activities

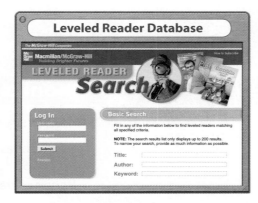

Leveled Reader Database

- Leveled Reader Database
- Search titles by level, skill, content area, and more

Available on CD

LISTENING LIBRARY
Recordings of selections
- Literature Big Books
- Read-Aloud Big Books
- Leveled Readers
- ELL Readers

NEW ADVENTURES WITH BUGGLES AND BEEZY
Phonemic awareness and phonics activities

Leveled Reader Activities

Approaching **On Level** **Beyond** **ELL**

See inside cover of all Leveled Readers.

Literacy Workstations

See lessons on pages 348–349.

Managing the Class

What do I do with the rest of my class?

Reading

Objectives

- Read and discuss a book with a partner
- Read a book and retell the story

Phonics/Word Study

Objectives

- Sort pictures by matching initial sounds with the letters *Aa*, *Pp*, and *Ss*
- Write and trace words with the letters *a, m, p, s*

Reading — **Buddy Reading** — 20 Minutes

Read and talk about a book with a partner.

❶ Read a book. ❷ Talk about it.

Do More
- Talk about the front cover and back cover with a partner.
- Write about the book.

For more book titles, go to the Meet the Author/Illustrator page on www.macmillanmh.com

9

© Macmillan/McGraw-Hill

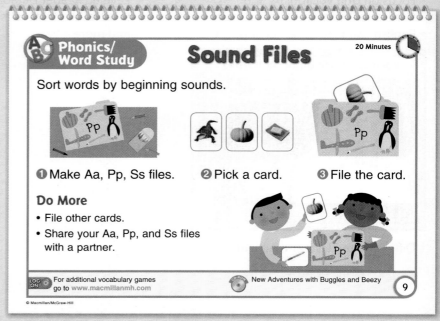

Phonics/Word Study — **Sound Files** — 20 Minutes

Sort words by beginning sounds.

❶ Make Aa, Pp, Ss files. ❷ Pick a card. ❸ File the card.

Do More
- File other cards.
- Share your Aa, Pp, and Ss files with a partner.

For additional vocabulary games go to www.macmillanmh.com

New Adventures with Buggles and Beezy

9

© Macmillan/McGraw-Hill

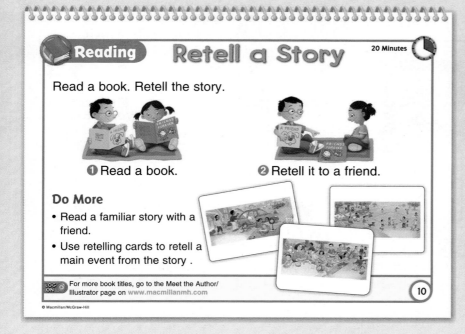

Reading — **Retell a Story** — 20 Minutes

Read a book. Retell the story.

❶ Read a book. ❷ Retell it to a friend.

Do More
- Read a familiar story with a friend.
- Use retelling cards to retell a main event from the story .

For more book titles, go to the Meet the Author/Illustrator page on www.macmillanmh.com

10

© Macmillan/McGraw-Hill

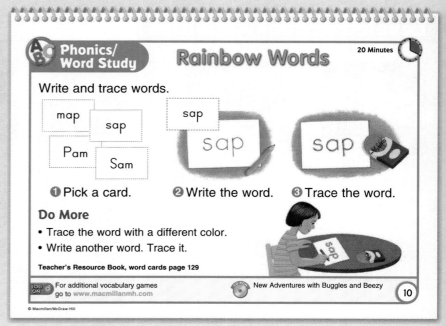

Phonics/Word Study — **Rainbow Words** — 20 Minutes

Write and trace words.

map sap sap Pam Sam sap sap

❶ Pick a card. ❷ Write the word. ❸ Trace the word.

Do More
- Trace the word with a different color.
- Write another word. Trace it.

Teacher's Resource Book, word cards page 129

For additional vocabulary games go to www.macmillanmh.com

New Adventures with Buggles and Beezy

10

© Macmillan/McGraw-Hill

Literacy Workstations

Reading

Phonics/ Word Study

Writing

Science/ Social Studies

Literacy Workstation Flip Charts

Writing

Objectives
- Write words that contain *Pp*
- Form words with the letters *a*, *m*, *Pp*, and *Ss*

Content Literacy

Objectives
- Recognize that sound travels
- Demonstrate an understanding of what a friend is through role play

---

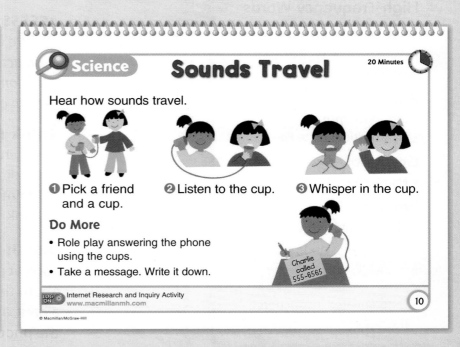

Writing — **Writing with Pp** — 20 Minutes

Make a P. List Pp words.

❶ Make a P.   ❷ Write words with Pp.   ❸ Paste the P.

Do More
- Write more words with p, a, and s.
- Use the words in sentences.

9

© Macmillan/McGraw-Hill

Science — **Sounds Travel** — 20 Minutes

Hear how sounds travel.

❶ Pick a friend and a cup.   ❷ Listen to the cup.   ❸ Whisper in the cup.

Do More
- Role play answering the phone using the cups.
- Take a message. Write it down.

Charlie called 555-6565

LOG ON — Internet Research and Inquiry Activity
www.macmillanmh.com

10

© Macmillan/McGraw-Hill

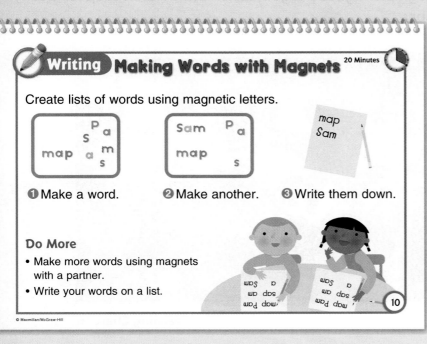

Writing — **Making Words with Magnets** — 20 Minutes

Create lists of words using magnetic letters.

❶ Make a word.   ❷ Make another.   ❸ Write them down.

Do More
- Make more words using magnets with a partner.
- Write your words on a list.

10

© Macmillan/McGraw-Hill

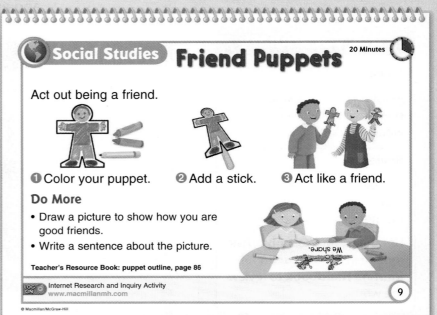

Social Studies — **Friend Puppets** — 20 Minutes

Act out being a friend.

❶ Color your puppet.   ❷ Add a stick.   ❸ Act like a friend.

Do More
- Draw a picture to show how you are good friends.
- Write a sentence about the picture.

Teacher's Resource Book: puppet outline, page 86

LOG ON — Internet Research and Inquiry Activity
www.macmillanmh.com

9

© Macmillan/McGraw-Hill

DAY 1
At a Glance

WHOLE GROUP

Oral Language
- Build Background

✔ **Comprehension**
- Read *Friends All Around*
- Strategy: Ask Questions
- Skill: Compare and Contrast

✔ **High-Frequency Words**
- Introduce *a*

✔ **Phonemic Awareness**
- Phoneme Isolation

✔ **Phonics**
- Introduce /p/*p*
- Handwriting: Write *Pp*

Grammar
- Naming Words (Nouns)

Writing
- Shared Writing: A List

SMALL GROUP

- Differentiated Instruction, pages 394–419

Oral Vocabulary

Week 2

assist	game
honest	pleasant
world	

Review

complete	favorite
friend	hobby
partner	

Use the **Define/Example/Ask** routine in the **Instructional Routine Handbook** to review the words.

Oral Language

 Talk About It

Build Background: *What Is a Friend?*

INTRODUCE THE THEME

Tell children that this week they will be talking and reading books about how friends in different parts of the **world** share activities, such as playing music. The world is our planet Earth.

Write the following question on the board: *Who can be a friend?* Track the print as you read aloud the question. Point out the difference between a letter and a word. Then ask children to point to the second word. Prompt children to answer the question.

ACCESS PRIOR KNOWLEDGE

- Have children discuss ways friends have fun together. *A* **game** *is an activity you play for fun. Each game has its own rules. What kinds of games do you play with your friends? Do you know any games from other places in the world?*

Think Aloud Let's look at this picture. It is two friends or sisters playing a game. I see a ball stuck to the circle that the girl is holding. She is in a wheelchair. There are trees and grass around. (Point to the ball, wheelchair, grass, and trees.) Where do you think they are? What game are they playing?

DISCUSS THE PHOTOGRAPH

Look at and discuss the photograph with children. Ask children about things they do in different places with their friends, such as at a park, at a street fair, or at a library. Talk about what else the girls in the photograph might do together. Remind children to speak clearly and audibly.

Teaching Chart 16

Share the Big Book

Listening Comprehension

PREVIEW Display the cover. *Children are standing in a circle. There is a map of the **world** under them. Let's read about what friends from all over the world do together.*

Read the title and the author's name aloud as you track the print. *Do you think the children are friends? Why?*

GENRE Tell children that this book is **expository** and tells facts about real people and places. Expository text is also called nonfiction.

Big Book

STRATEGY Ask Questions

EXPLAIN/MODEL Tell children that asking themselves questions as they read and listen to a book can help them to understand it.

Think Aloud I'll ask myself what these children might like to do together. I wonder if they all like the same things or if some of them like different things. I'll try to answer these questions.

SKILL Compare and Contrast

EXPLAIN/MODEL Tell children that thinking about how people and things in a story are the same or different can help us understand it. Paying attention to **details**, or parts of the story, helps us find out how people and things are the same or different.

Think Aloud Some of the children on the cover are boys and some are girls. Each child looks a little different from the others.

Read the Big Book

SET PURPOSE Have children ask themselves questions to help them gain information about how the friends are the same and different. Use the **Define/Example/Ask** routine to teach the story words on the inside back cover.

Respond to Literature

MAKE CONNECTIONS *How were some friends the same? In what ways are you like the kids from around the world?* Have them draw an activity from the book.

Objectives

- Discuss the theme
- Recognize the difference between a letter and a printed word
- Use oral vocabulary words *game* and *world*
- Listen and respond to a book
- Ask questions; compare and contrast
- Make connections to the larger community

Materials

- Teaching Chart 16
- Big Book: *Friends All Around*

ELL

Use the **Interactive Question-Response Guide** for *Friends All Around*, **ELL Resource Book** pages 42–47, to guide children through a reading of the book. As you read this book, make meanings clear by pointing to pictures, demonstrating word meanings, paraphrasing text, and asking questions.

Digital Learning

Story on **Listening Library Audio CD**

Objectives

- Read the high-frequency word *a*
- Identify the word *a* in text and speech
- Review the high-frequency words *we, can, the, like*

Materials

- High-Frequency Word Cards: *a, can, like, the, we*
- Teaching Chart 17

High-Frequency Words

 a

a

INTRODUCE Display the **High-Frequency Word Card** for **a**. Use the **Read/Spell/Write** routine to teach the word.

- **Read** Point to and say the word *a*. *I see* a *book.*

- **Spell** *The word* a *is spelled* a. Explain that *a* is a word with just one letter: *a. Let's read and spell* a *together.*

- **Write** *Now let's write the word* a *on our papers. Let's spell aloud the word as we write it:* a.

SPIRAL REVIEW

REVIEW *we, can, the, like* Display each card and have children read the word.

can	like
we	the

READ THE RHYME AND CHIME Instruct children to point to *a*. Then add *a* to the class Word Wall. Repeat the rhyme together for fluency.

A Pal
You are a friend.
You are my pal.
A pal for always,
A pal for now!

High-Frequency Word: a
Phonics: /p/p

Unit 2
Rhyme and Chime

Friends Week 2 17

Teaching Chart 17

For Tier 2 instruction, see page 394.

TIME TO MOVE!

Using color words and *a*, have children move to objects you name. For example: *Skip to a red block. Walk to a yellow truck.*

Phonemic Awareness

Phoneme Isolation

Model

Display the **Photo Card** for *pig*.

Today we are going to learn a new sound. Listen for the sound at the beginning of *pig*: /p/. *Pig* has /p/ at the beginning. Say the sound with me: /p/. What is the sound?

Let's pat our heads when we hear a word that begins with /p/!

Read the "A Pal" Rhyme and Chime again. Have children pat their heads each time they hear /p/.

You are my friend.
You are my pal.
A pal for always,
A pal for now!

Review /s/, /a/

Display the Photo Card for *seal*.
Repeat for *alligator*.

This is a *seal*. The beginning sound in *seal* is /s/. Listen: /sss/, *seal*. (**Stretch the beginning sound.**) What is the sound?

Guided Practice/Practice

Display and name each Photo Card. Children identify the initial sound. Guide practice with the first card.

Continue orally with the words *pan, as, sun, pet, past, song, at, soak*.

Say the name of the picture with me. Tell me the sound you hear at the beginning of the word.

Quick Check

Can children identify initial /p/ in a word?

During **Small Group Instruction**

If No → Approaching Level Provide additional practice, page 395.
If Yes → On Level Children blend words with /p/ and /s/, page 396.
Beyond Level Children blend words with /p/ and /s/, page 397.

Objectives
- Isolate initial sound /p/
- Review initial /s/ and /a/

Materials
- Photo Cards: *alligator, ant, ax, pen, pie, pig, seal, soap, sock*

ELL

Pronunciation Display and have children name Photo Cards from this and prior lessons to reinforce phonemic awareness and word meanings. Point to the card for *pig* and ask: *What do you see?* (a pig) What is the sound at the beginning of the word *pig*? (/p/) Repeat with other Photo Cards.

Objectives

- Match the letter *p* to the sound /p/
- Recognize the difference between a letter and a printed word
- Handwriting: write *Pp*

Materials

- Sound-Spelling Card: *Piano*
- Teaching Chart 17
- Word-Building Cards
- Handwriting
- Handwriting Teacher's Edition
- Activity Book, p. 14
- Practice Book, p. 47

ELL

Variations in Languages
Speakers of Hmong may have difficulty perceiving and pronouncing /p/. Use the Approaching Level Phonics lessons for additional pronunciation and decoding practice.

 Sound Pronunciation

See **Sound Pronunciation CD** for a model of the /p/ sound. Play this for children needing additional models.

Phonics

✔ Introduce /p/*p*

Model

Display the *Piano* **Sound-Spelling Card**.

This is the *Piano* card. The sound is /p/. The /p/ sound is spelled with the letter *p*. Say it with me: /p/. This is the sound you hear at the beginning of the word *piano*. Listen: /p/, /p/, /p/, *piano*.

What is the name of this letter? What sound does it stand for?

Read "A Pal." Point out that the word *Pal* in the title begins with the letter *P*. Model placing a self-stick note below the letter *P* in *Pal*. Show children the difference between a letter and a word.

Teaching Chart 17

Guided Practice/Practice

Read the rhyme. Stop after each line. Children place self-stick notes below words that begin with *p*. Guide practice with *pal* in line 2.

Repeat with initial *m*.

Let's put a sticky note below the word in the line that begins with *p*. The word *pal* begins with the letter *p*.

Let's put a sticky note below words in the line that begin with the letter *m*. The word *my* begins with the letter *m*.

Corrective Feedback

If children have difficulty with /p/, write the word *pig* on the board. Circle the *p*. *The letter* p *stands for the /p/ sound. Say the sound as I point to the letter.*

Build Fluency: Sound-Spellings

 SPIRAL REVIEW Display the following **Word-Building Cards**: *a, m, s, p*. Have children chorally say each sound. Repeat and vary the pace.

Handwriting: Write *Pp*

MODEL Model holding up your writing hand. Say the handwriting cues below as you write the capital and lowercase forms of *Pp* on the board. Then trace the letters on the board and in the air.

Straight down. Go back to the top. Around and in at the dotted line.

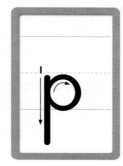

Straight down, past the bottom line. Circle around all the way.

PRACTICE Ask children to hold up their writing hand.

- Say the cues together as children trace with their index finger the letters you wrote on the board.

- Have children write *P* and *p* in the air as they say /p/.

- Distribute handwriting practice pages. Observe children's pencil grip and paper position, and correct as necessary. Have children say /p/ every time they write the letter *p*.

For Tier 2 instruction, see page 395.

Activity Book, page 14
Practice Book, page 47

> ✏️ **Daily Handwriting**
> Check that children form letters starting at the top and moving to the bottom. See **Handwriting Teacher's Edition** for ball-and-stick and slant models.

Objective

- Recognize and use words that name things (nouns)

Materials

- Photo Cards: *ax, jet, pen, rock, sun*
- Big Book: *Friends All Around*

Grammar

Naming Words (Nouns)

MODEL Remind children that they have been learning about naming words, which are called nouns. Instruct children that naming words can name people, places, animals, or things. *Today we will talk about words that name things.* Turn to page 13 of *Friends All Around* and read the sentence. Ask children which word names a thing. Then point to the bicycle in the photo and have children say its name again. Repeat for pages 18 and 19.

- Use the words *bicycles*, *books*, and *computers* to start a list and have children add other names of things.

- Say sentences and have children say the naming word that is a thing: *Patrick and Jeff played a* **game**. *What did they play?* (a game) *The dog chewed on a bone. What did the dog chew?* (a bone)

PRACTICE Show **Photo Cards** of *ax, sun, jet, rock,* and *pen*.

- Have children identify each picture. Model saying sentences about the photographs, such as:

- After each sentence, ask children which word names a thing.

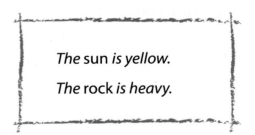

The sun *is yellow.*

The rock *is heavy.*

- Have children take turns choosing Photo Cards and saying complete sentences using the nouns. Ask children to tell you the noun they used. Then have them write the noun.

Writing

Shared Writing: A List

BRAINSTORM

Remind children that in *Friends All Around*, they read about some of the things that friends have fun doing together around the **world**. *What are some of the **games** and activities that friends did together?*

WRITE

- Create a list as shown below. Read the heading aloud as you track the print. Have children repeat.

- Model by rereading pages 8–9. *Some friends dance in a parade, and some friends dance in a show, so I will write* dance in a parade *and* dance in a show *on the list.*

- Continue by reading pages 10–11, 16–17, and 18–19. Have children suggest what to write on the list.

- Read the completed list aloud. Have children repeat after you. Point out the high-frequency word *a*.

- Point out how the words are written one under the other on the list. *A list helps us remember information and ideas.*

- Save the lists to refer to in other writing activities this week.

Things Friends Do Together

dance in a parade
dance in a show
ride horses
ride bikes
make a snowman
make a snow bear
jump rope
jump with a ball

Write About It

Have children draw a picture of something they use when they play with a friend. Tell them to include as many details as they can. Help children label their pictures.

Objective
- Write a list

Materials
- Big Book: *Friends All Around*

5-Day Writing

Picture Web	
DAY 1	Shared: A List
DAY 2	Interactive: A Word Web
DAY 3	Independent: Prewrite and Draft Picture Webs
DAY 4	Independent: Revise and Edit a Picture Web
DAY 5	Independent: Publish and Present

ELL

Prewriting Planning
Provide the **Big Book** for children. Have them point to and name things they use and share in games and activities with friends. List the things children name and help them label their pictures.

Transitions That Teach

While children line up, have them name some things people all over the **world** do.

WHOLE GROUP

Oral Language
- Build Robust Vocabulary

✓ **Comprehension**
- Reread *Friends All Around*
- Strategy: Ask Questions
- Skill: Compare and Contrast
- Fluency: Echo-Read

Vocabulary
- Number Words
- Story Word: *computers*

✓ **Phonemic Awareness**
- Phoneme Blending

✓ **Phonics**
- Review /p/*p*, /m/*m*, /a/*a*
- Blend with /p/*p*
- Pre-decodable Reader:
  I Am a Doctor

Writing
- Interactive Writing: A Word Web

SMALL GROUP

- Differentiated Instruction, pages 394–419

Oral Vocabulary

Week 2

assist	game
honest	pleasant
world	

Review

complete	favorite
friend	hobby
partner	

Use the **Define/Example/Ask** routine in the **Instructional Routine Handbook** to review the words.

Oral Language

 Talk About It

Build Robust Vocabulary

INTRODUCE WORDS

Tell children that the **Big Book** *Friends All Around* shows friends all over the world. *The world is our planet Earth and the people, animals, and things on it. I dream about traveling to different places around the world. Where in this world would you like to visit? What games or fun activities can you think of that are played in other parts of the world?* Guide children to speak in complete sentences. Read pages 2–13.

Vocabulary Routine

Use the routine below to discuss the meaning of each word.

Define: The **world** is our planet Earth and the people, animals, and things on it. Say the word with me.
Example: The globe is a model of our world.
Ask: What part of the world do we live in?

Define: **Games** are activities people play for fun. Say the word with me.
Example: Hide-and-seek and tag are our favorite games.
Ask: What games do you play with your friends?

CREATE A CHART

Use the Venn diagram on **Teaching Chart G2**. Label the circles. Read the chart together as you track the print. *Friends all over the world dance, so I will write* dance *in the center. Dance is a word that names an action. The friends in Mexico are dancing in a parade. I will write* dance in a parade *in one circle. The children like to dance in a show, so I will write* dance in a show *in the other circle.* Have children help you complete the Venn diagram by naming other games friends play. Identify action words with children.

Some Friends
dance in a parade
ride a bike

dance
ride

Other Friends
dance in a show
ride a horse

Listen for Rhyme

IDENTIFY RHYME

Remind children that words rhyme when they have the same ending sounds. *The word* pat *rhymes with* sat. Tell them *pat* and *sat* end with the sounds /at/. Ask: *What words rhyme with* pat *and* sat?

Have children listen for the rhyming words as they hear and recite "Sam, Sam."

RHYME ABOUT FRIENDS

Play the rhyme "Sam, Sam," using the **Listening Library Audio CD**. Then teach children the words and recite the poem together. Ask children to name pairs of words that rhyme. (*do/you; seen/green; pass/grass*)

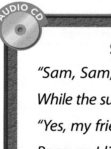

Sam, Sam

"Sam, Sam, come and play,
While the sun shines bright as day."
"Yes, my friend, that's what I'll do,
Because I like to play with you."

"Sam, Sam, have you seen
Pam and Matt on the green?"
"Yes, my friend, I saw them pass,
Skipping over the nice cut grass."

Objectives

- **Use oral vocabulary words** *game* and *world*
- **Complete a diagram**
- **Orally generate rhyme**
- **Identify rhyme**

Materials

- **Big Book:** *Friends All Around*
- **Graphic Organizer; Teaching Chart G2**
- **Listening Library Audio CD**

Digital Learning

Rhyme on Listening Library Audio CD

ELL ENGLISH LANGUAGE LEARNERS

Beginning	Intermediate	Advanced
Confirm Understanding Review oral vocabulary from prior lessons using the **Big Book** *Friends All Around*. For example, display pages 6–7. Say: *Friends play music together. What do these friends do?* (play music) Repeat with other pages.	**Enhance Understanding** Display the same page from the **Big Book** and ask: *What do these friend do?* (These friends play music together.) *What kind of music do you think they play?* Guide children to answer in complete sentences.	**Share Preferences** Ask: *What do you like to do with a friend?* Prompt children to add details to their answers.

Objectives

- Ask and respond to questions
- Compare and contrast

Materials

- Big Book: *Friends All Around*
- Retelling Cards
- Activity Book, pp. 15–16
- Practice Book, p. 48

Big Book

Digital Learning

Story on **Listening Library Audio CD**

ELL

Gesture and Talk
Use gesturing and talking to help make the text comprehensible.

pp. 2–3

same age, different age:
Select two children who are the same age. *How old are you? You are the same age.* Then have a child stand beside you. Point to the two of you and say: *We are different ages.*

Reread the Big Book

Listening Comprehension

CONCEPTS ABOUT PRINT Display the cover and read the title aloud with children as you track the print. Ask children to tell what they remember about the story.

 STRATEGY Ask Questions

Explain to children that a good way to understand a story is to ask questions to compare and contrast the people, places, and other things in it. *As we reread the book, let's think of questions about how people, places, and things are the same and how they are different. Then let's find the answers to our questions.*

 SKILL Compare and Contrast

Tell children that yesterday they found out that some books tell how things are alike and different. *Let's look at the details on pages 8 and 9. How are the costumes different?* Today we are going to read the **Big Book** again and talk about ways that friends can be alike and different around the **world**. Display and read page 3.

Think Aloud I see that these friends are different ages. I'll ask myself how these friends are the same. I see that the boy and the man both like to play the guitar. I also see that the girl and the baby are wearing similar clothes.

Read the Big Book and use the prompts on the inside covers.

pages 2–3

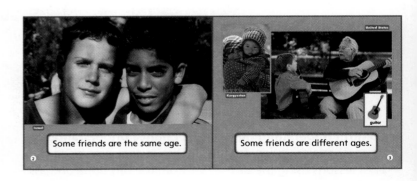

Develop Comprehension

pages 4–5

✔ COMPARE AND CONTRAST

Think Aloud One thing that is the same about all the pictures on these pages is that someone is learning something.

Some friends teach each other.

Some friends learn together.

pages 6–7

✔ ASK QUESTIONS

Think Aloud I'll ask myself what is the same about the friends in the photos. I see that they all like to play music. I wonder what is different. I see that they are playing different types of instruments.

Some friends play fast music.

Some friends play slow music.

pages 8–9

✔ COMPARE AND CONTRAST

■ *How are the friends in these pictures alike?* (They are all dancing.) *How are they different?* (Some are in a parade, but some are in a show.)

Some friends dance in a parade.

Some friends dance in a show.

pages 10–11

✔ ASK QUESTIONS

■ *On page 11, what are the people in the photographs doing together?* (climbing a rock; reading a book)

Some friends listen to each other.

Some friends help each other.

Comprehension

Ask Questions

- (page 8) I will ask myself how the friends are helping each other. I see that in the photo on the left the friends are helping each other to climb a big rock. In the other photo, the girl is helping her friend to read the book.

Compare and Contrast

- (pages 6–7) The instruments that the children are playing are similar to one another because they all make music. How are they different from each other?

- (pages 14–15) The friends on the left page made a man. The friends on the right page made a bear. How are the man and the bear similar to each other?

Story Word

(page 8) Computer

About the Author: Miela Ford

Miela Ford has written a number of children's books, many of which contain her own photographs. Her first book included photographs by her mother, the famous photographer Tana Hoban.

**Big Book
Inside Back Cover**

ELL

pp. 4–5
teach, learn: Show children how to draw a simple shape, such as a triangle. Have children try to copy the shape on paper or in the air. Point to yourself and say: *I teach.* Point to children and say: *You learn.*

pp. 6–7
fast music, slow music: Lead children in singing a stanza of a familiar song, such as "Row, Row Your Boat," rapidly. Say *fast.* Then lead them in singing the same stanza slowly and say *slow.*

pp. 8–9
dance: Lead children in dancing. *Do you like to dance?*

pp. 10–11
listen: Lead children in repeating the song they sang previously. As they sing, turn your head toward them and cup your ear. When they finish, point to your ear and say *listen!*

Text Evidence

Compare and Contrast

Explain When children answer a question about a selection, they often need to find text evidence to support their answer. *When figuring out what is alike and different, look for details in both the text and illustrations.*

Discuss Read pages 12–13. *Point to the children wearing helmets. How is that different from the children on horses?*

ELL

pp. 12–13
horses, bicycles: Lead children in pretending to gallop on horses. Say: *We ride horses.* Then have children sit in their chairs and pretend to pedal bikes. Say: *ride bicycle.*

pp. 14–15
snowman: Act out putting on a coat and mittens, opening a door and going outside, being cold, rolling snowballs, and putting them on top of each other to build a snowman. Repeat the sequence and have children join you in pretending. Show the *snow* **Photo Card** to provide a visual for *snow.*

pp. 16–17
jump with a rope, jump with a ball: Act out jumping rope. Say: *jump with a rope.* Act out playing soccer. Say: *jump with a ball.* Repeat phrases several times in random order and invite children to act out what you say.

pp. 18–19
share: Have two children share a book.

Develop Comprehension

pages 12–13

COMPARE AND CONTRAST
- *What is the same about what the friends on these pages are doing together?* (They are all riding something.) *What is different?* (Some are riding horses, but some are riding bikes.)

Some friends ride horses together.

Some friends ride bicycles together.

pages 14–15

ASK QUESTIONS
- *What is the same about what the friends on these pages are making?* (Possible answer: They are all making something from snow.)

Some friends make a snowman.

Some friends make a snow bear.

pages 16–17

CULTURAL PERSPECTIVES
Think Aloud Friends live and play **games** together all around the **world**. The friends in the first photograph live in Spain. The friends in the second photograph live in Suriname.

Some friends jump with a rope.

Some friends jump with a ball.

pages 18–19

COMPARE AND CONTRAST
- *What is the same about what the friends on these pages are doing together?* (Possible answer: They are all reading something.)

Some friends share books.

Some friends share computers, too.

pages 20–21

IDENTIFY SETTING

- *Where is each scene taking place?*

pages 22–23

REREAD
Think Aloud There is a word I don't know, *argue*. The children look upset with each other. *Argue* must mean "to disagree and be upset with each other."

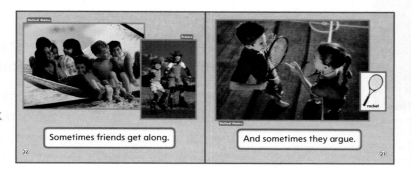

page 24

IDENTIFY CHARACTER
Think Aloud All friends care about each other. That means that friends like each other and think about how each other feels.

Respond to Literature

TALK ABOUT IT Have children refer to the book as they answer questions. Help them to speak audibly and in complete sentences.

- *What activities do friends around the **world** do together?* (They dance, ride bikes, play games, and share books.) LOCATE

- *How are the friends on pages 2 and 24 alike?* (They have arms around each other.) *How are they different?* (different clothes, different location, different ages) COMBINE

- *Why does the author think it is okay for friends to be different?* (The author shows friends doing different things.) CONNECT

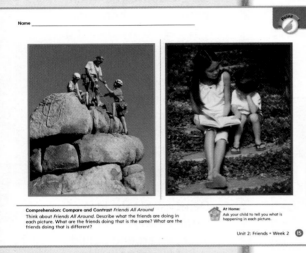

Activity Book, pages 15–16
Practice Book, page 48

Retelling Rubric

4 **Excellent**

Retells the selection without prompting, using detailed information, and referring to text structure and features. Clearly describes the main idea.

3 **Good**

Retells the selection with little guidance, using some details, and occasionally referring to text structure and features. Generally describes the main idea.

2 **Fair**

Retells the selection with some guidance, using limited details. Partially describes the main idea.

1 **Unsatisfactory**

Retells the selection only when prompted, using limited details. Does not describe the main idea.

Retell

Retelling Cards

GUIDED RETELLING

Remind children that as they listened to *Friends All Around*, they used the words and the photographs to help them understand the story. Now they will retell important facts of the story using the photographs on the cards.

- Display **Retelling Card 1**. Based on children's needs, use either the Modeled, Guided, or ELL prompts. The ELL prompts contain support for English Language Learners based on levels of language acquisition.

- Repeat the procedure with the rest of the Retelling Cards, using the prompts to guide children's retelling.

- Discuss the story. *The topic of a book is what it is about. What is this book about?* (friends) *A big idea of the book is that friends are the same in some ways. What is one way that friends can be the same?* (Possible answer: They can be the same age.) *The other big idea of the book is that friends are different in some ways. What is one way that friends can be different?* (Possible answer: They sometimes like to do different things, such as talking, climbing, or reading.)

- *How are you and your friends the same as and different from other friends around the* ***world****?*

Fluency: Echo-Read

MODEL Reread the sentence on page 2 of *Friends All Around*, emphasizing the word *same*. Reread the sentence on page 3, emphasizing the word *different*. Then reread pages 4–12 and have children echo-read as you track the print.

Quick Check
Can children find details to compare and contrast to understand a story? Can children retell important facts from a text?

Vocabulary

Number Words

Chant the following jingle:

One *apple—Crunch!*

Two *pears—Munch!*

Three *lemons—just squeeze, please!*

Repeat each line and ask children what word tells the number.

■ Place pictures of fruits on a table. Discuss the numbers of each kind of fruit: *I see* two *pears. There is* one *apple. How many lemons do you see?*

■ Have children arrange the pictures into groups, with each group containing a different number. For example, three pears, two apples, one lemon. Give each child a turn counting the items in a group and saying the numbers aloud.

NAME NUMBER WORDS Have children page through the **Big Book** *Friends All Around*. Ask them to count the number of friends they see on each page.

Story Word: *computers*

Read page 19 and ask children to point to the computer in the photograph. Ask children to describe what a computer is and how people use it for **games**, for writing, and for organizing. Explain that when computers were first created, they were mostly used for doing math. Another word for solving math problems is *compute*. That is how computers got their name.

TIME TO MOVE!

Give children directions that include number words: *Take two big steps. Make three jumps. Make one hop. Stretch two times.*

Objectives

• **Use number words**
• **Sort pictures into groups**
• **Learn the story word** *computers*

Materials

• **Big Book:** *Friends All Around*
• **3 each: pictures of apples, pears, and lemons**

Digital Learning

LOG ON For children who need additional language support and oral vocabulary development, use the activities found at **www.macmillanmh.com.**

ELL

Reinforce Meaning Display classroom materials on a table, such as one book, two sheets of paper, and three crayons. Count each group of items with children. Then have partners make similar groups and take turns counting the items. Ask the partners how many of each they have.

Objectives

- Orally blend sounds to form words
- Blend with /p/, /m/, /a/, /s/
- Identify and write letters for initial sounds
- Build fluency

Materials

- Puppet
- Word-Building Cards
- pocket chart

Phonemic Awareness

✓ Phoneme Blending

Model

Use the **Puppet** to model how to blend the sounds in the word *Pam*.

Repeat the routine with *pot*.

Happy is going to say the sounds in a word. Listen to Happy as he says each sound: /p/ /a/ /m/. Happy can blend these sounds together: /paaammm/, *Pam*. Say the sounds with Happy: /p/ /a/ /m/, /paaammm/, *Pam*. Now say the word with Happy: *Pam*.

Guided Practice/Practice

Say the sounds. Children blend the sounds to form words. Guide practice with the first word, using the same routine.

Happy is going to say the sounds in a word. Listen carefully to Happy as he says each sound. You will repeat the sounds, then blend them to make a word.

/p/ /i/ /g/	/p/ /i/ /t/	/m/ /a/ /n/
/p/ /i/ /n/	/a/ /n/ /t/	/p/ /a/ /n/

Phonics

✓ Review

p	m	a

Model

Hold up **Word-Building Card** *p*.

Repeat the routine with the letters *m, s,* and *a*.

This is the letter *p*. The letter *p* stands for the /p/ sound. What is the letter? What sound does it stand for?

Say the word. Write the letter *p*.

Repeat with *mat, sat, at*.

Listen as I say a word: *pig*. *Pig* has the /p/ sound at the beginning. The letter *p* stands for /p/. I'll write *p*.

Guided Practice/Practice

Say each word. Children write the letter that stands for the initial sound. Guide practice with the first word.

Listen as I say each word. Write the letter that stands for the beginning sound.

put	man	set	ant	mix
ax	pick	pay	mitt	sing

Build Fluency: Sound-Spellings

Display the following **Word-Building Cards**: *a, m, s, p*. Have children chorally say each sound. Repeat and vary the pace.

Blend with /p/*p*

Model

Place **Word-Building Card** *P* in the pocket chart.

This is the letter *p*. The letter *p* stands for the /p/ sound. Say /p/.

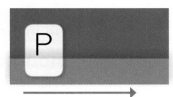

Place Word-Building Card *a* next to *P*. Move your hand from left to right below the letters.

This is the letter *a*. The letter *a* stands for the /a/ sound. Listen as I blend the two sounds together: /paaa/. Now you blend the sounds with me: /paaa/.

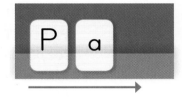

Place Word-Building Card *m* next to *Pa*. Move your hand from left to right.

Repeat with *sap*.

This is the letter *m*. The letter *m* stands for the /m/ sound. Listen as I blend the three sounds together: /paaammm/, *Pam*. Now you blend the sounds with me: /paaammm/, *Pam*.

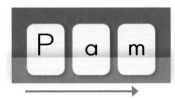

Guided Practice/Practice

Children blend sounds to form words. Guide practice with the first word.

| am | Pam | Sam |
| map | sap | |

ELL

Sound-Letter Relationships Distribute Word-Building Cards for *a, m, s, p* to reinforce that these letters represent the sounds /a/, /m/, /s/, /p/. Name familiar words with these sounds. Each time you say a word have children repeat it and ask them to show you the correct letters.

Objectives

- Review the words *a, like, the*
- Reread for fluency

Materials

- Pre-decodable Reader: *I Am a Doctor*
- High-Frequency Word Cards: *a, like, the*
- pocket chart

Pre-decodable Reader

Read *I Am a Doctor*

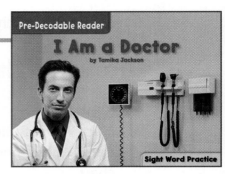
I Am a Doctor

 REVIEW HIGH-FREQUENCY WORDS Display **High-Frequency Word Cards** for **a**, **like**, and **the** in the pocket chart. Review words using the **Read/Spell/Write** routine.

MODEL CONCEPTS ABOUT PRINT *I hold the book so that the cover is on the front and the words are not upside down. I open the book by turning the cover. Then I turn each page as I read it.*

PREDICT *The title is* I Am a Doctor. *When I look through the pages, I see people dressed for different jobs. This book is* expository, *which is also called* nonfiction. *That means the events in the book happen in real life. What jobs do you think are in this book?*

FIRST READ Point out the rebus and discuss what it stands for. Have children point to each word, sounding out the decodable words and saying the sight words quickly. Children should chorally read the story the first time through.

DEVELOP COMPREHENSION Ask the following: *What were some of the jobs in the book? Which job would you like to do? Why?*

SECOND READ Have partners reread the book together. Circulate, listen in, and provide corrective feedback.

I am a doctor. 2

I am a vet. 3

I am a police officer. 4

I am a firefighter. 5

I am a chef. 6

I am a teacher. 7

I am a principal. 8

Pre-decodable Reader

Writing

Interactive Writing: A Word Web

REVIEW

■ Display and read the list children created for the Shared Writing activity as you track the print. Have children repeat after you.

WRITE

■ Say: *Today we are going to make a word web about a **game** friends play together.*

■ Display page 17 of *Friends All Around. What game are these friends playing?* (soccer)

■ Draw a word web. *These friends are playing soccer, so I will write* soccer *in the center circle.* Say the word aloud and track the print.

■ Have children suggest things you need for a game of soccer.

■ Collaborate with children to write the names of the items in the other circles. Have children help by writing all of the letters they know.

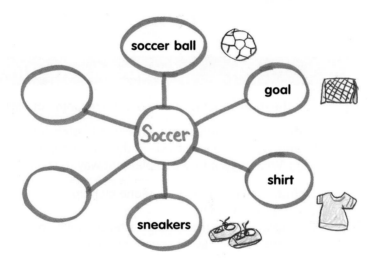

■ Read the word web aloud as you track the print. Point out that the web contains information about one game friends play together.

■ To extend the lesson, have children suggest sentences about how you use each item and record their ideas.

Write About It

Have children draw a picture in their Writer's Notebook of something they like to play. Help them write a caption for their drawing using the sentence frame *I like* _____.

Objectives

• Complete a word web
• Use letter knowledge to write letters in a word

Materials

• Shared Writing from Day 1
• Big Book: *Friends All Around*

5-Day Writing

Picture Web	
DAY 1	Shared: A List
DAY 2	Interactive: A Word Web
DAY 3	Independent: Prewrite and Draft Picture Webs
DAY 4	Independent: Revise and Edit a Picture Web
DAY 5	Independent: Publish and Present

ELL

Reinforce Meaning Ask children to draw and describe sports or games they have played. Have them name things they need to play these sports or games. List the things on the board and read the list together.

Transitions That Teach

While lining up for recess, have children describe the **games** they like to play.

DAY 3
At a Glance

WHOLE GROUP

Oral Language
- Build Robust Vocabulary
- Oral Vocabulary Cards: "Brer Turtle Helps Out"

✓ **Comprehension**
- Read "Making Friends" and "The Fight"

✓ **High-Frequency Words**
- Review *a*

✓ **Phonemic Awareness**
- Phoneme Isolation

✓ **Phonics**
- Review /p/*p*, /s/*s*
- Blend with /p/*p*

Grammar
- Naming Words (Nouns)

Writing
- Independent Writing: Prewrite and Draft Picture Webs

SMALL GROUP

- Differentiated Instruction, pages 394–419

Additional Vocabulary

To provide 15–20 minutes of additional vocabulary instruction, see Oral Vocabulary Cards 5-Day Plan. The pre- and posttests for this week can be found in the **Teacher's Resource Book**, pages 216–217.

Oral Language

 Talk About It ## Build Robust Vocabulary

BUILD BACKGROUND

Introduce the story "Brer Turtle Helps Out" using **Oral Vocabulary Card 1** and read the title aloud. *This is a story about being a good friend. Part of being a good friend is being helpful.* Ask children to tell what they think will happen in the story.

■ Read the story on the back of the cards. Pause at each oral vocabulary word and read the definition. You may wish to check children's understanding using the Paraphrase, Identify Story Elements, and Compose Sentences prompts.

Oral Vocabulary Cards

Vocabulary Routine

Use the routine below to discuss the meaning of each word.

Define: Something or someone nice is **pleasant**. Say the word with me.
Example: Taking a bike ride in the park is a pleasant way to spend the day.
Ask: What is your idea of a pleasant way to spend the day?

Define: You can **assist** someone by helping that person do something. Say the word with me.
Example: I assist the librarian after school by putting the books away.
Ask: How do you assist your family at mealtime?

Define: An **honest** person obeys the rules and tells the truth. Say the word with me.
Example: When your parent asks you a question, it is important to be honest.
Ask: If you break your friend's toy by accident, what would be an honest thing to do?

 SPIRAL REVIEW

■ Use the routine on Cards 2 and 4 to review the words **world** and **game**.

■ Review last week's words: *compete, favorite, friend, hobby,* and *partner.*

Listen for Rhythm

IDENTIFY RHYTHM

Remind children that rhythm is a regular or steady beat. Children will identify the beat by playing the game with a partner.

RHYME ABOUT FRIENDSHIP

Tell children that they will say a rhyme about a **game** friends play. Play the rhyme "Pat-a-Cake" and have children recite the poem and play the game with a partner.

Repeat the rhyme without the recording and pause before the words *can* and *me* for children to fill in the words that rhyme. Explain that *man* and *can*, and *P* and *me* rhyme. Then ask children which of these word pairs rhyme: *man/can, me/see, cake/hat, sat/can.*

Pat-a-Cake

Pat-a-cake, pat-a-cake, baker's man,

Bake me a cake as fast as you can.

Pat it and shape it and mark it with a P,

And bake it in the oven for Pam and me.

Objectives

- **Listen and respond to a folktale**
- **Use oral vocabulary words** *assist, game, honest, pleasant,* and *world*
- **Identify rhyming pairs of words**

Materials

- **Oral Vocabulary Cards: "Brer Turtle Helps Out"**

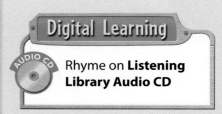

Digital Learning

Rhyme on **Listening Library Audio CD**

Objectives

- Read and respond to a poem
- Predict based on title and illustrations
- Identify rhythm
- Use skills and strategies to comprehend, analyze, and evaluate poetry

Materials

- Big Book of Explorations, Vol. 1: "Making Friends" and "The Fight," pp. 26–28

Vocabulary

wiggled to move in short movements

puffed to swell up or out

Poetry

Genre

Big Book of Explorations

LITERARY TEXT: POETRY Tell children that today they will listen to two poems about friendship. *In "Brer Turtle Helps Out," Brer Rabbit and Brer Wolf had a fight. One of the poems we will read will be about two other friends having a fight and then making up.*

LITERARY ELEMENT: RHYME

Explain/Model Tell children that there are different kinds of poems. *Some poems rhyme and some poems do not rhyme.* Tell children that they will hear one poem that rhymes and one poem that does not.

■ Point to the picture of the two girls on page 27.

Think Aloud As I read the first poem, I will pay close attention to the words. This will help me understand the story within the poem. In the second poem, "The Fight" I will listen for rhyming words. Rhyming words can add rhythm and also help me understand what the writer is saying.

READ "MAKING FRIENDS" AND "THE FIGHT"

Preview and Predict Point to the contrasting pictures of the smiling girls on page 27 and the upset alligators on page 28. Read the title of each poem and the author's name. Ask children to predict what each poem might be about.

Vocabulary Ask children to use prior knowledge to explain the words *wiggled* and *puffed*. As they listen to the poem, guide them to tell about why the author used them.

Set Purpose Tell children that the first poem is a short story about how two girls became friends. Have children listen for how it happens. In the second poem, have children listen for words that rhyme and for the rhythm of the poem. Reread the second poem and have children clap the rhythm.

Read the poems aloud as you track the print.

pages 26–27

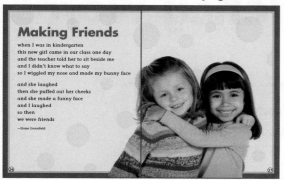

page 28

Retell and Respond

Talk About It Ask children to talk about the two poems.

- *How did the two poems make you feel? Which words in the poem tell you how the two girls in "Making Friends" become friends?*

- *What are some words that rhyme in "The Fight"?*

- *Do you think children all around the **world** meet each other, fight, and make up in the same way?*

Connect to Content

Social Studies Activity:
Friends Everywhere

- Provide books and pictures of children playing together from around the world.

- Have children talk about how all children help each other and play together. Guide them to draw and label pictures of friends: *We play **games**.*

Write About It
Have children draw a picture of their faces when they make a new friend and when they are angry with a friend.

ELL

Beginning

Reinforce Words Before you read "Making Friends," pantomime wiggling your nose, making a bunny face, laughing, and puffing out your cheeks. Before you read "The Fight," pantomime having an argument with a friend and crying. Have children repeat the phrases as you pantomime.

Intermediate

Role-Play Ask children to demonstrate introducing themselves to someone new. Model saying: *Hi, my name is _____.* Then have children act out making up with a friend by having one say: *I'm sorry* and *Want to play?* The other child can respond: *I'm sorry, too. Let's play.*

Advanced

Summarize Have children use their own words to retell and explain one of the poems.

Objective

- Read the high-frequency word *a*

Materials

- High-Frequency Word Cards: *a, I, like, we*
- index card with: period mark
- pocket chart
- Photo Cards: *balloon, doll, jump rope, kitten, penguin*
- Activity Book, pp. 17–18
- Practice Book, pp. 49–50

High-Frequency Words

  a

 a

SPIRAL REVIEW **REVIEW** Display the **High-Frequency Word Card** for **a**. Review the word using the **Read/Spell/Write** routine.

Repeat the routine for the words **I**, **like**, and **we**.

APPLY Build sentences in the pocket chart using High-Frequency Word Cards and **Photo Cards**. Read each sentence aloud, then have children chorally read it as you track the print with your finger. Use the sentence below and the following: *I like a doll. I like a penguin.*

| I | like | a | 🎈 | . |

READ FOR FLUENCY Chorally read the Take-Home Book with children. Then have them reread the book to review high-frequency words and build fluency.

Quick Check

Can children read the word *a*?

During **Small Group Instruction**

If No → **Approaching Level** Provide additional practice with high-frequency words, page 404.

If Yes → **On Level** Children are ready to read the Take-Home story.

Beyond Level Children are ready to read the Take-Home story.

 **TIME TO MOVE!**

I can see a red thing in our room. Ask a volunteer to walk to a red object, point to it, and say: *This is a red thing.* Model the activity a second time, using color names children have learned, and then have partners take turns seeing and finding colored objects.

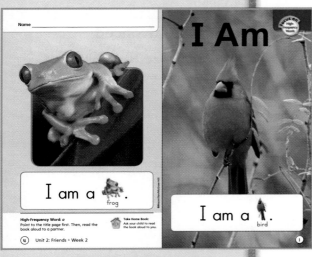

Activity Book, pages 17–18
Practice Book, pages 49–50

Phonemic Awareness
Phoneme Isolation

Objective
- **Listen for initial and final /p/**

Materials
- **Sound Box**
- **WorkBoard Sound Boxes; Teacher's Resource Book, p. 136**
- **markers**

Model

Display the **Sound Box**.

Listen for /p/ in the word *pen*. Say the word with me: *pen*. The /p/ sound is at the beginning of *pen*. I will put a marker in the first box because I hear /p/ at the beginning of *pen*.

Listen for /p/ in *nap*. **(Clearly enunciate and emphasize the ending sound.)** Say the word with me: *nap*. The /p/ sound is at the end of *nap*. I will put the marker in the last box because I hear /p/ at the end of *nap*.

Repeat the routine with the words *pit* and *lip*.

Guided Practice/Practice

Distribute Sound Boxes and markers. Children identify the position of /p/ in words. Guide practice with the first word, using the routine.

Listen to each word. Say the word and then place a marker in the Sound Box to show where you hear /p/.

pen	cup	pear	pan	pat	soap
trip	pie	pig	map	pod	dip
top	cap	stop	peach	pet	rip

For Tier 2 instruction, see page 404.

Objectives

- Review sound-spellings for /p/p, /s/s
- Blend with /p/p
- Read words with p
- Read simple one-syllable words

Materials

- Big Book: *Friends All Around*
- Word-Building Cards
- pocket chart

Phonics

Review /p/p, /s/s

p   s

Model

Display page 11 of the **Big Book** *Friends All Around*. Read the text. Have children echo-read.	I'll find a word that ends with the letter *p*.
Frame the word *help*.	*Help* ends with the letter *p*. Say the word with me: *help*. (Emphasize /p/ at the end of the word.)
Repeat with *s* on page 13 with the words *some* and *bicycles*.	

Guided Practice/Practice

Repeat using page 16.	Who can find a word that ends with the letter *p*?
Guide children to find and frame the word *jump*.	Yes, *jump* ends with the letter *p*. Say the word with me: *jump*.
Repeat with the letter *s* using page 18 with the words *some* and *books*.	

Build Fluency: Sound-Spellings

Display the following **Word-Building Cards**: *a, m, p, s*. Have children chorally say each sound. Repeat and vary the pace.

For Tier 2 instruction, see page 405.

Blend with /p/p

Model

Use the pocket chart and the **Word-Building Cards**.

This letter is *m*. The letter *m* stands for the /m/ sound. Say /m/.

Place Word-Building Card *a* next to *m*. Move your hand from left to right.

This letter is *a*. The letter *a* stands for the /a/ sound. Listen as I blend the two sounds together: /mmmaaa/. Now blend the sounds with me: /mmmaaa/.

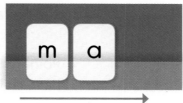

Place Word-Building Card *p* next to *ma*. Move your hand from left to right.

Repeat with *Pam*.

This letter is *p*. The letter *p* stands for the /p/ sound. Listen as I blend the three sounds together: /mmmaaap/, *map*. Now you blend the sounds with me: /mmmaaap/, *map*.

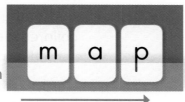

Guided Practice/Practice

Children blend words. Guide them as needed.

am   map   Pam
Sam   sap

Read Words

Apply
Write the words and the sentences. Guide practice with the first word, using the **Sound-by-Sound Blending Routine**.

Read the sentences with children.

> am
> Pam
> map
> I am Pam.
> I like the map.

Corrective Feedback

Blending: Sound Error Model the sound that children missed, then have them repeat the sound. For example, for the word *Pam*, say: *My turn*. Tap under the letter *m* in the word *Pam* and say: *Sound? What's the sound?* Then return to the beginning of the word. Say: *Let's start over*. Blend the word with children again.

Grammar

Naming Words (Nouns)

MODEL Use the **Big Book** *Friends All Around* to review naming words, which are called nouns. Instruct children that naming words can name people, places, animals, or things. *Today we will talk about words that name things.* Turn to page 3 of *Friends All Around* and point to the guitar. Say: *This is a* guitar. *What is the name of this instrument?* (guitar) Explain to children that the word *guitar* is a noun.

- Point to items around the classroom (table, clock, books, etc.) and have children tell you what they are. Explain that these are all naming words that name things.

PRACTICE Page through the Big Book and have children point to different things on the pages, for example, a watering can, a tree, or the pair of glasses that the boy is wearing on page 4. Have children identify what they pointed to. If children do not know what something is, identify it for them.

- Have children make sentences using the things children identified in the Big Book pages. For example: *The kids planted the* tree. If children need help, supply a sentence frame, such as: *The boy is playing a __drum__.*

- Have children say the word or words in each sentence that names a thing. Then have them make up sentences of their own using the things identified in the Big Book or the things identified in the classroom.

ELL

Basic and Academic Language As children identify things in the Big Book, list them on the board and illustrate them. Then pair English Language Learners with fluent speakers and have partners make up sentences with the listed words. Write their sentences, read them together, and ask: *What word in your sentence is the name of a thing? What are words that name things called?*

Writing

Independent Writing: Picture Webs

Display and read the web that children created on Day 2.

BRAINSTORM
Tell children that they will begin to make their own picture web about things friends like to do together. *What are some things you like to do with your friends?*

■ List children's ideas on a chart and add a small drawing next to each one.

PREWRITE
Draw a picture web and print *Play a Board* **Game** in the center. Read it aloud as you track the print. Write *chips, counters, board,* and *table* at the ends of the lines. Share what you wrote with children and track the print as you read it. Point out that these words are all nouns. Have children chorally repeat the words.

■ Have children select an activity to write about.

DRAFT
Have children write their names on the top of the paper. Ask them to draw a circle in the center. Tell them to illustrate and write the name of an activity in the circle. They can use the web and list you created as a model.

■ Have children add a small drawing for each item.

■ Collect and save children's work to use again tomorrow.

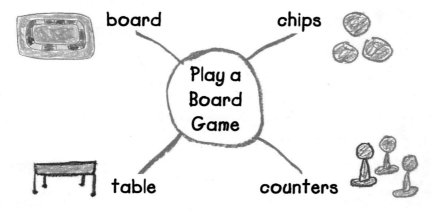

Write About It
Ask children to draw in their Writer's Notebook a picture of an indoor game they like to play with their friends. Help children label their drawings. Point out the noun in the label.

Objectives
- Complete an individual picture web
- Write words
- Use letter knowledge to write letters in a word

Materials
- children's writing from Day 2

5-Day Writing

Picture Web	
DAY 1	Shared: A List
DAY 2	Interactive: A Word Web
DAY 3	Independent: Prewrite and Draft Picture Webs
DAY 4	Independent: Revise and Edit a Picture Web
DAY 5	Independent: Publish and Present

ELL

Use New Language Ask questions to help children complete the picture web. *What do you need to play a board game? Do you need chips? Let's write and draw a picture of chips at the end of a line on the picture web.*

Transitions That Teach

While lining up, have children tell about something that they can do to **assist** others.

WHOLE GROUP

Oral Language
- Build Robust Vocabulary

✦ **Comprehension**
- Read Aloud: "The Lion and the Mouse"

Vocabulary
- Number Words
- Story Word: *computers*

✦ **Phonemic Awareness**
- Phoneme Blending

✦ **Phonics**
- Picture Sort
- Blend with /p/*p*
- Pre-decodable Reader: *A Map*

Writing
- Independent Writing: Revise and Edit a Picture Web

SMALL GROUP

- Differentiated Instruction, pages 394–419

Oral Language

 Talk About It ## Build Robust Vocabulary

HOW FRIENDS HELP

Discuss ways friends **assist**, or help, one another. *Friends can do many things to assist one another. When you help friends, they know that you care.*

- Have children share ways they can assist someone who is younger, older, bigger, or smaller than they are.

CREATE A LIST

Write the heading for a list like the one shown below.

Think Aloud Sometimes I help friends by cheering them up when they are sad. Other times I help them learn a new **game**. Helping friends makes me feel good.

Help children name other ways friends can help one another. Add their ideas to the list. Read aloud the words as you track them.

How Friends Assist Each Other

| tie a friend's shoes |
| cheer up a sad friend |
| get help when a friend is hurt |
| teach a friend a new game |
| help a friend clean the room |
| share a snack |

ELL ENGLISH LANGUAGE LEARNERS

Beginning	Intermediate	Advanced
Confirm Understanding Demonstrate how to assist by helping a child tie his or her shoe. Then have children help or assist you with classroom chores such as putting books away.	**Add Details** Prompt children to add details as they tell about ways to assist a friend. *What do you say to a friend who is sad? How do you help a friend learn a game?*	**Share Experiences** Ask children to tell how they can help a friend who gets hurt. Have children dictate their responses for you to write on the board and share with the class.

Listen for Rhyme

IDENTIFY RHYME

Remind children that words rhyme when they have the same ending sounds. *The word* cap *rhymes with* lap. Tell children *cap* and *lap* end with the sounds: /aaap/, *ap*.

FRIENDSHIP RHYME

Tell children that they will recite the rhyme "Sam, Sam" that they learned earlier in the week. Replay the rhyme and have children join in.

Repeat the rhyme, pausing before the words *day, you, green,* and *grass*. Have children finish the line by saying the rhyming word.

Repeat the word pairs: *play/day, do/you, seen/ green,* and *pass/grass*.

Sam, Sam

"Sam, Sam, come and play,
While the sun shines bright as day."

"Yes, my friend, that's what I'll do,
Because I like to play with you."

"Sam, Sam, have you seen
Pam and Matt on the green?"

"Yes, my friend, I saw them pass,
Skipping over the nice cut grass."

Objectives

- Discuss the theme
- Use oral vocabulary words *assist, game, honest, pleasant,* and *world*
- Recognize and generate rhyme

Digital Learning

Rhyme on **Listening Library Audio CD**

Objective

- **Listen and respond to a fable**

Materials

- Read-Aloud Anthology: "The Lion and the Mouse," pp. 37–40

ELL

Act Out Lead children in acting out being a large lion and a small mouse. Stretch tall and hold out your arms while saying: *Roar! I am a big lion!* Then crouch down and whisper: *I am a tiny mouse.* Have children repeat the actions and sentences.

Readers Theater

BUILDING LISTENING AND SPEAKING SKILLS
Distribute copies of "Who Helped the Lion?," Read-Aloud Anthology pages 160–162. Have children practice performing the play throughout the unit. Assign parts and have children present the play or perform it as a dramatic reading at the end of the unit.

Interactive
Read Aloud

Listening Comprehension

GENRE: LITERARY TEXT/FICTION
Explain that this selection is a **fable**. Tell children that a fable is a very old story that usually has a lesson at the end. Remind children that "The Bundle of Sticks" is also a fable. See the **Read-Aloud Anthology** for more information about fables.

Read Aloud

CULTURAL PERSPECTIVES
Tell children that "The Lion and the Mouse" is another Aesop's fable. Animals are the main characters in most of the stories by Aesop. Point out the area of the **world** where Aesop traveled (Greece and Turkey).

READ "THE LION AND THE MOUSE"

- **MODEL ASKING QUESTIONS** Use the Think Alouds provided at point of use in the fable for the strategy.

- **MODEL FLUENT READING** Read aloud the fable with fluent expression. Stop occasionally so that children can predict what will happen next. Point out that how you read the dialogue helps the listener understand what the characters say and how they feel.

- **EXPAND VOCABULARY** See page 37 of the Read-Aloud Anthology to teach new words using the **Define/Example/Ask** routine.

Respond to Literature

TALK ABOUT IT Ask children to retell what happened in the fable.

- *Describe the lion. Describe the mouse. How are they different?*

- *How did the little mouse help the big lion?*

- *What did you learn from this story? When have you been able to help someone bigger?*

Write About It

Have children draw a picture of the tiny mouse helping the huge lion. Help them write a label or a sentence.

Vocabulary

Number Words

REVIEW NUMBERS

Display the number cards in the pocket chart one at a time as you guide children in counting from one to five. Point to each card and say a sentence using the number word. For example: *I see* one *red shirt. I see* two *windows.*

Distribute a number card to each child and read the card together. Tell children that they will listen to a story and sort out the number words. *Each time you hear a number word, hold up the matching card.* Read the following story:

> A boy and his grandfather went to the zoo to see animals from around the **world**. They saw one *gorilla jumping up and down.* Then, they passed four *monkeys in a tree. Next, they saw* two *lions eating lunch and* three *zebras running away. Then, they passed* five *penguins waddling.*

one | two | three | four | five

Story Word: *computers*

Display page 19 of the **Big Book** *Friends All Around* and ask children what they think the children are doing on the computers. *What are some of the different ways people use computers? What kinds of **games** might the children be playing? Where are some of the different places we might find computers?*

TIME TO MOVE!

Choose a group of five children. Have the first child demonstrate a movement of his or her choice, such as a jumping or standing on one leg. The rest of the class repeats the movement. The second child demonstrates a movement, and the class repeats it. When all five children have done an action, put all five movements together. Use number words to keep the order of the movements.

Objectives

- Identify and use number words
- Review story word *computers*
- Follow oral directions

Materials

- index cards with *one, two, three, four,* and *five* written on them
- pocket chart
- Big Book: *Friends All Around*

ELL

Reinforce Meaning Display the index cards on a table. Have children put the correct number of crayons or paper clips on top of each card. Read the cards and have children repeat.

Objectives

- Blend sounds to form words
- Sort picture names with initial *a, p, s*
- Blend with *s, m, p, a*
- Read simple one-syllable words

Materials

- Puppet
- Word-Building Cards
- pocket chart
- Photo Cards: *anchor, ant, apple, ax, paint, pea, pizza, pig, seal, sock, sun, soup*
- Activity Book, p. 20
- Practice Book, p. 52

Phonemic Awareness

✔ Phoneme Blending

Model

Use the **Puppet** to model how to blend the word *pat*.

Repeat the routine with *sat*.

Happy is going to say the sounds in a word. Listen as Happy says each sound: /p/ /a/ /t/. Happy can blend the sounds together: /paaat/, *pat*. Say the sounds with Happy: /paaat/. Now say the word with Happy: *pat*.

Guided Practice/Practice

Say the sounds. Children blend the sounds to say the words. Guide practice with the first word.

Happy is going to say the sounds in a word. Listen to Happy as he says each sound. Blend the sounds together to say the word.

/p/ /a/ n/	/p/ /a/ /d/	/m/ /a/ /p/
/k/ /a/ /p/	/s/ /a/ /t/	/t/ /a/ /p/

Phonics

✔ Picture Sort

Model

Show **Word-Building Card** *p* in the pocket chart.

This is the letter *p*. The letter *p* stands for the /p/ sound as in *pig*. Say the sound with me: /p/, /p/, /p/.

Follow the routine for *s* and *a*.

This is the letter *s*. The letter *s* stands for the /s/ sound as in *sun*. This is the letter *a*. *A* stands for the /a/ sound as in *apple*.

Hold up the **Photo Card** for *pizza*. Follow routine for *sock* and *ax*.

Here is the picture of a *pizza*. *Pizza* begins with /p/. I'll place *pizza* under the letter *p*.

Guided Practice/Practice

Children sort the Photo Cards. Guide practice with the next card, using the routine.

Build Fluency: Sound-Spellings

 SPIRAL REVIEW Display the following **Word-Building Cards**: *a, m, s, p*. Have children chorally say each sound. Repeat and vary the pace.

 ## Blend with /p/*p*

Model

Place **Word-Building Card** *s* in the pocket chart.

This letter is *s*. The letter *s* stands for the /s/ sound. Say /s/.

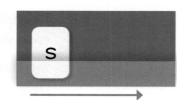

Place Word-Building Card *a* next to *s*. Move your hand from left to right as you blend the sounds.

This letter is *a*. The letter *a* stands for the /a/ sound. Listen as I blend the two sounds together: /sssaaa/. Now you blend the sounds with me. (/sssaaa/)

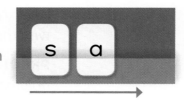

Place Word-Building Card *p* next to *sa*. Move your hand from left to right as you blend the sounds.

This letter is *p*. The letter *p* stands for the /p/ sound. Listen as I blend the three sounds together: /sssaaap/, *sap*. Now you blend the sounds with me. (/sssaaap/, *sap*)

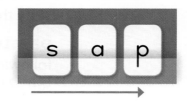

Repeat the routine with *map*.

Guided Practice/Practice

Children blend the words. Guide the practice with the first word.

Pam   am   Sam   map

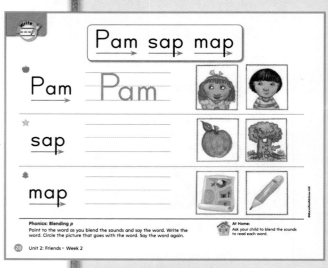

Activity Book, page 20
Practice Book, page 52

Objectives

- Read decodable words with /p/*p*
- Review the high-frequency words *a*, *I*, *like*, *the*, and *we*
- Reread for fluency

Materials

- Pre-decodable Reader: *A Map*
- High-Frequency Word Cards: *a*, *I*, *like*, *the*, *we*
- pocket chart

Pre-decodable Reader

Read *A Map*

A Map

 REVIEW Display **High-Frequency Word Cards** for **a**, **I**, **like**, **the**, and **we** in the pocket chart. Use the **Read/Spell/Write** routine to review each word.

MODEL CONCEPTS ABOUT PRINT Demonstrate book handling. *I hold the book so that the cover is on the front and the words are not upside down. I open the book by turning the cover. I read from left to right. Then I turn each page as I read it, starting with the first page and ending with the last page.*

PREDICT Have children describe the cover. *What is the father holding?* (map) *What will he use it for? What might happen in this story?*

FIRST READ Have children point to each word and say the high-frequency words quickly. Help them use syntactic and semantic cues to comprehend decodable text. Children should chorally read the story the first time through.

DEVELOP COMPREHENSION Check comprehension by using the following prompts: *Choose two places on the map. How are they the same? How are they different?*

SECOND READ Have partners reread the book together. Have children stop their partner and reread if the text does not make sense to them.

We like the map!

2

We like a .
pig

3

We like a 🎃 .
pumpkin

4

We like a 🐑 .
sheep

5

We like a 🥧 .
pie

6

We like a 🐕 .
puppy

7

We like the map!

8

Pre-decodable Reader

Writing

Independent Writing: A Picture Web

REVISE AND EDIT

Distribute children's picture webs. Have them reread their webs and check for the following:

- Does my picture web show something my friends and I like to do together?

- Did I write the name of the activity?

- Did I draw pictures to show the things we need?

Circulate and help children as they review and revise their picture webs. Have children share their webs with partners. Guide children to revise their webs based on partner and teacher feedback.

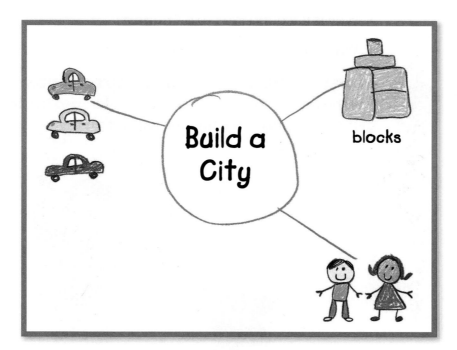

Build a City

blocks

Write About It

Ask children to draw an activity or **game** they have never tried but would like to try some day. Help them label their drawing.

Objectives

- Revise and edit children's picture web and drawings
- Use letter knowledge to write letters

Materials

- children's writing from Day 3

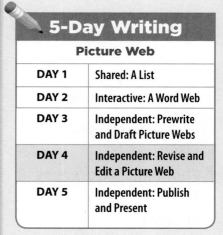

5-Day Writing	
Picture Web	
DAY 1	Shared: A List
DAY 2	Interactive: A Word Web
DAY 3	Independent: Prewrite and Draft Picture Webs
DAY 4	Independent: Revise and Edit a Picture Web
DAY 5	Independent: Publish and Present

ELL

Use New Language
Choose an activity from the **Big Book** for children to use. Draw a word web and write the activity in the center. Help children name things needed for the activity. Write them and illustrate them around the web.

Transitions That Teach

While children are getting ready to go, have them tell why it is important to tell the truth and be **honest**.

WHOLE GROUP

Oral Language
- Build Robust Vocabulary

✔ **Comprehension**
- Strategy: Ask Questions
- Skill: Compare and Contrast
- Read Across Texts

✔ **Vocabulary**
- Review High-Frequency Words
- Review Number Words
- Build Fluency

✔ **Phonemic Awareness**
- Phoneme Identity

✔ **Phonics**
- Review /p/p, /s/s, /m/m, /a/a
- Read Words
- Dictation

Writing
- Independent Writing: Publish and Present

SMALL GROUP

- Differentiated Instruction, pages 394–419

Review and Assess
Oral Language
Build Robust Vocabulary

REVIEW WORDS

Review this week's oral vocabulary words with children. Explain that all of the words can be used to discuss friendships. Talk about what games children play with friends. Ask: *How can children assist their friends?*

Use the following questions to check children's understanding:

- What **games** have you played this week?

- Where is a cold place in the **world**?

- Who can **assist** you when you are learning something new?

- Why is it a good idea to be **honest**?

- Who do you think is a **pleasant** person?

REVIEW SONGS AND RHYMES ABOUT FRIENDS

Say the rhyme "Pat-a-Cake" and ask children to join in and play the game. Have children name the words that rhyme. (*man, can*)

Review and Assess
Comprehension

STRATEGY Ask Questions

REFLECT ON THE STRATEGY Remind children that they have learned how to ask questions about the people, animals, and places or other things in the selections they have read. Have children ask questions they have about the selections the class read this week.

Think Aloud I can use the answers to these questions to compare an expository selection and a fable.

SKILL Compare and Contrast

Have children compare the friends in *Friends All Around* and "The Lion and the Mouse." Ask them to think about the **details** in the texts to help them compare and contrast.

- *How are the friends from around the **world** in* Friends All Around *alike? In what ways are they different?*

- *In what ways are the lion and the mouse in the fable different? Alike?*

- *Are the lion and the mouse like the friends in* Friends All Around? *How?*

Reading Across Texts

Explain that sometimes readers like to think about how a selection is like or unlike another selection or a poem.

- Create a chart like the one shown to compare the expository text *Friends All Around* with the fable "The Lion and the Mouse."

Friends All Around	The Lion and the Mouse
expository	fable
photographs	illustrations
tells about things friends can do together	a small mouse helps a big lion

Objectives

- Review the strategy and skill
- Compare and contrast genres and stories
- Listen to and share information

Materials

- Big Book: *Friends All Around*
- Read-Aloud Anthology: "The Lion and the Mouse," pp. 37–40
- Activity Book, p. 21

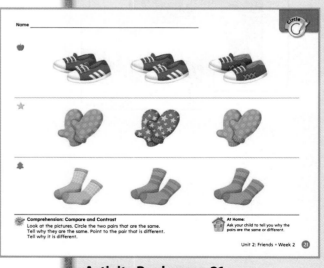

Activity Book, page 21

What Is a Friend? **389**

Objectives

- Review high-frequency words *a, can, like, the,* and *we*
- Review number words
- Build fluency

Materials

- High-Frequency Word Cards: *a, can, like, the, we*
- number words on index cards: *one, two, three, four, five*
- small colored tiles

Fluency

Connected Text Have children reread this week's **Pre-decodable Readers** with a partner. Circulate, listen in, and note those children who need additional instruction and practice reading this week's decodable and sight words.

Pre-Decodable Reader
I Am a Doctor
by *Tomika Jackson*

Pre-Decodable Reader
A Map
by Jeff Stanley • illustrated by Jared Lee

Sight Word Practice

Review and Assess
Vocabulary

 ## High-Frequency Words

Distribute one of the following **High-Frequency Word Cards** to each child: **a**, **like**, **the**, **we**, and **can**. Say: *When you hear the word that is on your card, stand and hold up your Word Card.*

- We *all live in* the **world**.
- *I* like the *book*.
- We can *go for* a *walk*.
- *I* can *run*.
- *My dog is* a *golden retriever*.

Build Fluency: Word Automaticity

Rapid Naming Display the High-Frequency Word Cards *can, we, the, like,* and *a*. Point quickly to each card, at random, and have children read the word as fast as they can.

a	like	the	we	can

Number Words

Display the number cards and name each number word. Then have children use a collection of small colored tiles to form sets. For example: 3 red, 3 blue, and 2 orange tiles or 1 red, 2 blue, 3 green, and 4 yellow tiles.

TIME TO MOVE!

Have children stand in a circle. Each child can give a direction that includes a number and an action, such as "three quick jumps" or "four quiet claps."

Review and Assess
Phonemic Awareness

Phoneme Identity

Guided Practice

Display the **Photo Cards** for *pie*, *pen*, and *pizza*.

I will say three picture names: *pie, pen,* and *pizza*. What are the names of these pictures? Say the names with me: *pie, pen, pizza*. What sound is the same in *pie, pen,* and *pizza*? Yes, the first sound, /p/, is the same.

Practice

Display sets of three Photo Cards. Children identify the sound at the beginning of the picture names in each set.

Use these sets of cards: *saw, soup, sock; penguin, pie, pumpkin; ant, apple, ax.*

Say the names of each set of pictures. Tell me what sound is the same in these picture names.

Objective
- **Recognize the same sound in different words**

Materials
- Photo Cards: *apple, ant, ax, pen, penguin, pie, pizza, pumpkin, saw, sock, soup*

Objectives

- Review sound-spellings /p/, /s/, /m/, /a/
- Read simple one-syllable words

Materials

- Word-Building Cards
- pocket chart
- 4 index cards with: *I, am, Pam,* period mark
- 4 index cards with: *I, like, Sam,* period mark
- Sound Box
- WorkBoard Sound Boxes; Teacher's Resource Book, p. 136
- markers
- Activity Book, p. 22

Activity Book, page 22

Review and Assess
Phonics

Build Fluency: Sound-Spellings

Rapid Naming Display the following **Word-Building Cards**: *a, m, p, s.* Have children chorally say each sound. Repeat and vary the pace.

 ## Read Words

Apply

Distribute the first set of cards: *I, am, Pam,* and the period. Have children stand in sequence.	Let's read the sentence together. *I am Pam.*
Repeat, using the other set of cards.	Let's read the sentence together. *I like Sam.*

Dictation

Dictate the following sounds: /m/, /a/, /s/, /p/. Have children write the letters.	Listen as I say a sound. Repeat the sound, then write the letter that stands for the sound. /m/ /a/ /s/ /p/
Then dictate words for children to spell. Model how to use the **Sound Boxes** to segment the word. Have them repeat. Write the letters and words on the board for children to self-correct.	Now let's write some words. I will say a word. I want you to repeat the word, then think about how many sounds are in the word. Use your Sound Boxes to count the sounds. Then write one letter for each sound you hear. am Sam map Pam sap

Review and Assess
Writing

Independent Writing: A Picture Web

PUBLISH

Explain to children that you will gather their picture webs to make a class book.

- Brainstorm ideas for a title, such as "My Friends and I Play Together."

- Have a few children work on a cover. Write the title on the cover.

- Make holes along the edges of the cover and each page. Bind the pages together with yarn.

PRESENT

Ask children to take turns reading their picture webs to the class and telling what the pictures show. Allow them to add descriptions to the pictures, such as: *My friends and I like to play a **game** in the pool.*

LISTENING, SPEAKING, AND VIEWING

- Remind children to speak clearly and to be good listeners when a classmate is speaking.

- Place the finished book in the Reading Workstation for everyone to enjoy. Children may wish to put a copy of their work in their Writing Portfolio.

Write About It

Ask children to draw a picture of something they like to do in a park or a playground. Help them label their drawing.

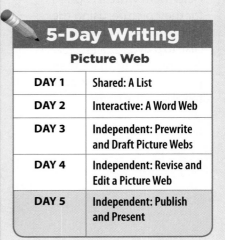

Objective

- Publish and present a piece of writing

Materials

- children's writing from Day 4

5-Day Writing

Picture Web	
DAY 1	Shared: A List
DAY 2	Interactive: A Word Web
DAY 3	Independent: Prewrite and Draft Picture Webs
DAY 4	Independent: Revise and Edit a Picture Web
DAY 5	Independent: Publish and Present

Transitions That Teach

While children wait in line, have them talk about ways they can be **pleasant** with one another.

ON YOUR OWN
Games with Friends

Have children draw a picture of a game that they like to play with friends. Help them write a caption for their picture, using the following sentence frame: *I like to play _____.*
Ask children to share their picture with the class and tell about the game.

ELL

Partners When pairing children to make up sentences, pair English Language Learners with children who are more proficient. Write their sentences, read them together, and point out the high-frequency words.

Approaching Level

Oral Language

Objective   Preteach oral vocabulary
Materials   • none

THEME WORDS: *game, world*

- Tell children the meanings for **game** and **world**. *A game is something you play for fun. A game has rules. Baseball and Simon Says are* games. *The* world *is where we live. The* world *is made up of Earth and everything on it. There are many countries in the* world. *If possible, show children a globe and explain that it is a model of the world.*

- Discuss the words with children. *What* games *do you like to play? What* games *would kids from around the* world *enjoy playing? What other parts of the* world *have you visited?*

- Have children use the following sentence frames to generate complete oral sentences using the vocabulary words: *My favorite game is _____. The best place in the world to visit is _____.*

High-Frequency Words

Objective   Preteach high-frequency words
Materials   • **High-Frequency Word Cards:** *a, can, I, like, the, we*

PRETEACH WORD: *a*

- Display the **High-Frequency Word Card** for **a**.

- **Read** Point to and say the word *a. This is the word* a. *A is a one-letter word that we use before other words. We often use* a *to talk about one thing. I have* a *friend. Let's play* a *game. This is* a *school.*

- **Spell** *The word* a *is spelled* a. Have children read and spell *a*.

- **Write** Finally, have children write the word *a*.

- Have children work with a partner to make up sentences using the word *a*. Ask them to talk about a game that they would like to learn.

HIGH-FREQUENCY WORDS REVIEW

Display the High-Frequency Word Cards **I**, **can**, **we**, **like**, and **the**, one card at a time, as children chorally read and spell the word. Mix and repeat. Note words children need to review.

Tier 2

Approaching Level

Phonemic Awareness

Objective Identify initial sound /p/
Materials
- **Photo Cards:** pen, penguin, piano, pie, pizza, pumpkin
- **Sound-Spelling Card:** Piano

PHONEME ISOLATION

Model
- Display the **Photo Card** for pen. *This is a pen. Listen for the beginning sound in* pen: /p/, /p/, /pen/. Pen *begins with* /p/.
- Display the Piano **Sound-Spelling Card**. Point to the articulation picture. *Watch how the lips close and press together and then quickly open to say /p/. When I say /p/, a puff of air comes out of my mouth.*

Guided Practice/Practice
- Display the Photo Cards. Have children take turns selecting a picture, naming it, and saying the initial sound of the picture name: *This is a _____. _____ begins with /p/.*

Phonics

Objective Recognize words that begin with /p/p
Materials
- **Photo Cards:** pen, penguin, piano, pie, pizza, pumpkin
- **Sound-Spelling Card:** Piano • **Word-Building Cards**

PRETEACH: RECOGNIZE /p/p

Model
- Display Photo Cards for pie and piano and the Piano Sound-Spelling Card. Say: *The name of this letter is* p. P *stands for the /p/ sound that you hear at the beginning of* pie. *I will place the* p **Word-Building Card** *on the picture of the pie because* pie *begins with /p/. Repeat with* piano.

Guided Practice/Practice
- Display the Photo Cards on a table. Say: *This is the picture of a pen. What sound do you hear at the beginning of* pen? *What letter stands for /p/? Let's place a* p *on the pen because* pen *begins with /p/. Repeat with remaining Photo Cards for /p/p.*
- For additional practice, point out objects in the classroom with names that begin with /p/ (puzzle, paper, pen, pencil, etc.). Hold the p card next to each while children say the name chorally.

SOUND-SPELLINGS REVIEW

Tier 2

Display Word-Building Cards for *p, s, a,* and *m,* one at a time. Have children chorally say the sound. Repeat and vary the pace.

Corrective Feedback

Mnemonic Display the Piano Sound-Spelling Card. Say: *This is the* Piano *Sound-Spelling Card. The sound is /p/. The /p/ sound is spelled with the letter* p. *Say /p/ with me: /p/. This is the sound at the beginning of* piano. *What is the letter? What is the sound? Which word begins with /p/?* Piano *is the word we can use to remember the sound for* p, /p/.

ON YOUR OWN

What I Like

Extend phonics by having children draw pictures of things that they like with names that begin with /p/p. Help children label their pictures.

What I Like
puppy
pizza

ELL

Sound-Letter Relationships Provide additional practice in pronouncing the /p/ sound and naming the letter *p* as children point to it.

Puppet

On Level

High-Frequency Words

Objective Review high-frequency words *a*, *like*, *the*, and *we*
Materials • **High-Frequency Word Cards:** *a*, *like*, *the*, *we*

REVIEW: *a, like, the, we*

- Display the **High-Frequency Word Card** for **a**.

- **Read** Point to and say the word *a*. *This is the word* a. *It is a one-letter word we use before other words. I am a teacher. This is a school. We read a book.*

- **Spell** *The word* a *is spelled* a. Have children read and spell *a*.

- **Write** Finally, have children write the word *a*.

- Repeat with **like**, **the**, and **we**. Then have partners make up complete sentences using the words *a*, *like*, *the*, and *we*. Direct children to use sentence frames to talk about things they like: *We like a _____. We like the _____.*

Phonemic Awareness/Phonics

Objectives Blend sounds in words with /p/; Recognize initial /p/p, /s/s, /a/a, /m/m
Materials • **Puppet** • **Word-Building Cards**

PHONEME BLENDING

Model

- Hold up the **Puppet**. *Listen as Happy says the sounds in a word: /p/ /a/ /m/, Pam. What is the word? Now let's blend with Happy: /p/ /a/ /m/, Pam. Repeat with* pat.

Practice

- *Listen as Happy says the sounds in a word.* Have children blend the following sounds. Guide practice with the first word.

/p/ /a/ /d/	/m/ /a/ /p/	/p/ /i/ /t/	/s/ /i/ /p/
/p/ /a/ /l/	/n/ /a/ /p/	/s/ /i/ /n/ /k/	/s/ /a/ /n/ /d/

REVIEW /p/p, /s/s, /a/a, /m/m

Model

- Display **Word-Building Card** *p*. *The name of this letter is* p. P *stands for the /p/ sound we hear at the beginning of* piano. *What is the sound? I'll hold up the* p *card because* piano *begins with /p/.* Repeat with *s* and *sun*, *a* and *apple*, *m* and *map*.

- Say: *pet, mug, sink, ant, alligator, sail, money, pan, mop, ax,* and *pig*. Children hold up the corresponding small Word-Building Card and say the initial sound. Guide practice with the first two words.

Beyond Level

High-Frequency Words/Vocabulary

Objective Introduce high-frequency words and expand oral vocabulary

Materials • none

ACCELERATE

- Write *pull* and *fly* on the board.

- **Read** Point to and say the word *pull*. *This is the word* pull. *It means "to move." I pull my brother in a wagon.* Demonstrate pulling.

- **Spell** *The word* pull *is spelled* p-u-l-l. Have children read and spell *pull*.

- **Write** Finally, have children write the word *pull*.

- Repeat the routine with *fly*.

- Have children work with a partner to make up oral sentences using the words *pull* and *fly*. Ask them to talk about things they like to do with friends.

EXPAND ORAL VOCABULARY

- **Synonyms** Review the meaning of the oral vocabulary word *assist* with children. Then explain that a *synonym* is a word that means the same thing as another word.

- Say: *A synonym for the word* assist *is* help. *When you* help *people, you make it easier for them to do something. My brother* helps *me rake leaves. Crossing guards* help *you cross the street safely.*

- Have children take turns using the new word *help* in sentences. Then tell children they will work with a partner to name the different ways they help or assist people at home or school.

Phonics

Objectives Blend words with /p/*p*; review sound-letter correspondence

Materials
- **Sound-Spelling Card:** *Piano* • **Word-Building Cards**
- **Sound-Spelling WorkBoards**

ENRICH

- Happy will say and then blend sounds in a word: /p/ /a/ /s/ /t/, /paaassst/, past. Say the sounds and have children blend and say the words: /p/ /i/ /n/ /k/, /p/ /a/ /th/, /ch/ /i/ /p/, /l/ /a/ /m/ /p/.

- Display **Word-Building Cards** *a, b, c, ck, d, f, g, h, i, j, k, l, m, n, p, qu, r, s, t, v, w, x, y, z*. Point to the letters or spellings one at a time and say the name and the sound with children. Have children repeat the name and sound as they write the letter or spelling several times on their **WorkBoards**.

ON YOUR OWN

Pull or Fly

Ask children to draw a picture to show something that they can pull or something that they can fly. Have them write *pull* or *fly* below their picture.

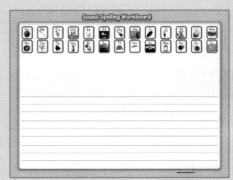

Sound-Spelling WorkBoard

ELL ENGLISH LANGUAGE LEARNERS

Oral Language Warm-Up

Content Objective Learn theme vocabulary
Language Objective Repeat and demonstrate rhyme to demonstrate understanding
Materials • Listening Library Audio CD • Visual Vocabulary Resources

BUILD BACKGROUND KNOWLEDGE

All Language Levels

- Continue developing vocabulary around the unit theme "Friends" using the rhyme "Pat-a-Cake." Display a picture of friends playing together, such as a picture from *Friends All Around*. Teach the word *game* as you point to friends playing ball in the picture. Have children repeat the word three times.

- Play "Pat-a-Cake" on the **Listening Library Audio CD**. Demonstrate the actions as you sing the rhyme.

- Then teach children the actions of partners clapping as they sing the rhyme. Explain that this is like playing a game together. Emphasize key words that rhyme such as *man, can,* and *me*.

- Play the rhyme several times until children begin to correctly repeat the rhyme and clap together in rhythm.

- Ask children to tell about other games they play with friends. Build on their responses to model speaking in complete sentences. For example: *You play tag with your friends.*

Academic Language

Language Objective Use academic language in classroom conversations

All Language Levels

- This week's academic words are **boldfaced** throughout the lesson. Define the word in context and provide a clear example from the selection. Then ask children to generate an example of a word with a similar meaning.

Academic Language Used in Whole Group Instruction

Oral Vocabulary Words	Vocabulary and Grammar Concepts	Strategy and Skill Words
assist	number words	ask
game	naming words	questions
honest		compare
pleasant		contrast
world		noun

Cognates

Help children identify similarities and differences in pronunciation and spelling between English words and Spanish cognates:

Cognates

honest	*honesto*

ENGLISH LANGUAGE LEARNERS

Vocabulary

Language Objective Demonstrate understanding and use of key words by identifying and describing games friends play

Materials • **Visual Vocabulary Resources**

PRETEACH KEY VOCABULARY

All Language Levels

Use the **Visual Vocabulary Resources** to preteach the weekly oral vocabulary words *assist, game, honest, pleasant,* and *world.* Focus on one or two words per day. Use the following routine that appears in detail on the cards.

- Define the word in English and provide the example given.
- Define the word in Spanish, if appropriate, and indicate if the word is a cognate.
- Display the picture and explain how it illustrates or demonstrates the word. Engage children in structured partner-talk about the image, using the key word.
- Ask children to chorally say the word three times.
- Point out any known sound-spellings or focus on a key aspect of phonemic awareness related to the word.

PRETEACH FUNCTION WORDS AND PHRASES

All Language Levels

Use the Visual Vocabulary Resources to preteach the function words and phrases *into (walk into)* and *out of (walk out of).* Focus on one word per day. Use the detailed routine on the cards.

- Define the word in English and, if appropriate, in Spanish. Point out if the word is a cognate.
- Refer to the picture and engage children in talk about the word. For example, children will partner-talk using sentence frames, or they will listen to sentences and replace a word or phrase with the new function word.
- Ask children to chorally repeat the word three times.

TEACH BASIC WORDS

Beginning/Intermediate

Use the Visual Vocabulary Resources to teach the basic words *racket, ball, bat, mitt, puck,* and *stick (softball* or *hockey).* Teach these "things friends use to play" words using the routine provided on the card.

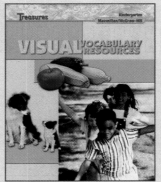

Visual Vocabulary Resources

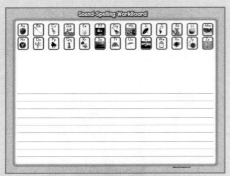

Sound-Spelling WorkBoard

ELL

Partners When pairing children to make up sentences with the word *a*, pair English Language Learners with children who are more proficient. Write their sentences, read them together, and point out the word *a*.

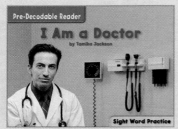

Pre-decodable Reader

Approaching Level

High-Frequency Words

Objective	Reteach high-frequency words
Materials	• **High-Frequency Word Cards:** *a, like* • **Sound-Spelling WorkBoards**

RETEACH WORD: *a*

Tier 2

- Distribute a **WorkBoard** to each child. Then display the **High-Frequency Word Card** for **a**.

- Use the **Read/Spell/Write** routine to reteach the word. Point to and say the word. *This is the word* a. *It is a one-letter word we use before other words. I am a teacher. I have a pen. I have a book.* A *is spelled with the letter* a. Have children read and spell *a*. Then have them write the word on their WorkBoards.

- Have children work with a partner to make up sentences using the word *a*. Ask them to talk about a job they would like to have one day.

CUMULATIVE REVIEW

Display the High-Frequency Word Cards **can**, **I**, **like**, **the**, and **we**, one card at a time, as children chorally read and spell the word. Mix and repeat. Note words children need to review.

Pre-decodable Reader

Objective	Teach Pre-decodable Reader *I Am a Doctor*
Materials	• **Pre-decodable Reader:** *I Am a Doctor*

I Am a Doctor

- Display the cover and read the title. Open to the title page and point out the title. *Let's read the title together.* Have children read each high-frequency word and sound out the word *Am* as you run your finger under it. Help them pronounce *Doctor*. Then read the title again. *What do you think we will read about in this book?*

- Page through the book. Ask children what they see in each photograph. Have children find the words *I*, *am*, and *a*. Point out and name each rebus.

- Read the book chorally with children. Have children point to each word or rebus as they read it. Provide corrective feedback as needed.

- Have children point to people in the photographs and use the word *a* to name them: *a doctor, a vet, a police officer, a firefighter, a cook, a teacher, a principal.*

- After reading, ask children to recall things they read about.

Puppet

Approaching Level

Phonemic Awareness

Objective Blend sounds in words with /p/
Materials • **Puppet**

PHONEME BLENDING

Tier **2**

Model

■ Hold up the **Puppet**. *Listen as Happy says the sounds in a word. First, he'll say each sound: /p/ /a/ /m/. Then, he will blend the three sounds together to say the word: /p/ /a/ /m/, /paaammm/,* Pam. *The word is* Pam. *What is the word?*

Guided Practice/Practice

■ *Happy will say the sounds in another word: /p/ /i/ /g/. Now you say the sounds with Happy: /p/ /i/ /g/. Let's blend the sounds together: /p/ /i/ /g/, /piiig/,* pig. *What's the word?*

■ Guide practice with the first word using the same routine.

/p/ /a/ /t/	/p/ /i/ /t/	/p/ /a/ /d/
/p/ /i/ /n/	/p/ /a/ /l/	/p/ /i/ /l/
/p/ /a/ /k/	/p/ /a/ /n/	/p/ /a/ /s/

Phonics

Objective Reinforce letter-sound correspondence for /p/*p*
Materials • **Sound-Spelling Card:** *Piano* • **Word-Building Cards**
  • **Sound-Spelling WorkBoards**

RETEACH /p/*p*

Model

■ Display the *Piano* **Sound-Spelling Card**. *The letter* p *stands for the /p/ sound as in* piano. *What is this letter? What sound does it stand for?* Repeat with *pen.*

■ Trace *p* on a **Word-Building Card**. *I will say a sentence. We will trace* p *on our cards when we hear /p/.* Say: *Pete put purple pencils in Pat's desk.*

Guided Practice/Practice

■ Distribute **WorkBoards**. Say: *pig, moon, pop, pull, sock, pet, pat, pen, what, best, pan.* Children write *p* on their WorkBoard when they hear a word with /p/. Guide them with the first two words.

CUMULATIVE REVIEW

Display Word-Building Cards for *p, s, a,* and *m,* one at a time. Have children chorally say the sound. Repeat and vary the pace.

Corrective Feedback

If children cannot discern initial /p/, review the word *Pam.* Have children stop at the first sound and repeat /p/, /p/, /p/ before saying *Pam.*

Sound-Spelling WorkBoard

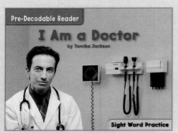

Pre-decodable Reader

Pre-decodable Reader

On Level

Pre-decodable Reader

Objective   Reread *I Am a Doctor* to develop fluency
Materials   • **Pre-decodable Reader:** *I Am a Doctor; A Map*

REREAD FOR FLUENCY

- Ask children to look back at the photographs in *I Am a Doctor*. Have them use their own words to retell what the book is about.

- Have children reread a page or two of *I Am a Doctor*. Work with them to read with accuracy and expression. Model reading a page. Point out how you use your voice to add expression to your reading. *When I read, "I am a doctor," I emphasize* doctor *by saying the word a little stronger than the other words. I want to show that the person on this page is talking about his job.*

- Provide time to listen as children read their page(s). Comment on their accuracy and expression and provide corrective feedback by modeling proper fluency.

- Use the same routine for **Pre-decodable Reader** *A Map* on Day 4.

Beyond Level

Pre-decodable Reader

Objective   Reread *I Am a Doctor* to reinforce fluency
Materials   • **Pre-decodable Reader:** *I Am a Doctor; A map*

REREAD FOR FLUENCY

- Ask children to look back at the photographs in *I Am a Doctor* and use their own words to retell what the book is about.

- Listen as children read. Comment on their expression and accuracy. Modeling proper fluency if needed.

- Use the same routine for **Pre-decodable Reader** *A Map* on Day 4.

INNOVATE

- Have children add pages to the book by drawing pictures of other jobs that people have. Have them write captions for their pictures. For example, a child might draw a picture of a nurse and write: *I am a nurse.* Help children write the job names.

ELL ENGLISH LANGUAGE LEARNERS

Access to Core Content

Content Objective Develop listening comprehension

Language Objective Discuss text using key words and sentence frames

Materials • **ELL Resource Book,** pp. 42–47

PRETEACH BIG BOOK/TRADE BOOK

All Language Levels

Use the Interactive Question-Response Guide on **ELL Resource Book** pages 42–47 to introduce children to *Friends All Around*. Preteach half of the selection on Day 1 and half on Day 2.

■ Use the prompts provided in the guide to develop meaning and vocabulary. Use the partner-talk and whole-class responses to engage children and increase student talk.

■ When completed, revisit the selection and prompt children to talk about the photos. Provide sentence starters as needed and build on children's responses to develop language.

ELL Resource Book

Big Book

Beginning	Intermediate	Advanced
Use Visuals During the Interactive Reading, select several pictures. Describe them and have children summarize what you said.	**Summarize** During the Interactive Reading, select a few lines of text. After you read them and explain them, have children summarize the text.	**Expand** During the Interactive Reading, select a larger portion of text. After you read it and explain it, have children summarize the text.

Approaching Level

High-Frequency Words

Objective Recognize high-frequency words *a, like, the, we*
Materials • **High-Frequency Word Cards:** *a, like, the, we* • **Word-Building Cards**

 REVIEW WORDS: *a, like, the, we*

- Display the **High-Frequency Word Card** for **a**. Say the word and have children repeat it. Point to the letter and have children name it.

- Distribute small **Word-Building Card** *a*. Point out that the word *a* has only one letter.

- Repeat the above routines with the words **like**, **the**, and **we**. Have children form each word with small Word-Building Cards.

- Ask a question with the word *a: Who is a teacher?* Have children use *a* to answer the question. Continue with the other words.

CUMULATIVE REVIEW

Display the High-Frequency Word Cards for *a, like, the,* and *we,* one card at a time, as children chorally read and spell the word. Mix and repeat. Note words children need to review.

Phonemic Awareness

Objective Identify initial and final /p/p
Materials • **Photo Cards:** *map, mop, paint, pen, penguin, piano, pie, pizza, pumpkin, rope, soap, soup, top, up* • **Sound Boxes** • markers
• **WorkBoard Sound Boxes; Teacher's Resource Book**, p. 136

PHONEME ISOLATION

Tier 2

Model

- Use the **Sound Boxes**. Display the **Photo Card** for *pen. Listen for the beginning sound in* pen: */peeennn/,* pen. Pen *begins with* /p/. *I'll place a marker in the first box to show that I hear* p *at the beginning of* pen.

- Display the Photo Card for *map. Listen for the end sound in* map: */mmmaaap/,* map. Map *ends with* /p/. *I'll place a marker in the last box to show that I hear* /p/ *at the end of* map.

Guided Practice/Practice

- Distribute Sound Boxes and markers. Display the Photo Cards. Children take turns selecting a picture and naming it. Have children listen for /p/ and place the marker in the first or last box as they say: *This is (a) _____. I hear /p/ at the _____ of _____.*

ELL

Extra Practice During the Cumulative Review, pair children and have partners take turns reading and spelling the high-frequency words.

Approaching Level

Phonics

Objectives Review blending with /p/*p*; build fluency
Materials   • **Word-Building Cards** • pocket chart

Tier 2

REVIEW SKILLS: BLEND SOUNDS

Model

- Place **Word-Building Card** *s* in the pocket chart. *The name of this letter is* s. *The letter* s *stands for the /s/ sound. Say /s/. What is the letter? What is the sound?*

- Place *a* next to *s*. *The name of this letter is* a. *Follow the above routine for* a. *Move your hand from left to right below the letters. Now listen as I blend the two sounds together: /sssaaa/.*

- Place *p* next to *sa*. *Follow the above routine for* p. *Listen as I blend the three sounds together: /sssaaap/,* sap. *Let's blend the word together: /s/ /a/ /p/, /sssaaap/,* sap.

Guided Practice/Practice

- Distribute small Word-Building Cards *s*, *a*, and *p*. Guide practice as children say each letter sound. Have them blend the sounds to say the word *sap*. Then build and blend *map* and *Pam*.

Build Fluency

- Write *sap*, *Pam*, *am*, and *map* on the board. Have children blend the words as quickly as they can.

Pre-decodable Reader

Objective Preteach Pre-decodable Reader *A Map*
Materials • **Pre-decodable Reader:** *A Map*

PRETEACH *A Map*

- Display the cover of the book and read the title. Open to the title page and point out the title. *Let's read the title together. Look at the cover picture. What does the dad have? What is the boy doing? What do you think will happen in this book?*

- Page through the book. Ask children to describe each picture. Have them point to the high-frequency word *a*.

- Read the book chorally with children. Have them point to each word or rebus as they read it. Provide corrective feedback.

- Ask children to use *We*, *like*, *the*, and *a* to talk about what they like in the book. *We like a pumpkin, too. We like a pie, too. We like a puppy, too. We like the map!*

- After reading, ask children to recall things they read about.

Pre-decodable Reader

ON YOUR OWN

Draw a Place

Have children choose a place shown on the map in the book and draw a picture of themselves there. Provide this frame: *I like a _____.*

I like a pumpkin.

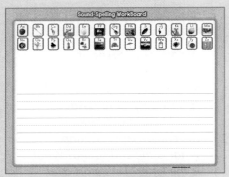

Sound-Spelling WorkBoard

On Level

Phonics

Objective	Review recognizing initial and final /p/ and blending /p/*p*, a/*a*, /m/*m*, and /s/*s*
Materials	• **Word-Building Cards** • pocket chart • **Sound-Spelling WorkBoards**

REVIEW /p/p

Model

■ Display **Word-Building Card** *p. The name of this letter is* p. *This letter stands for the /p/ sound you hear at the beginning of* piano. *What is the sound? I'll hold up the* p *card because* piano *begins with /p/.* Repeat with final *p* and the word *map*.

Guided Practice/Practice

■ **Blend Words** Place Word-Building Cards *a* and *m* in the pocket chart. Point to each letter for children to identify. Move your hand from left to right below the letters as you blend the word. *Now listen as I blend the two sounds together: /aaammm/,* am. *What's the word?* Repeat with *Pam, Sam, map, sap.*

■ Have children write *a* and *m* several times on their **WorkBoards** as they say /a/, /m/. Repeat with /p/ and /s/.

Corrective Feedback

Sound Error If children cannot give the sounds for final blends, model each sound. For example: /nnn/ /d/. Say each sound slowly and gradually faster to blend the two sounds together: /nnnd/. Have children repeat. Then repeat the Guided Practice activity.

Beyond Level

Phonics

Objectives	Introduce final blends; blend and read words
Materials	• none

ACCELERATE

■ Write *sand, ant,* and *past* on the board. Draw a line under *nd, nt,* and *st* in each word. *When two consonants appear at the end of the word, the sounds of the letters are often blended.* Point to *nd* in *sand. Say: The letter* n *stands for /n/ as in* nest. *The letter* d *stands for /d/ as in* dolphin. *I can blend these sounds together: /n/ /d/, /nnnd/. The sound is /nd/.* Blend the entire word with children: /s/ /a/ /n/ /d/, /sssaaannnd/, sand. Repeat with *ant* and *past*.

■ Help children read words with final blends. Write these words on the board: *and, band, hand, land, sand; list, fist, mist; fast, last, past, cast.* Model blending as needed.

ELL ENGLISH LANGUAGE LEARNERS

Big Book of Explorations

Access to Core Content

Content Objective Develop listening comprehension
Language Objective Discuss text using key words and sentence frames
Materials • **ELL Resource Book**, pp. 42–49

PRETEACH BIG BOOK OF EXPLORATIONS

> **All Language Levels**

Use the Interactive Question-Response Guide on **ELL Resource Book** pages 48–49 to preview the **Big Book of Explorations** selections "Making Friends" Preteach half of the selection on Day 1 and half on Day 2.

Grammar

Content Objective Identify nouns
Language Objective Speak in complete sentences, using sentence frames
Materials • **Listening Library Audio CD** • **Photo Cards**

NAMING WORDS (NOUNS)

> **All Language Levels**

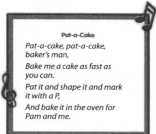

Pat-a-Cake

Pat-a-cake, pat-a-cake, baker's man,
Bake me a cake as fast as you can.
Pat it and shape it and mark it with a P,
And bake it in the oven for Pam and me.

- Review nouns. Remind children that nouns can name people, places, and things. Point to things around the room (desk, chair, pencils) and name them. Have children repeat.

- Play "Pat-a-Cake" from the **Listening Library Audio CD**. Tell children to listen for naming words that name things. Say that things are items they can touch or see.

- Point out the naming words that name things: *cake* and *oven*. Explain that there are other naming words that name people, such as *Pam* and *man*. Display **Photo Cards** of familiar things, such as *car, book, bus, balloon, pen, kite, window, star, snow*. Point to each photo and name it. Have children repeat.

PEER DISCUSSION STARTERS

> **All Language Levels**

- Distribute Photo Cards of things friends play with together discussed this week, such as *bike, book, jump rope, ball, snow*.

- Pair children and have them complete the sentence frame *We play with a _____*. Ask them to expand by providing as many details as they can. For example: *It is _____*. Circulate, listen in, and take note of each child's language use and proficiency.

Puppet

Approaching Level

Phonemic Awareness

Objective Blend sounds to form words
Materials • **Puppet**

PHONEME BLENDING

Tier 2

Model

- Hold up the **Puppet**. *Happy is going to say the sounds in a word. Listen as Happy says the sounds in* pan: /p/ /a/ /n/. *Now Happy will blend the sounds together:* /paaannn/, pan. *Say the sounds with Happy:* /paaannn/. *Say the word with Happy:* pan. *Repeat with* map.

Guided Practice/Practice

- Have the Puppet say /s/ /a/ /p/. Have children blend the sounds with the Puppet and say the word: /sssaaap/, *sap*. Then have the Puppet say the sounds for the following words. Have children blend each word.

/p/ /a/ /t/	/l/ /a/ /p/	/t/ /i/ /p/
/t/ /a/ /p/	/l/ /i/ /p/	/p/ /i/ /t/
/t/ /a/ /m/	/p/ /i/ /p/	/p/ /i/ /k/
/m/ /o/ /p/	/p/ /a/ /n/	/p/ /a/ /m/

Phonics

Objective Blend with /p/*p*, /s/*s*, /m/*m*, and /a/*a* to read words
Materials • **Word-Building Cards** • pocket chart

BLEND SOUNDS IN CVC WORDS

Tier 2

Model

- Place **Word-Building Cards** *m*, *a*, and *p* in the pocket chart. *The name of this letter is* m. *The letter* m *stands for the* /m/ *sound. Say* /m/. *The name of this letter is* a. *The letter* a *stands for the* /a/ *sound. Say* /a/. *The name of this letter is* p. *The letter* p *stands for the* /p/ *sound. Say* /p/.
- *Now let's put the three sounds together to say a word:* /mmmaaap/, map. *Blend the sounds in the word with me:* /mmmaaap/, map.

Guided Practice/Practice

- Distribute small Word-Building Cards *m*, *a*, *p*. Have children form *map* and blend the sounds together to say the word: /mmmaaap/, *map*. Repeat with *sap, Pam, am,* and *Sam*. Guide practice as necessary.

Corrective Feedback

Blending Error Say: *My turn.* Model blending. Then lead children in blending the sounds. Say: *Blend the sounds with me.* Then say: *Your turn. Blend.* Have children chorally blend. Return to the beginning of the word. Say: *Let's start over.*

ELL

Extra Practice Provide additional practice in pronouncing and blending sounds that do not transfer directly to the native language of some children, such as the short vowel /a/.

Approaching Level

Leveled Reader Lesson 1

Objective   Read *Animal Friends* to apply skills and strategies

Materials   • **Leveled Reader:** *Animal Friends*

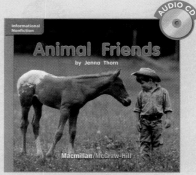

Leveled Reader

BEFORE READING

- **Preview** Read the title and the name of the author. *What animal friend do you see on the cover?* Turn to the title page and point out that it also has the title and the name of the author. *What do you think you will learn about animal friends?*

- **Model Concepts About Print** Demonstrate book handling for children. Guide them as they follow along with their books. *I hold the book so that the cover is on the front and the words are not upside down. I open the book by turning the cover. Then I turn each page as I read it, starting with the first page and ending with the last page at the back of the book.*

- **Review High-Frequency Words** Write **I**, **like**, and **a** and read the words aloud. Guide children as they name the letters in each word. Have children find *I*, *like*, and *a* in the book. Ask them to point to and read the words.

- **Page Through the Book** Name unfamiliar items and identify the rebus pictures.

- **Set a Purpose for Reading** *Let's find out about animal friends.*

DURING READING

- Remind children to use the rebuses and photographs to gain information and to look for the high-frequency words *I*, *like*, and *a*. Show children how to self-correct. *On page 2, I look at the rebus picture and I think, "I like a dog." Then I look at the photograph and see that the boy is holding a small dog. The small dog is a puppy. I think the word is* puppy. *"I like a puppy." That matches the photograph.*

- Monitor children's reading and provide help as needed.

AFTER READING

- Ask children to point out words that they had trouble reading and to share strategies they used to help them.

- Have children turn to a partner and ask each other questions. Tell children to respond in complete sentences.

- Ask children to retell important facts and to share personal responses. *Did the book make you think of an animal you would like as a friend? What animal is it? How can it be a friend?*

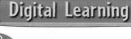
Digital Learning

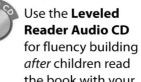
Use the **Leveled Reader Audio CD** for fluency building *after* children read the book with your support during Small Group time.

ON YOUR OWN
Animal Graph

Provide index cards for each child to draw his or her favorite animal from *Animal Friends*. Create a picture graph on chart paper. List the animal names down the chart. Have children place their picture next to the animal name. Count the pictures to find the favorite.

Leveled Reader

ELL

Retell Use the Interactive Question-Response Guide Technique to help English Language Learners understand *We Can Share*. As you read, make meaning clear by pointing to pictures, demonstrating word meaning, paraphrasing text, and asking children questions.

ON YOUR OWN

P Is for *Pizza*

Have children draw a picture of a silly pizza that they could share with a friend. Have them put *p* toppings on their pizza, such as pretzels, pickles, and peanuts, and label the toppings.

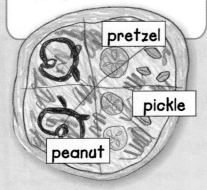

On Level

Leveled Reader Lesson 1

Objective Read *We Can Share* to apply skills and strategies
Materials • **Leveled Reader:** *We Can Share*

BEFORE READING

- **Preview** Read the title and the name of the author. *Who do you see on the cover? What are the friends sharing?* Turn to the title page. Point out that it also has the title and name of the author. Then open and page through the book. Name unfamiliar items and identify the rebuses. *What do you think you will read about in this book?*

- **Model Concepts About Print** Demonstrate book handling. *I hold the book so that the cover is on the front and the words are not upside down. I turn the cover to open the book. Then I turn each page as I read it.*

- **Review High-Frequency Words** Write **we**, **can**, **like**, and **a** on chart paper. Have children find each word in the title or in the text of the book. Have them point to each word as they read it.

- **Set a Purpose for Reading** *Let's find out what friends can share.*

DURING READING

- Have children turn to page 2 and begin by whisper-reading the first two pages.

- Remind children to look for the new high-frequency word and to use the rebus pictures and photographs.

- Monitor children's reading and provide help. Stop during the reading and ask open-ended questions to facilitate discussion, such as: *What things are good to share? What is the author showing and telling us about sharing with friends?*

AFTER READING

- Ask children to point out words they had trouble reading and to share strategies they used to figure them out. Reinforce good behaviors. For example: *Jon, I noticed that you follow the words with your finger and read from left to right.*

- Have children turn to a partner and ask each other questions about the story. Tell children to respond in complete sentences.

- **Retell** Have children retell important facts from the text. Help them make a personal connection. *What things have you shared with friends? Why do you think sharing is fun?*

Beyond Level

Leveled Reader Lesson 1

Objective   Read *I Like My Friends* to apply skills and strategies
Materials   • **Leveled Reader:** *I Like My Friends*

Leveled Reader

BEFORE READING

- **Preview** Read the title and the name of the author. *What are the children on the cover doing?* Turn to the title page and point out that it also has the title and the name of the author. *What are the children doing in this photograph? What do you think this book is about?*

- **Introduce Story Words** Point to the word *wagon* on page 2. Read the sentence. Have children use the photograph to explain what a *wagon* is. Repeat with *donkey* on page 5.

- **Set a Purpose for Reading** *Let's find out what friends do with each other and for each other.*

DURING READING

- Remind children that when they come to an unfamiliar word, they can look for familiar chunks in the word, break the word into syllables and sound out each part, or think about what the word might mean. If the word does not sound right or make sense in the sentence, children can self-correct.

- Monitor children's reading and provide help as needed.

AFTER READING

- Ask children to point out words they had trouble reading and to share the strategies they used to figure them out.

- Have children turn to a partner and ask each other questions about the story. Tell children to respond in complete sentences.

- Ask children to retell important facts from the book. Help them share personal experiences. *Can you tell us about things you've done with friends? Now tell us how you have helped friends.*

- **Evaluate** *Think about what makes somebody a good friend. Then finish this sentence: A good friend is somebody who _____.*

- As a preparation for writing an acrostic about themselves, have children work in pairs to list ways they try to be a good friend.

- **Model** Write *FRIEND* vertically on the board. Tell children they will use their list to write an acrostic about themselves. Explain that they will use each letter of *friend* as the start of an adjective or phrase that describes how they are a good friend. To model the activity, write *Funny* or *Friendly* next to the letter *F*.

I Am a Friend

Have children write the sentence *I am a friend*. Then have them draw a picture to show one way that they can be friends with someone.

I am a friend.

Leveled Reader

Vocabulary

Preteach Vocabulary Use the routine in the **Visual Vocabulary Resources**, pages 309–310, to preteach the ELL Vocabulary listed on the inside front cover of the Leveled Reader.

ELL ENGLISH LANGUAGE LEARNERS

Leveled Reader

Content Objective Read to apply skills and strategies
Language Objective Retell information using complete sentences
Materials • **Leveled Reader:** *We Like It*

BEFORE READING

All Language Levels

- **Preview** Read the title *We Like It*. Ask: *What's the title? Say it again.* Repeat with the author's name. Point to the cover photo and say: *I see two girls with something in their hands.* Point to the girls and their hands as you name them. *They are eating peaches. Now turn to a partner and tell about this picture.*

- **Page Through the Book** Use simple language to tell about the photo on each page. Immediately follow up with questions, such as: *Is this a pie? Is this a peach or a pear?*

- **Review Skills** Use the inside front cover to review the phonics skill and high-frequency words.

- **Set a Purpose** Say: *Let's read to find out about what the friends like to eat.*

DURING READING

All Language Levels

- Have children whisper-read each page, or use the differentiated suggestions below.

- **Retell** Stop after every two pages and ask children to state what they have learned so far. Reinforce language by restating children's comments when they have difficulty using story-specific words. Provide differentiated sentence frames to support children's responses and engage children in partner-talk where appropriate.

Beginning	Intermediate	Advanced
Echo-Read Have children echo-read after you.	**Choral-Read** Have children choral-read with you.	**Choral-Read** Have children choral-read.
Check Comprehension Point to pictures and ask questions such as: *Do you see a pretzel? Point to a pretzel the girl is eating.*	**Check Comprehension** Ask questions/prompts such as: *What are the children doing in this photo? What are some kinds of fruit these friends like?*	**Check Comprehension** Ask: *How are all of the things these friends like the same? How are they different? Which foods in this book do you like?*

ELL ENGLISH LANGUAGE LEARNERS

AFTER READING

All Language Levels

Book Talk Children will work with peers of varying language abilities to discuss their books for this week. Display the four **Leveled Readers** read this week: *I Like My Friends* (Beyond Level), *We Can Share* (On Level), *Animal Friends* (Approaching Level), and *We Like It* (English Language Learners).

Ask the questions and provide the prompts below. Call on children who read each book to answer the questions or respond to the prompt. If appropriate, ask children to find the pages in the book that illustrate their answers.

- Who are the friends in your book?
- What do the friends do together?
- What do they like?
- How are these friends like yours? What do they do that is different from your friends?
- What do you like in this the book? Tell about it.

Develop Listening and Speaking Skills Tell children to remember the following:

- Share information in cooperative learning interactions. Remind children to work with their partners to retell the story and complete any activities. Ask: *What happened next in the story?*

- Employ self-corrective techniques and monitor their own and other children's language production. Children should ask themselves: *What parts of this passage were confusing to me? Can my classmates help me clarify a word or sentence that I don't understand?*

- Use high-frequency English words to describe people, places, and objects.

- Narrate, describe, and explain with specificity and detail. Ask: *Where did the story take place? Can you describe the setting? What else did you notice?*

- Express opinions, ideas, and feelings on a variety of social and academic topics. Ask: *What do you think about the characters in the story?*

Approaching Level

Phonemic Awareness

Objective Recognize the same sound in different words

Materials
- **Photo Cards:** *alligator, ant, apple, map, moon, mouse, pen, piano, pumpkin, saw, seal, soap*

PHONEME IDENTITY

Tier 2

Model
- Display **Photo Cards** for *pen, piano,* and *pumpkin. What are the names of these pictures? Say the names with me:* pen, piano, pumpkin. *What sound is the same at the beginning of* pen, piano, *and* pumpkin? *Yes, /p/ is the same. It is the first sound in all the words.*

Guided Practice/Practice
- Display the Photo Cards for *map, moon, mouse. Let's name these pictures:* map, moon, mouse. *Tell me what sound is the same in these picture names. Yes, /m/ is the same. It is the first sound in all the words. Repeat with* saw, seal, soap *and* alligator, ant, apple.

Phonics

Objective Identify initial and final /p/*p* and build fluency

Materials
- **Photo Cards:** *map, mop, pen, penguin, piano, pie, pizza, pumpkin, rope, soap, soup, top* • **Word-Building Cards** • pocket chart
- **Sound-Spelling WorkBoards**

BUILD FLUENCY: LETTER-SOUND CORRESPONDENCE

Tier 2

Model
- Place **Word-Building Card** *p* in the top row of the pocket chart. Place the Photo Cards facedown in a stack. Pick the first card, name the picture, and tell whether it begins or ends with the /p/ sound. Then place it in the pocket chart under *p*.

Guided Practice/Practice
- Have each child choose a Photo Card, say the name of the picture, identify whether the name begins or ends with /p/*p*, and place it in the pocket chart under the *p* card. Guide practice with the first Photo Card.

Build Fluency
- Display the card for *p*. Have children name the letter as quickly as they can. Then ask them to write the letter *p* on their **WorkBoards** several times as they say /p/.

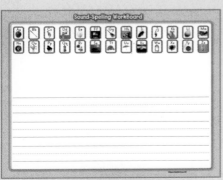

Sound-Spelling WorkBoard

Approaching Level

Leveled Reader Lesson 2

Objective Reread *Animal Friends* to reinforce fluency, phonics, and comparing and contrasting

Materials • **Leveled Reader:** *Animal Friends*

FOCUS ON FLUENCY

- Tell children that you will read one page of the book and they should read that page right after you. They should follow along in their books and try to read at the same speed and with the same expression that you use.

SKILL COMPARE AND CONTRAST

- *Look at the photographs on pages 2 and 3, and 6 and 7. Look at the **details** in the photo. How are the puppy and the pony alike? How are these animal friends different?*

REREAD BOOKS

- Distribute copies of previously read **Leveled Readers**. Tell children that rereading the books will help them develop their skills.

- Circulate and listen in as children read. Stop them periodically and ask them how they are figuring out words or checking their understanding.

High-Frequency Words

Objective Review high-frequency words *a*, *like*, *the*, and *we*

Materials • **High-Frequency Word Cards:** *a*, *like*, *the*, *we*

BUILD WORD AUTOMATICITY: *a, like, the, we*

- Distribute copies of the **High-Frequency Word Card** for **a**. Say the word and have children repeat it. Have children name the letter in the word. Repeat with the words **like**, **the**, and **we**.

- **Build Fluency** Use the High-Frequency Word Cards to review previously taught words. Repeat, guiding children to read more rapidly.

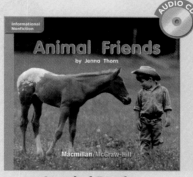

Leveled Reader

Meet Grade-Level Expectations

As an alternative to this day's lesson, guide children through a reading of the On Level Leveled Reader. See page 410. Because both books contain the same vocabulary, phonics, and comprehension skills, the scaffolding you provided will help most children gain access to this more challenging text.

ON YOUR OWN

All About Animals

Have children draw a picture of an animal friend. Have them complete a sentence frame to tell about the picture: *I like a _____.* Provide models of animal names for children to copy.

I like a puppy.

Leveled Reader

ON YOUR OWN

Same or Different?

Have children draw a picture of something they like that they can also share with a friend. Have them write the caption *I like a _____.* Then have partners show their picture to each other and discuss how the things they like are the same or different. Have children meet with a new partner to repeat the process.

On Level

Leveled Reader Lesson 2

Objective   Reread to apply skills and strategies to retell a selection
Materials   • **Leveled Reader:** *We Can Share*

BEFORE READING

- Ask children to look through *We Can Share* and recall what the book is about. Reinforce vocabulary by repeating children's sentences using more sophisticated language. For example: *Yes, the children in the book share things. They have fun sharing things to eat, such as fruit and pizza.*

DURING READING

- Have children join you in a choral-reading of the book. Model reading with expression. *When I read page 2, I emphasize the word* pear *by saying the word a little stronger. I use the same emphasis when I read* pie *on page 3. I say these words with emphasis to draw attention to what the children in the book like to share.* Have children use the same kind of expression when they read.

- Assign each child a page. Have children practice by whisper-reading. *Follow along as other children read, and be ready to come in when it is your turn. Remember, use lots of expression.*

AFTER READING

- Have children retell the important facts. Ask: *What questions did you ask yourself as you read the book?*

- *In what way are all the children in the book alike? What is different about the things that the children are sharing?*

Beyond Level

Leveled Reader Library

Leveled Reader Lesson 2

Objective Reread to apply skills and strategies to retell a selection

Materials • **Leveled Reader:** *I Like My Friends*

BEFORE READING

- Have children look back at *I Like My Friends* and recall what the book is about. Ask: *How are the children in the book alike? What are some of the different things the children do with friends?*

DURING READING

- Assign each child a page to read aloud. Have children practice by whisper-reading. *Follow along as each child reads, and be ready to come in when it is your turn. Remember, use lots of expression.*

AFTER READING

- Explain that we can ask questions about a book to help us understand it. Model the strategy: *When I began reading the book, I asked myself:* What do friends like to do together? *As I read the first page, I found out that friends can pull a wagon together. Then I asked:* What else can friends do together? *I read on to find out.* What questions did you ask as you read?

- Have children share some of the questions they asked. Have them tell how they found the answers to their questions.

Expand Vocabulary

Objectives Learn and apply the meaning of the new words *wagon* and *donkey*; brainstorm names of other things to ride in or on

Materials • **Leveled Reader:** *I Like My Friends*

ENRICH: *wagon, donkey*

Gifted Talented

- Write *wagon* and *donkey* on cards. Display *wagon* and read the sentence on page 2: *I like to pull a wagon.* Have children point to the *wagon*. Ask: *What can you put in a wagon?*

- Ask children to use the photograph to describe what a *wagon* is. (something on wheels that can be pulled) Point out that the words *wagon* and *donkey* are both nouns. Both words name something. Both words are nouns. Ask children to use *wagon* in sentences. Repeat with *donkey*.

- Point out that friends can ride in a wagon or on a donkey together. Have children brainstorm names of other things that friends can ride in or on together. Record responses in a web labeled "We Like to Ride with Friends."

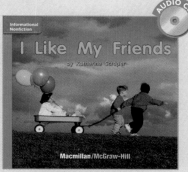
Leveled Reader

ON YOUR OWN

Ask and Answer

Have partners write and illustrate a question and answer: *Can a friend _____? A friend can _____.* One child writes the question and the other writes the answer. They collaborate on the drawing.

ELL

Partners When children write and illustrate a question and answer, pair English Language Learners with children who are more proficient.

ELL ENGLISH LANGUAGE LEARNERS

Fluency

Content Objectives Reread Pre-decodable Readers to develop fluency; develop speaking skills

Language Objective Tell a partner what a selection is about

Materials • **Pre-decodable Readers:** *I Am a Doctor; A Map*

REREAD FOR FLUENCY

Beginning

- Review the high-frequency words **a**, **like**, **can**, and **I** using the **Read/Spell/Write** routine.

Intermediate/Advanced

- Use each word in a sentence that illustrates its use, such as: *I can hop.* Act out hopping. *I like music.* Act out listening to and enjoying music. *I can read a book.* Act out reading a book.

All Language Levels

- Guide children through a choral-reading of *I Am a Doctor* and *A Map*. Model reading the sentence "I am a doctor." Point out how you used your voice to add expression to your reading by emphasizing the word *doctor* to show that it is an important word in the sentence. Model reading the sentence again and have children chorally repeat.

DEVELOP SPEAKING/LISTENING SKILLS

All Language Levels

- Have children reread *I Am a Doctor* and *A Map* to a partner. Remind them to listen carefully and follow along in their book as their partner is reading. Work with children to read with accuracy and appropriate expression.

- Ask children to tell their partner about the pictures on each page. Then have the other partner describe the pictures. Circulate, listen in, and provide additional language as needed.

Beginning	Intermediate	Advanced
Confirm Understanding Ask partners to tell you which is their favorite picture in the book. Prompt them to explain why it is their favorite picture.	**Share Preferences** Ask partners to tell you which is their favorite picture in the book. Prompt them to explain why it is their favorite picture.	**Compare and Contrast** Have partners compare two different pictures and describe them. Prompt them to explain how they are alike and different.

ELL
ENGLISH LANGUAGE LEARNERS

High-Frequency Words

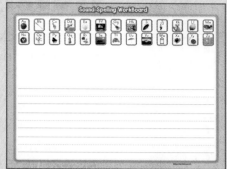

Sound-Spelling WorkBoard

Content Objective Spell high-frequency words correctly

Language Objective Write in complete sentences, using sentence frames

Materials • **Sound-Spelling WorkBoards** • **Sound-Spelling Cards** • **Photo Cards**

Beginning/Intermediate

■ Write the high-frequency word **a** on the board. Have children copy the word on their **WorkBoards**. Then help them say, then write, a sentence for the word. Provide the sentence starter *I see a _____.*

Advanced

■ Children should first orally state their sentence. Correct as needed. Then they can draw a picture to complete the sentence. For children who are ready, help them spell words using their growing knowledge of English sound-spelling relationships. Model how to segment the word children are trying to spell and attach a spelling to each sound. Use the **Sound-Spelling Cards** to reinforce the spellings for each English sound.

Writing

All Language Levels

■ Dictate the following sound and ask children to write the letter: /p/. Have them write the letter five times as they say /p/. Demonstrate correct letter formation, as needed.

■ Then display a set of **Photo Cards**. Select at least five cards whose picture names begin with /p/ (*pen, pie, pumpkin, peach, penguin*) and three whose picture names begin with /m/ (*mop, moon, mouse*).

■ Say the name of each card, stretching the initial sound to emphasize it. You may also need to reinforce the meaning of each picture and model correct mouth formation when forming the sound. Use the articulation pictures and prompts on the back of the small Sound-Spelling Cards for support. Tell children that if the picture name begins with /p/, you want them to write the letter *p* on their WorkBoards.

Phonemic Awareness/ Phonics

For English Language Learners who need more practice with this week's phonemic awareness and phonics skills, see the Approaching Level lessons. Focus on minimal contrasts, articulation, and those sounds that do not transfer from the child's first language to English. For a complete listing of transfer sounds, see pages T10–T31.

Weekly Assessment

Use your Quick Check observations and the assessment opportunities identified below to evaluate children's progress in key skill areas.

Skills	Quick Check Observations	Pencil and Paper Assessment
✔ **PHONEMIC AWARENESS/ PHONICS** /p/p	353	Activity Book, pp. 14, 20, 22 Practice Book, pp. 47, 52
✔ **HIGH-FREQUENCY WORDS** *a*	374	Activity Book, pp. 17–18 Practice Book, pp. 49–50
✔ **COMPREHENSION** Compare and Contrast	364	Activity Book, pp. 15–16, 21 Practice Book, p. 48

Quick Check Rubric

Skills	1	2	3
✔ **PHONEMIC AWARENESS/ PHONICS**	Does not connect the sound /p/ with the letter *Pp* and has difficulty blending the CVC words *Pam, map,* and *sap.*	Usually connects the sound /p/ with the letter *Pp* and blends the CVC words *Pam, map,* and *sap* with only occasional support.	Consistently connects the sound /p/ with the letter *Pp* and blends the CVC words *Pam, map,* and *sap.*
✔ **HIGH-FREQUENCY WORDS**	Does not identify the high-frequency words.	Usually recognizes the high-frequency words with accuracy, but not speed.	Consistently recognizes the high-frequency words with speed and accuracy.
✔ **COMPREHENSION**	Does not compare and contrast using pictures and text.	Usually compares and contrasts using pictures and text.	Consistently compares and contrasts using pictures and text.

DIBELS LINK

PROGRESS MONITORING
Use your DIBELS results to inform instruction.
IF...
Initial Sound Fluency (**ISF**)   0–7

THEN...
Evaluate for Intervention

TPRI LINK

PROGRESS MONITORING
Use your TPRI scores to inform instruction.
IF...
Phonemic Awareness   Still Developing
Graphophonemic Knowledge   Still Developing
Listening Comprehension   Still Developing

THEN...
Evaluate for Intervention

End-of-Week Assessment

Diagnose		Prescribe
Review the assessment answers with children. Have them correct their errors. Then provide additional instruction as needed.		
PHONEMIC AWARENESS/ PHONICS /p/*p*	**IF...** **Quick Check Rubric:** Children consistently score 1 or **Pencil and Paper Assessment:** Children get 0–2 items correct	**THEN...** Reteach Phonemic Awareness and Phonics Skills using **Phonemic Awareness** or **Phonics Intervention Teacher's Editions**. SPIRAL REVIEW Use the Build Fluency lesson in upcoming weeks to provide children practice reading words with /p/*p*.
HIGH-FREQUENCY WORDS *a*	**Quick Check Rubric:** Children consistently score 1 or **Pencil and Paper Assessment:** Children get 0–2 items correct	Reteach High-Frequency Words using the **Phonics Intervention Teacher's Edition**. SPIRAL REVIEW Use the High-Frequency Words lesson in upcoming weeks to provide children practice reading the word *a*.
COMPREHENSION Skill: Compare and Contrast	**Quick Check Rubric:** Children consistently score 1 or **Pencil and Paper Assessment:** Children get 0–2 items correct	Reteach Comprehension Skill using the **Comprehension Intervention Teacher's Edition**.

Response to Intervention

To place children in Tier 2 or Tier 3 Intervention use the *Diagnostic Assessment*.

- Phonemic Awareness
- Phonics
- Vocabulary
- Comprehension
- Fluency

Week 3 ★ At a Glance

Priority Skills and Concepts

 ### Comprehension
- **Genre:** Fiction, Expository, Folktale
- **Strategy:** Ask Questions
- **Skill:** Identify Character
- **Skill:** Make Predictions

 ### High-Frequency Words
- *a* , *like*

Oral Vocabulary
- Build Robust Vocabulary:
  grateful , *include* , *problem* , *solve* , *thoughtful*

Fluency
- Echo-Read
- Word Automaticity
- Sound-Spellings

 ### Phonemic Awareness
- **Phoneme Isolation**
- **Phoneme Categorization**
- **Phoneme Blending**

 ### Phonics
- *Ss, Pp*

Grammar
- **Naming Words (Nouns)**

Writing
- **Sentences**

Key   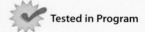 Tested in Program    Review Skill

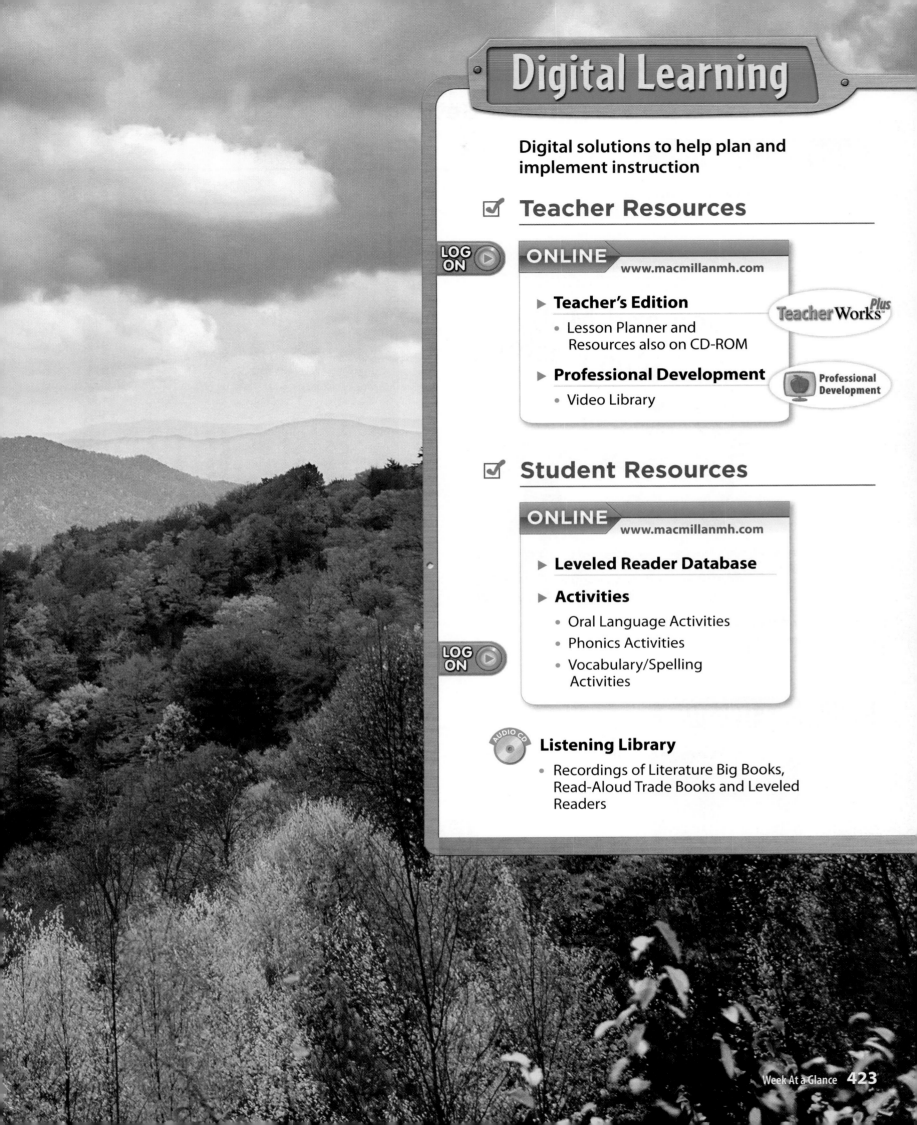

Digital Learning

Digital solutions to help plan and implement instruction

☑ Teacher Resources

LOG ON ▶

ONLINE
www.macmillanmh.com

▶ **Teacher's Edition**

Teacher Works *Plus*

• Lesson Planner and Resources also on CD-ROM

▶ **Professional Development**

Professional Development

• Video Library

☑ Student Resources

ONLINE
www.macmillanmh.com

▶ **Leveled Reader Database**

▶ **Activities**

• Oral Language Activities
• Phonics Activities
• Vocabulary/Spelling Activities

LOG ON ▶

Listening Library

• Recordings of Literature Big Books, Read-Aloud Trade Books and Leveled Readers

Theme: Getting Along

Student Literature

A mix of fiction and nonfiction

Trade Book

Genre Fiction

Big Book of Explorations

Genre Expository

Support Literature

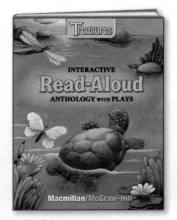

Interactive Read-Aloud Anthology

Genre Folktale

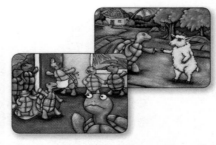

Oral Vocabulary Cards
- Listening Comprehension
- Build Robust Vocabulary

Pre-decodable Readers

Resources for Differentiated Instruction

Leveled Readers

GR Levels Rebus-C

Genre	Fiction

- Same Theme
- Same Vocabulary/Phonics
- Same Comprehension Skills

Approaching Level

On Level

Beyond Level

ELL

Leveled Reader Database
Go to www.macmillanmh.com.

Practice

Activity Book

Practice Book

ELL Practice Book

Response to Intervention

Tier 2

- Phonemic Awareness
- Phonics
- Vocabulary
- Comprehension
- Fluency

Tier 3

Unit Assessment

Assess Unit Skills

- Phonemic Awareness
- Phonics
- High-Frequency Words
- Listening Comprehension

HOME-SCHOOL CONNECTION

- Family letters in English and Spanish
- Take-home stories and activities

Go to **www.macmillanmh.com** for Online Lesson Planner

TeacherWorks *Plus*
All-In-One Planner and Resource Center

Professional Development
Video Library

Trade Book

Simon and Molly
plus Hester
Lisa Jahn-Clough

WHOLE GROUP

WHOLE GROUP	DAY 1	DAY 2
ORAL LANGUAGE	**? Focus Question** Do you always like what a friend does? Build Background, 434	**? Focus Question** What happens when a friend does not like what you like?
• Oral Vocabulary	**Oral Vocabulary** *grateful, include, problem, solve, thoughtful*, 434	**Oral Vocabulary** *grateful, include, problem, solve, thoughtful*, 442 Color Words, 449
• Phonemic Awareness	✔ **Phonemic Awareness** Phoneme Isolation, 437	✔ **Phonemic Awareness** Phoneme Categorization, 450
WORD STUDY		
• Phonics	✔ **Phonics** Review /s/s, /p/p, 438 Handwriting: Review *Ss, Pp*, 439 Activity Book, 24 Practice Book, 47	✔ **Phonics** Review /s/s, /p/p, /m/m, /a/a, 450 Blend with /a/a, /p/p, /m/m, /s/s, 451
• High-Frequency Words	✔ **High-Frequency Words** *a*, *like*, 436	✔ **Review High-Frequency Words**, 452
READING		
• Listening Comprehension • Apply Phonics and High-Frequency Words • Fluency	**Share the Trade Book** *Simon and Molly plus Hester* **Strategy:** Ask Questions, 435 ✔ **Skill:** Identify Character, 435 Trade Book	**Reread the Trade Book** *Simon and Molly plus Hester* **Strategy:** Ask Questions, 444 ✔ **Skill:** Identify Character, 444 Retell, 448 **Pre-decodable Reader:** *I Like, We Like*, 452 Activity Book, 25 Practice Book, 54 **Fluency** Echo-Read, 448 Trade Book
LANGUAGE ARTS		
• Writing • Grammar	**Shared Writing** Lists, 441 **Grammar** Naming Words (Nouns), 440	**Interactive Writing** Sentences, 453
ASSESSMENT		
• Informal/Formal	**Quick Check** Phonemic Awareness, 437	**Quick Check** Comprehension, 448

 SMALL GROUP Lesson Plan ▷ **Differentiated Instruction 428–429**

Priority Skills

Half-Day Kindergarten

Teach Core Skills
Focus on tested skill lessons, other lessons, and small group options as your time allows.

Phonemic Awareness/Phonics	High-Frequency Words	Oral Vocabulary	Comprehension
Review /s/s, /p/p	*a, like*	Color and Number Words	**Strategy:** Ask Questions
			Skill: Identify Character

DAY 3

❓ Focus Question What is a way you and your friend can help in your community?

Oral Vocabulary *grateful, include, problem, solve, thoughtful,* 454

Oral Vocabulary Cards: "The Turtle and the Sheep"

Phonemic Awareness
Phoneme Blending, 459

Phonics
Review /s/s, /p/p, /m/m, /a/a, 460
Blend with /s/s, /p/p, /m/m, /a/a, 460
Read Words, 461

High-Frequency Words
like, a, 458
Activity Book, 27–28
Practice Book, 55–56
Read for Fluency, 458

Read the Big Book of Explorations
"Helping Hands," 29–32

Text Feature:
Use Labels, 456

Big Book of Explorations

Independent Writing
Prewrite and Draft a Sentence, 463
Grammar
Naming Words (Nouns), 462

Quick Check High-Frequency Words, 458

DAY 4

❓ Focus Question When have you worked together with friends to get a job done?

Oral Vocabulary *grateful, include, problem, solve, thoughtful,* 464

Number Words, 467

Phonemic Awareness
Phoneme Blending, 468

Phonics
Cumulative Review, 468
Blend with /a/a, /m/m, /p/p, /s/s, 469
Activity Book, 29–30
Practice Book, 57

Review High-Frequency Words, 470

Interactive Read Aloud
Listening Comprehension, 466

Read Aloud: "The Little Red Hen"

Pre-decodable Reader:
Pam, 470

Read Aloud

Independent Writing
Revise and Edit a Sentence, 471

Quick Check Phonics, 469

DAY 5
Review and Assess

❓ Focus Question Which story about friends did you like best?

Oral Vocabulary *grateful, include, problem, solve, thoughtful,* 472

Color and Number Words, 474

Phonemic Awareness
Phoneme Categorization, 475

Phonics
Build Fluency, 476
Read Words, 476
Dictation, 476
Activity Book, 32

High-Frequency Words
can, we, the, like, a, 474

Read Across Texts
Strategy: Ask Questions, 473
Skill: Identify Character, 473
Activity Book, 31

Fluency Word Automaticity, 474

Independent Writing
Publish and Present Sentences, 479

Weekly Assessment, 504–505

Differentiated Instruction

What do I do in small groups?

Teacher-Led Small Groups

Independent Activities

Focus on Skills

IF... children need additional instruction, practice, or extension based on your Quick Check observations for the following priority skills

 Phonemic Awareness
Phoneme Isolation, Blending, Categorization

 Phonics
Ss and *Pp*

 High-Frequency Words
a , *like*

 Comprehension
Strategy: Ask Questions
Skill: Identify Character

THEN...

Approaching	Preteach and
ELL	Reteach Skills
On Level	Practice
Beyond	Enrich and Accelerate Learning

 Suggested Small Group Lesson Plan

	DAY 1	**DAY 2**
Approaching Level Tier 2 • **Preteach/Reteach** **Tier 2 Instruction**	• Oral Language, 478 • High-Frequency Words, 478 **ELL** High-Frequency Words Review, 478 • Phonemic Awareness, 479 • Phonics, 479 **ELL** Sound-Spellings Review, 479	• High-Frequency Words, 484 **ELL** • Pre-decodable Reader, 484 • Phonemic Awareness, 485 • Phonics, 485
On Level • **Practice**	• High-Frequency Words, 480 • Phonemic Awareness/Phonics, 480 **ELL**	• Pre-decodable Reader, 486
Beyond Level • **Extend/Accelerate** **Gifted and Talented**	• High-Frequency Words/Vocabulary, 481 **ELL** Expand Oral Vocabulary, 481 • Phonics, 481	• Pre-decodable Reader, 486
ELL • **Build English Language Proficiency** • **See ELL in other levels.**	• Oral Language Warm-Up, 482 • Academic Language, 482 • Vocabulary, 483	• Access to Core Content, 487

Small Group

Focus on Leveled Readers

**Levels
Rebus–C**

Approaching

On Level

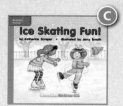
Beyond

ELL

Additional Leveled Readers

Leveled Reader Database
www.macmillanmh.com

Search by

- Comprehension Skill
- Content Area
- Genre
- Text Feature
- Guided Reading Level
- Reading Recovery Level
- Lexile Score
- Benchmark Level

Subscription also available

Manipulatives

Sound-Spelling WorkBoards

Sound-Spelling Cards

Photo Cards

High-Frequency Word Cards

Visual Vocabulary Resources

DAY 3

- High-Frequency Words, 488 **ELL**
- Phonemic Awareness, 488
- Phonics, 489
- Pre-decodable Reader, 489

- Phonics, 490 **ELL**

- Phonics, 490

- Access to Core Content, 491
- Grammar, 491

DAY 4

- Phonemic Awareness, 492
- Phonics, 492 **ELL**
- Leveled Reader Lesson 1, 493

- Leveled Reader Lesson 1, 494 **ELL**

- Leveled Reader Lesson 1, 495
  Synthesize, 495

- Leveled Reader, 496–497

DAY 5

- Phonemic Awareness, 498
- Phonics, 498 **ELL**
- Leveled Reader Lesson 2, 499
- High-Frequency Words, 499

- Leveled Reader Lesson 2, 500

- Leveled Reader Lesson 2, 501 **ELL**
- Expand Vocabulary, 501

- Fluency, 502
- High-Frequency Words, 503
- Writing, 503

Managing the Class

What do I do with the rest of my class?

- Activity Book
- Practice Book
- ELL Practice Book
- Leveled Practice Activities
- Literacy Workstations
- Online Activities
- Buggles and Beezy

Classroom Management Tools

Weekly Contract

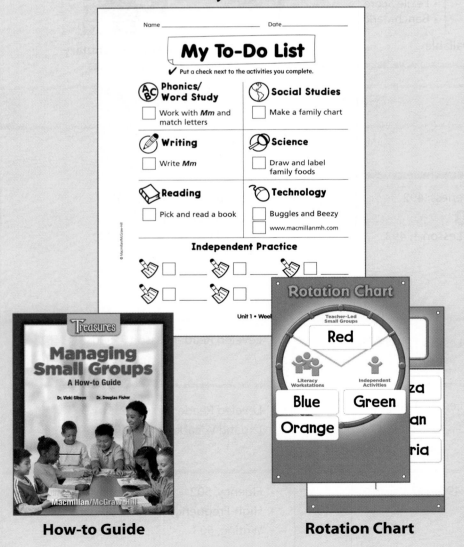

How-to Guide

Rotation Chart

Phonics Activities

- Match Letters
- Match Letters to Sounds
- Blend Words

Meet the Author/Illustrator

Lisa Jahn-Clough

- Lisa has taught both writing and illustrating for many years at a college in Maine.
- Lisa lives in Portland, Maine, but was born on a small farm in Rhode Island.
- Lisa's father was a zoologist and she even had a pet monkey, named Zepher, when she was young.

Other books by Lisa Jahn-Clough
- Jahn-Clough, Lisa. *Simon and Molly Plus Hester*. Boston, MA: Houghton Mifflin, 2001.
- Jahn-Clough, Lisa. *My Friend and I*. Boston, MA: Houghton Mifflin, 1999.

- Read Other Books by the Author or Illustrator

Practice

Activity Book

Practice Book

ELL Practice Book

Independent Activities

ONLINE INSTRUCTION www.macmillanmh.com

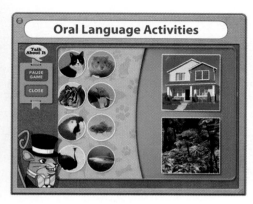

Oral Language Activities

- Focus on Unit Vocabulary and Concepts
- English Language Learner Support

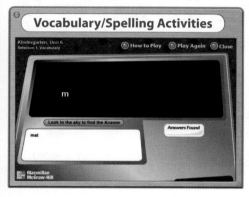

Vocabulary/Spelling Activities

- Differentiated Lists and Activities

Leveled Reader Database

- Leveled Reader Database
- Search titles by level, skill, content area, and more

Available on CD

LISTENING LIBRARY
Recordings of selections
- Literature Big Books
- Read-Aloud Trade Books
- Leveled Readers
- ELL Readers

NEW ADVENTURES WITH BUGGLES AND BEEZY
Phonemic awareness and phonics activities

Leveled Reader Activities

Approaching

On Level

Beyond

ELL

See inside cover of all Leveled Readers.

Literacy Workstations

Reading

Phonics/ Word Study

Writing

Science/ Social Studies

See lessons on pages 432–433.

Managing the Class

What do I do with the rest of my class?

Reading

Objectives

- Choose a book to read independently
- Read a book and add a page to book to create a new ending

Phonics/Word Study

Objectives

- Identify words that begin with letters *Aa*, *Mm*, *Pp*, and *Ss*
- Blend sounds to form words with the letters *a*, *m*, *P*, and *S*

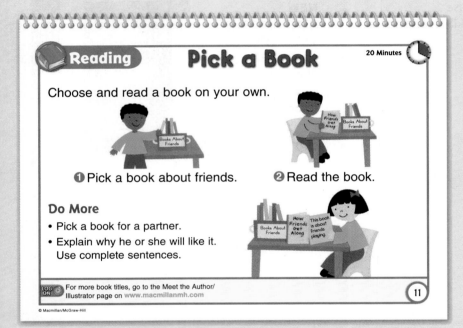

Reading — **Pick a Book** — 20 Minutes

Choose and read a book on your own.

❶ Pick a book about friends. ❷ Read the book.

Do More
- Pick a book for a partner.
- Explain why he or she will like it. Use complete sentences.

For more book titles, go to the Meet the Author/ Illustrator page on www.macmillanmh.com 11

© Macmillan/McGraw-Hill

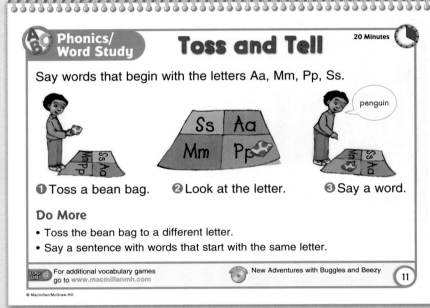

Phonics/ Word Study — **Toss and Tell** — 20 Minutes

Say words that begin with the letters Aa, Mm, Pp, Ss.

penguin

❶ Toss a bean bag. ❷ Look at the letter. ❸ Say a word.

Do More
- Toss the bean bag to a different letter.
- Say a sentence with words that start with the same letter.

For additional vocabulary games go to www.macmillanmh.com — New Adventures with Buggles and Beezy 11

© Macmillan/McGraw-Hill

Reading — **Read It, Add to It** — 20 Minutes

Read a book. Add a new page.

The End ?

The friends play.

❶ Read the book. ❷ What could happen next? ❸ Write a new page.

Do More
- Share your new page with a friend.
- Work with your friend to write another new page.

For more book titles, go to the Meet the Author/ Illustrator page on www.macmillanmh.com 12

© Macmillan/McGraw-Hill

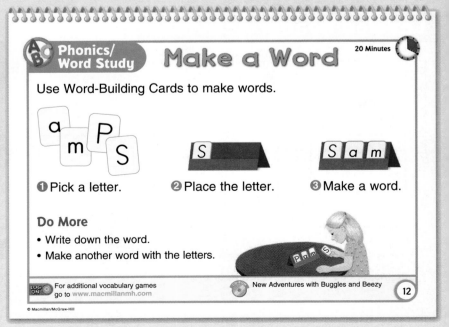

Phonics/ Word Study — **Make a Word** — 20 Minutes

Use Word-Building Cards to make words.

a P m S — S — S a m

❶ Pick a letter. ❷ Place the letter. ❸ Make a word.

Do More
- Write down the word.
- Make another word with the letters.

For additional vocabulary games go to www.macmillanmh.com — New Adventures with Buggles and Beezy 12

© Macmillan/McGraw-Hill

Literacy Workstations

 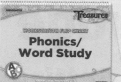  

Reading

Phonics/ Word Study

Writing

Science/ Social Studies

Literacy Workstation Flip Charts

Writing

Objectives

- Write and illustrate sentences: *We like* _____.
- Write dialogue for two friends

Content Literacy

Objectives

- Mix different colors of clay to make new colors
- Use pictures to talk about happy and sad feelings

Writing — We Like It! 20 Minutes

Write about what you and a friend like.

We like _____.   We like __toys__.   We like __toys__.

❶ Write the sentence. ❷ Finish the sentence. ❸ Draw a picture.

Do More
- Read your partner's sentence.

11

© Macmillan/McGraw-Hill

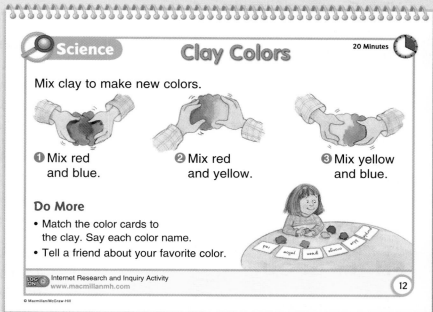

Science — Clay Colors 20 Minutes

Mix clay to make new colors.

❶ Mix red and blue. ❷ Mix red and yellow. ❸ Mix yellow and blue.

Do More
- Match the color cards to the clay. Say each color name.
- Tell a friend about your favorite color.

LOG ON — Internet Research and Inquiry Activity
www.macmillanmh.com

12

© Macmillan/McGraw-Hill

Writing — What Friends Say 20 Minutes

Write what two friends friends might say to each other.

I like you. I like you too.   I like you. I like you too.

❶ Draw two friends. ❷ What might they say? ❸ Write it down.

Do More
- Write more of what the two friends might say. Use complete sentences.
- Share with a partner.

12

© Macmillan/McGraw-Hill

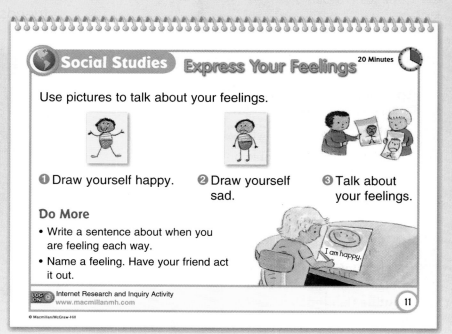

Social Studies — Express Your Feelings 20 Minutes

Use pictures to talk about your feelings.

❶ Draw yourself happy. ❷ Draw yourself sad. ❸ Talk about your feelings.

Do More
- Write a sentence about when you are feeling each way.
- Name a feeling. Have your friend act it out.

LOG ON — Internet Research and Inquiry Activity
www.macmillanmh.com

11

© Macmillan/McGraw-Hill

WHOLE GROUP

Oral Language
- Build Background

✓ **Comprehension**
- Read *Simon and Molly plus Hester*
- Strategy: Ask Questions
- Skill: Identify Character

✓ **High-Frequency Words**
- Introduce *a, like*

✓ **Phonemic Awareness**
- Phoneme Isolation

✓ **Phonics**
- Review /s/s, /p/p
- Handwriting: Review *Ss, Pp*

Grammar
- Naming Words (Nouns)

Writing
- Shared Writing: Lists

SMALL GROUP

- Differentiated Instruction, pages 478–503

Oral Vocabulary

Week 3

grateful include problem
solve thoughtful

Review

assist games honest
pleasant world

Use the **Define/Example/Ask** routine in the **Instructional Routine Handbook** to review the words.

Oral Language

 Talk About It ## Build Background: *Getting Along*

INTRODUCE THE THEME

Tell children that this week they will read about friends who solve **problems**, or difficulties, together. Not having enough game pieces for all of the children who want to play a game is a problem friends might have.

Write the following question on the board: *Do you always like what a friend does?* Track the print as you read it aloud. *Watch as I point to each word. Point to the space between each word in the sentence. I will start with the word* Do. *Say each word after me as we point to and read it again.* Hold up a finger for each word that you say.

ACCESS PRIOR KNOWLEDGE

- Ask children to describe what can happen to cause a problem between friends. *A problem is something that causes trouble and has to be fixed. Have you had a problem with your friends? How did you* **solve** *or fix the problem?*

Think Aloud Let's look at the children in this photograph. All of them are holding onto or reaching for the same toy. (**Point to the children and toy.**) There are three children who want to play with one toy.

DISCUSS THE PHOTOGRAPH

The children want to play with the same toy. What could the friends do to solve their problem? How might they play together? Have children dictate a story in sequence about a problem they had with their friends. Discuss how they solved the problem.

Teaching Chart 18

Share the Trade Book

Listening Comprehension

PREVIEW Display the cover. *I see three children playing outside. Two of them are making the same movement. Maybe they are dancing.* Point to the children as you talk. *Now let's read about some friends.*

Read the title and the name of the author/illustrator as you track the print.

GENRE Tell children that this book is **fiction**, a story that did not really happen.

Trade Book

 STRATEGY Ask Questions

EXPLAIN/MODEL Tell children that asking themselves questions about the characters in a story can help them to understand it.

Think Aloud The title is *Simon and Molly plus Hester.* I ask myself: Who are the children on the cover? The boy and the girl are playing together. Are they Simon and Molly? Who is the other girl? I think that she is Hester. When I read, I will find out.

 SKILL Identify Character

EXPLAIN/MODEL Tell children that knowing what the characters, or people and animals, do and say helps us understand the story better.

Think Aloud Hester looks like she is joining Simon and Molly. I wonder how Simon and Molly will **solve** the **problem** when Hester wants to play with them.

Read the Trade Book

SET PURPOSE Tell children to ask themselves questions about the three characters and what they do. Use the **Define/Example/Ask** routine to teach the story words on the inside back cover.

Respond to Literature

MAKE CONNECTIONS *Has a situation like this ever happened to you? How did you resolve it?* Have children draw themselves doing something with Simon, Molly and Hester.

Objectives

- Discuss the theme
- Demonstrate awareness of word boundaries
- Use oral vocabulary words *solve* and *problem*
- Listen to and respond to a story
- Ask questions/identify characters
- Make connections to the larger community

Materials

- Teaching Chart 18
- Read-Aloud Trade Book: *Simon and Molly plus Hester*

ELL

Use the **Interactive Question-Response Guide** for *Simon and Molly plus Hester*, **ELL Resource Book** pages 50–57, to guide children through a reading of the book. As you read this book, make meaning clear by pointing to pictures, demonstrating word meanings, paraphrasing text, and asking questions.

Digital Learning

Story on **Listening Library Audio CD**

Objectives

- Identify the words *a* and *like* in text and speech
- Review the high-frequency words *can, I, the, we*
- Identify and use words that name actions

Materials

- High-Frequency Word Cards: *a, can, I, like, the, we*
- Teaching Chart 19

ELL

Reinforce Meaning Display the **High-Frequency Word Cards** *a, can, I, like, the, we*. Use the words in simple sentences such as, *I like to sing*. As you say each sentence, point to the words and use gestures to convey meaning. Have children repeat the sentences.

High-Frequency Words

 a, like

| a | like |

REVIEW Display the **High-Frequency Word Card** for **like**.
Use the **Read/Spell/Write** routine to teach the word.

- **Read** Point to and say the word *like*. *I like ice cream.*

- **Spell** *The word* like *is spelled* l-i-k-e. *What's the first sound in* like? *That's right. The first sound in* like *is /l/. That's why the first letter is* l. *After the* l, *I see an* i, k, *and* e. *Let's read and spell* like *together.*

- **Write** *Now let's write the word* like *on our papers. Let's spell aloud the word as we write it:* like, l-i-k-e. Repeat the routine with **a**.

REVIEW *I, the, we, can* Display each card and have children read the words. Repeat several times.

READ THE RHYME AND CHIME
Ask children to point to *like* and *a*. Repeat the rhyme together for fluency. Add *like* and *a* to the class Word Wall.

| I | the |
| we | can |

We Like Some Fun

We like a picnic.
We like a party.
We like silly songs.
We all get along!

High-Frequency Words: like, a
Phonics: /s/s, /p/p

Unit 2
Rhyme and Chime

Friends Week 3 19

Teaching Chart 19

For Tier 2 instruction, see page 478.

 **TIME TO MOVE!**

Have children stand in a circle while you stand in the middle. Chant and clap the words *We like to…* Then call out a word to finish the sentence, such as *wiggle*. Children can wiggle as they say the word. Repeat with other action words.

Phonemic Awareness

Phoneme Isolation

Model

Display the **Photo Card** for *sun*.

Listen for the sound at the beginning of *sun*: /sss/, *sun*. *Sun* has /s/ at the beginning. Say the sound with me: /sss/. What is the sound? (/s/) We'll make a sizzling sun with our arms when we hear /s/ at the beginning of a word.

Repeat the routine, using the Photo Card for *piano*.

Read "We Like Some Fun." Have children form circles with their arms every time they hear /s/.

We like a picnic.

We like a party.

We like silly songs.

We all get along!

Repeat for initial /p/.

We'll say the Rhyme and Chime again and point up when we hear words that begin with /p/.

Display and name the Photo Cards one at a time.

Listen to this riddle about a Photo Card. You eat this with a spoon, and it begins with /s/. I use a spoon to eat *soup*, and *soup* begins with /s/.

Guided Practice/Practice

Children solve riddles.

Guide practice with the first riddle.

Create more riddles for the rest of the Photo Cards.

You write with this, and it begins with /p/. (pen)

This animal lives in the ocean, and its name begins with /s/. (seal)

Quick Check

Can children identify initial /s/ and /p/ in words?

During **Small Group Instruction**

If No → **Approaching Level** Provide additional practice, page 479.

If Yes → **On Level** Review /s/ and /p/, page 480.

Beyond Level Review /s/ and /p/, page 481.

Objective

- **Isolate the beginning /s/ and /p/ sounds in words**

Materials

- **Photo Cards:** *pea, penny, piano, pie, pig, pizza, saw, seal, six, soap, soup, sun*

ELL

Pronunciation Display and have children name **Photo Cards** from this and prior lessons to reinforce phonemic awareness and word meanings. Point to a card and ask: *What do you see?* (the sun) *What is the sound at the beginning of the word* sun? (/s/). Repeat with the Photo Card for *piano* and others with initial sounds /s/ and /p/.

Objectives

- Review sound-spellings for /s/s, /p/p
- Handwriting: form *Ss* and *Pp* legibly

Materials

- Sound-Spelling Cards: *Piano, Sun*
- Teaching Chart 19
- Word-Building Cards
- Handwriting
- Handwriting Teacher's Edition
- Activity Book, p. 24
- Practice Book, p. 53

Phonics

✓ Review /s/s, /p/p

Model

Display the *Sun* **Sound-Spelling Card**.

Repeat for the letter *p*, using the *Piano* Sound-Spelling Card.

This is the *Sun* card. The sound is /s/. The /s/ sound is spelled with the letter *s*. Say it with me: /s/. This is the sound at the beginning of the word *sun*. Listen: /sss/ . . . *un*, *sun*.

What is the name of this letter? What sound does this letter stand for?

Reread the "We Like Some Fun" Rhyme and Chime. Reread the title. Point out that the word *Some* begins with the letter *S*. Model placing a self-stick note below the letter *S* in *Some*.

We Like Some Fun

We like a picnic.
We like a party.
We like silly songs.
We all get along!

Unit 2
Rhyme and Chime

High-Frequency Words: like, a
Phonics: /s/s, /o/p

Friends · Week 3 · 19

Teaching Chart 19

For Tier 2 instruction, see page 479.

Guided Practice/Practice

Read the rest of the rhyme. Children place a self-stick note below words that begin with *s* or *p*. Guide practice with *silly* in line 3.

Let's place a sticky note below any word in the line that begins with *s*. The word *silly* begins with *s*.

Which word begins with the letter *p*? The word *picnic* begins with the letter *p*.

Corrective Feedback

If children have difficulty with /s/s, write the word *sun* on the board. Circle the *s*. *The letter* s *stands for the sound at the beginning of* sun. *Say the sound as I point to the letter.* Repeat with *some* and *piano*.

Build Fluency: Sound-Spellings

 SPIRAL REVIEW Display the following **Word-Building Cards**: *a, m, p, s*. Have children chorally say each sound. Repeat and vary the pace.

Handwriting: Review *Ss, Pp*

MODEL Model holding up your writing hand. Say the handwriting cues from the **Handwriting Teacher's Edition** as you write the capital and lowercase forms of *Ss, Pp* on the board. Then trace the letters on the board and in the air.

 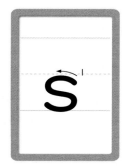 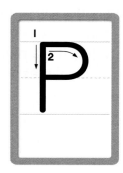 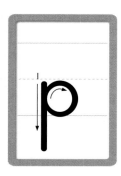

PRACTICE Ask children to hold up their writing hand.

- Say the cues together as children trace with their index finger the letters you wrote on the board.

- Have children write *S* and *s* in the air as they say /sss/. Repeat with *Pp*.

- Distribute handwriting practice pages. Observe children's pencil grip and paper position, and correct as necessary. Have children say /sss/ every time they write the letter *s* and say /p/ multiple times every time they write the letter *p*.

For Tier 2 instruction, see page 479.

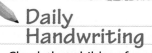
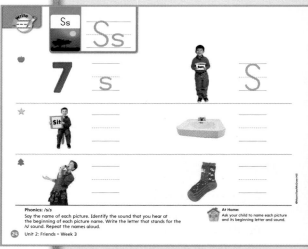
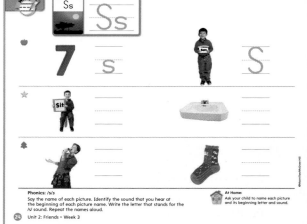

Activity Book, page 24
Practice Book, page 53

Objectives

- Recognize naming words (nouns), singular and plural
- Take turns speaking one at a time

Materials

- Photo Cards: *kangaroo, ladybug, ant, bat, fan*
- Read-Aloud Trade Book: *Simon and Molly plus Hester*

ELL

Basic and Academic Language Display the **Photo Cards** from this and prior lessons and pair English Language Learners with fluent English speakers. Have partners make up sentences with the Photo Card words and other nouns. Write their sentences, read them together, and say: *Tell me the naming word(s), or noun(s), in your sentence.*

Grammar

Naming Words (Nouns)

MODEL Remind children that they have been learning about words that name people, places, animals, and things. Read page 4 of the **Trade Book** *Simon and Molly plus Hester* and ask children to say the naming words in the sentences. *(two-wheeler, toast, butter)* Ask whether the naming words name people, things, animals, or places. Confirm that they name things.

Read page 5 and point out the word *friends*. Explain that this is a noun that names people. Also point out that it names more than one thing. It is a plural noun. Read page 8 and ask children to say the noun that names more than one. (airplanes)

- Show children the illustration on page 11 of the book. Ask them to tell you a word that names something in the picture, such as *boy, girl, plate, table, toast,* or *butter.*

PRACTICE

Show children a variety of **Photo Cards**.

- Have children identify who or what is in each picture. Model saying sentences about some of the photographs, such as:

> A kangaroo *likes to hop.*
>
> A ladybug *has spots.*

- Have children take turns selecting Photo Cards and making up sentences that use naming words. Ask children to use naming words that name one thing, person, place, or animal as well as naming words that name more than one. After each sentence, have children tell you the naming word(s). Then ask them to write the words.

Writing
Shared Writing: Lists

BRAINSTORM

Remind children that in *Simon and Molly plus Hester*, they learned that the friends had a **problem**. *Simon and Molly like to do the same things, but Hester likes to do different things. What are some things that Simon and Molly like to do? What does Hester like to do?*

WRITE

- Create two lists as shown below. Read the titles aloud as you track the print. Have children repeat.

- Read pages 6–7. *Molly and Simon like to ride her two-wheeler, so I will write* two-wheeler *on the list for Molly and Simon.*

- Continue by reading pages 8–9 and 10–11. Have children tell you what to write on each list.

Simon and Molly Like	Hester Likes
two-wheeler	paper airplanes
toast with butter	toast with butter + cinnamon sugar

- Read the completed lists aloud and have children repeat after you. Point out the high-frequency word *like*.

- Point out how the words are written one under the other. *A list helps us remember information and ideas.*

- Save the lists to refer to in other writing activities this week.

Write About It

Ask children to draw and label a picture of something the characters in the book like to do together.

Objectives

- Dictate information for lists to compare things that characters like
- Describe characters

Materials

- Read-Aloud Trade Book: *Simon and Molly plus Hester*

5-Day Writing

	Sentences
DAY 1	Shared: Lists
DAY 2	Interactive: Sentences
DAY 3	Independent: Prewrite and Draft a Sentence
DAY 4	Independent: Revise and Edit a Sentence
DAY 5	Independent: Publish and Present

ELL

Prewriting Planning
Provide the **Trade Book** for children to use. Show the cover and read the title. Ask children to describe the children on the cover. *What are the children doing?* (dancing/walking) *What is Hester holding?* (a flower)

Transitions That Teach

While preparing to leave the classroom, have children tell how they **solved** a problem.

Oral Language
- Build Robust Vocabulary

✔ **Comprehension**
- Reread *Simon and Molly plus Hester*
- Strategy: Ask Questions
- Skill: Identify Character
- Fluency: Echo-Read

Vocabulary
- Color Words
- Story Word: *two-wheeler*

✔ **Phonemic Awareness**
- Phoneme Categorization

✔ **Phonics**
- Review /a/*a*, /p/*p*, /s/*s*, /m/*m*
- Blend with /a/*a*, /p/*p*, /s/*s*, /m/*m*
- Pre-decodable Reader: *I Like, We Like*

Writing
- Interactive Writing: Sentences

SMALL GROUP

- Differentiated Instruction, pages 478–503

Oral Vocabulary

Week 3

grateful   include   problem
solve   thoughtful

Review

assist   games   honest
pleasant   world

Use the **Define/Example/Ask** routine in the **Instructional Routine Handbook** to review the words.

Oral Language

 Talk About It ## Build Robust Vocabulary

INTRODUCE WORDS

Tell children that today you are going to talk about the **Trade Book** *Simon and Molly plus Hester*. There are three characters in the story: *Simon, Molly, and Hester. Simon has a problem when Hester moves in. A problem is a difficult situation that needs to be fixed. Simon didn't want to share his friend with Hester. That was a problem. The friends find a way to solve the problem. What kind of problems have you solved with classmates?* Read pages 3–13 aloud. Have children ask and answer each other's questions about this topic.

Vocabulary Routine

Use the routine below to discuss the meaning of each word.

Define: A **problem** is a difficult situation that needs to be fixed. Say the word with me.
Example: Litter on the playground is a problem.
Ask: Have you ever had a problem with a friend? What was it?

Define: **Solve** means "to fix a problem or to find an answer to something." Say the word with me.
Example: Mom solved the problem of the missing shoe when she found it in our puppy's bed.
Ask: If three friends want to play different things, what is one way to solve the problem?

CREATE A CHART

Create a three-column chart. Label the columns as shown. Read aloud the words, tracking the print. Discuss what happens with the characters Simon, Molly, and Hester in the beginning, middle, and end of the story. Guide children to use complete sentences by recasting their responses. Add children's ideas to the chart.

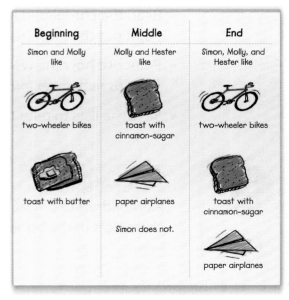

Beginning	Middle	End
Simon and Molly like	Molly and Hester like	Simon, Molly, and Hester like
two-wheeler bikes	toast with cinnamon-sugar	two-wheeler bikes
toast with butter	paper airplanes	toast with cinnamon-sugar
	Simon does not.	paper airplanes

Listen for Syllables

IDENTIFY SYLLABLES

Tell children that a syllable is a part of a word. Many words have one part or one syllable as in the word *play*. Others, such as *sunny,* have two parts or two syllables. Play the rhyme "Out to Play," using the **Listening Library Audio CD**. Then teach children the words and recite the rhyme together. Have children clap for each syllable they hear as they recite it aloud.

RHYME ABOUT FRIENDS

After reciting the rhyme chorally several times, ask: *Which words in "Out to Play" rhyme?* (play/day, along/song) *Do the words* ram *and* bat *rhyme?* (No. They don't end with the same sound.) *What do the friends in the rhyme like to do while they play?* (sing) *What clues in the rhyme tell us these friends get along?* (They play and sing together.)

Out to Play

Dad and Sam went out to play

On a hot and sunny day.

Pam and Matt both came along.

They played and sang this happy song.

Lamb and ram went out to play

On a hot and sunny day.

Cat and bat both came along.

They played and sang this happy song.

ELL
ENGLISH LANGUAGE LEARNERS

Beginning	**Intermediate**	**Advanced**
Confirm Understanding Review oral vocabulary from previous lessons using the **Trade Book** *Simon and Molly plus Hester.* For example, turn to page 4 and ask: *Show me Molly. Is Simon on a bike?*	**Enhance Understanding** Display the same page and ask: *Tell me things that Molly and Simon do together.* Display a later page and ask: *What different things does Hester like?* Guide children to answer in complete sentences.	**Discuss Characters** Ask partners to discuss how Simon changed from the beginning of the story to the end. Have children dictate sentences about how Simon changed.

Objectives

- Use oral vocabulary words *problem* and *solve*
- Discuss beginning, middle, and end
- Complete a chart
- Identify syllables in spoken words
- Distinguish orally presented rhyming word pairs from non-rhyming word pairs

Materials

- **Read-Aloud Trade Book:** *Simon and Molly plus Hester*
- **Listening Library Audio CD**

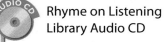

Rhyme on Listening Library Audio CD

Objectives

- Ask questions
- Identify character
- Respond to a story
- Retell a story
- Develop fluency

Materials

- Read-Aloud Trade Book: *Simon and Molly plus Hester*
- Activity Book, p. 25
- Practice Book, p. 54
- Retelling Cards

Simon and Molly plus Hester

Lisa Jahn-Clough

Trade Book

Digital Learning

Story on **Listening Library Audio CD**

ELL

Gesture and Talk Use gestures and other strategies to help make the text comprehensible.

p. 3

together: Ask two children to stand next to each other. Point to the pair and say: *You are together.* Have them stand apart from each other and say: *You are not together.* Have children repeat.

Reread the Trade Book

Listening Comprehension

CONCEPTS ABOUT PRINT Display the cover and read the title aloud with children as you track the print. Have children tell what they remember about the story.

 STRATEGY Ask Questions

Explain to children that they have been learning how to ask questions about the stories they listen to and read. *Name a question that you had about* Simon and Molly plus Hester *that has been answered. Share questions that have not been answered.*

 SKILL Identify Character

Tell children that yesterday they talked about the characters, people or animals in the story, and what they do. *Today you will hear the story again and think about how the characters feel.* Display pages 3–5.

Think Aloud I think Molly and Simon look like they are good friends. They do lots of things together. They look happy when they are together. They help **solve** each other's **problems**.

Read the **Trade Book** and use the prompts.

page 3

 PHONICS

- *I'll read the first sentence again. Which word begins with the sound that the letter s stands for?* (*Simon*)

Simon and Molly play together every day. Just the two of them.

pages 4–5

 IDENTIFY CHARACTER

Think Aloud I see that Molly and Simon share and do things for each other. Molly shares her bike with Simon, and Simon makes Molly toast. They are nice to each other.

Molly lets Simon ride her two-wheeler.

Simon makes Molly toast with butter.

They are the best of friends. Just the two of them.

Develop Comprehension

pages 6–7

SPIRAL REVIEW

MAKE PREDICTIONS

Think Aloud The last page said Molly and Simon are good friends. This page says "Until Hester moved in." The word *until* makes me predict they will not be good friends.

pages 8–9

ASK QUESTIONS

Think Aloud Molly and Hester want to do the same thing. Simon does not. I wonder how that makes Simon feel? Do you have any questions about the story?

pages 10–11

IDENTIFY CHARACTER

- *Who likes cinnamon-sugar toast?* (Molly and Hester) *Who likes plain toast?* (Simon)

pages 12–13

ASK QUESTIONS

- *Why doesn't Simon want to talk to Hester?* (He is mad at her for taking Molly away from him.)

CONCEPTS ABOUT PRINT

- *Point to the first sentence on this page.*

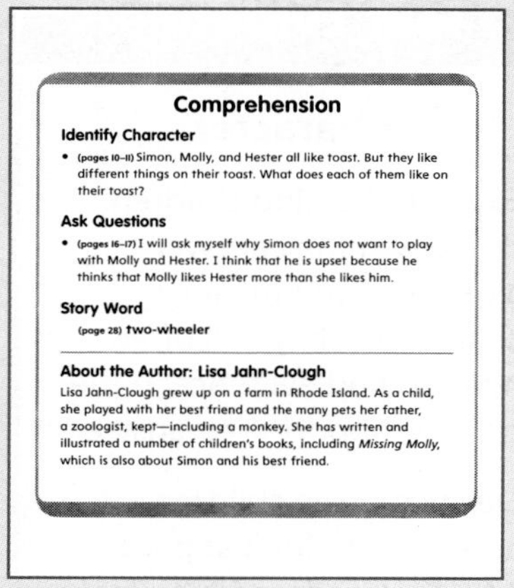

Comprehension

Identify Character

- (pages 10–11) Simon, Molly, and Hester all like toast. But they like different things on their toast. What does each of them like on their toast?

Ask Questions

- (pages 16–17) I will ask myself why Simon does not want to play with Molly and Hester. I think that he is upset because he thinks that Molly likes Hester more than she likes him.

Story Word

(page 28) two-wheeler

About the Author: Lisa Jahn-Clough

Lisa Jahn-Clough grew up on a farm in Rhode Island. As a child, she played with her best friend and the many pets her father, a zoologist, kept—including a monkey. She has written and illustrated a number of children's books, including *Missing Molly,* which is also about Simon and his best friend.

Trade Book Inside Back Cover

ELL

pp. 8–9

ride a bike, make paper airplanes: Act out riding a bike while saying *ride a bike.* Repeat for making a paper airplane. Have children act out which of the two activities they like better. Help children see that different people like to do different things. Describe each action and have children repeat.

pp. 12–13

fell over, Are you okay?: Act out getting on a bike and falling. Look distressed. Say: *Ouch!* Prompt children to say: *Are you okay?*

Text Evidence

Character

Explain Remind children that when they answer a question about story characters, they will often need to find evidence in the text to support their answer.

Discuss Have children listen to and look at pages 14–15. *How does Simon look and feel?* (He looks and feels very sad and worried.)

ELL

pp. 14–15

better than: Say: *Simon thinks Molly likes Hester more than him. He is worried that Molly likes Hester better than him. Which do you like better: milk or juice?* Prompt children to answer in complete sentences: *I like milk better than juice.*

pp. 16–17

go home: Draw an outline of a house on the board. Point to Simon on page 16, then point to your drawing. Say: *Simon has to go home. What is Simon doing?*

pp. 18–19

fly away: Act out throwing a paper airplane, then flying like a plane. Have children join you as they say *fly away.*

pp. 20–21, 22–23

don't know how: Ask children yes/no questions about what the characters can do: *Can Molly ride a bike? Can Simon ride a bike? Can Molly make paper planes? Can Simon make paper planes?* Contrast what they do and don't know how to do.

Develop Comprehension

pages 14–15

✓ IDENTIFY CHARACTER

- *How do you think Simon feels? Why does he feel that way?* (Possible answer: He feels sad and worried that Molly does not like him anymore.)

pages 16–17

CONCEPTS ABOUT PRINT

- *Point to the first sentence on this page. Point to the last word in that sentence.* (asked)

pages 18–19

✓ IDENTIFY CHARACTER

- *How can you tell that Simon does not like Hester?* (He wishes she would fly away.)

pages 20–21

✓ ASK QUESTIONS

- *What **problem** does Hester have? How might Simon and Molly help her to **solve** it? What other solutions can you think of?*

pages 22–23

VISUALIZE
Think Aloud This page doesn't show Simon, but I remember he is in a tree near where the girls are talking. In my mind, I can see him listening to what the girls say.

pages 24–25

IDENTIFY CHARACTER
- *How does Simon feel?* (He is happy. He just found out that Molly is still his best friend.)

CONCEPTS ABOUT PRINT
- *How many words are in this sentence?* (6)

pages 26–27

pages 28–29

IDENTIFY CHARACTER
- *How do Simon and Hester become friends?* (They become friends by helping each other.)

ELL

pp. 30–31
play together: Have children act out the things the three characters do together and say: *They play together.*

Retelling Rubric

4 Excellent

Retells the selection without prompting, in sequence, and using supporting details. Clearly describes the setting, main characters, and complete plot.

3 Good

Retells the selection with little guidance, in sequence, and using some details. Generally describes the setting, main characters, and plot.

2 Fair

Retells the selection with some guidance, mostly in sequence, and using limited details. Partially describes the setting, main characters, and plot.

1 Unsatisfactory

Retells the selection only when prompted, out of sequence, and using limited details. Does not describe the main characters or plot.

pages 30–31

ILLUSTRATOR'S CRAFT

■ *How does the illustrator let you know that Simon and Hester are friends now?* (The illustrator shows them doing things together and smiling at each other.)

page 32

AUTHOR'S PURPOSE

■ *What did the author want us to learn about making friends?* (Sometimes we can make friends with someone that we didn't like at first.)

Respond to Literature

TALK ABOUT IT Ask children to discuss the story.

■ *What did Hester want to do instead of ride a bike?* (make paper airplanes) LOCATE

■ *What does Simon want to do with Molly and Hester?* (He wants to ride a bike and have toast with butter.) CONNECT

■ *How are Simon and Hester different? How are they alike?* (They like to do different activities; they like to play.) COMBINE

Retell

GUIDED RETELLING

■ Display **Retelling Card 1**. Based on children's needs, use either the Guided, Modeled, or ELL prompts. The Modeled prompts contain support for ELLs based on levels of language acquisition.

Fluency: Echo-Read

MODEL Reread page 12. Use different voices for each character. Then reread pages 14–21 and have children echo-read.

Quick Check

Can children identify character to understand a story?

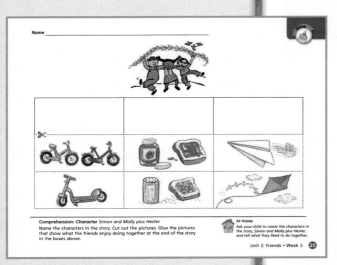

Activity Book, page 25
Practice Book, page 54

Vocabulary

Color Words

REVIEW COLORS

Display in the pocket chart a square of each color. Identify each color and have children say the color names with you.

Have children sort pictures of objects by color.

Give each child a square of colored paper. Say: *I am going to read some riddles. Hold up the matching color for the answer to each riddle.*

What's a rhyme for fellow? (*yellow*)

What's a rhyme for you? (*blue*)

What's a rhyme for slurple? (*purple*)

What's a rhyme for bread? (*red*)

What's a rhyme for bean? (*green*)

Story Word: *two-wheeler*

Reread page 4 of the **Trade Book** *Simon and Molly plus Hester.* Point out the picture of the two-wheeler and the written word. Explain that *two-wheeler* is another word for *bicycle*. The word is made up of two words, *two* and *wheeler*. Say: *A two-wheeler is a vehicle with two wheels.*

TIME TO MOVE!

Use colored chalk to make a "path" of colors outside. First, draw two lines of colored circles, side by side. To play, one child at a time jumps with two feet into the side-by-side circles. Children name the colors as they move along the path.

Objectives

- Identify and sort color words
- Orally generate rhymes in response to spoken words
- Learn the story word *two-wheeler*

Materials

- squares of colored paper: red, orange, yellow, green, blue, purple
- pictures of different colored objects
- pocket chart
- colored chalk
- Read-Aloud Trade Book: *Simon and Molly plus Hester*

Digital Learning

 LOG ON For children who need additional language support and oral vocabulary development, use the activities found at **www.macmillanmh.com**.

ELL

Guessing Game Gather children around a table. Hide a colored square behind your back. Say: *I am going to show one color.* Have a child guess what the color will be. When you hold up the square, have the child who guessed correctly tell the others what color it is. *The color is _____.*

Objectives

- Review initial /s/s, /p/p, /m/m, /a/a
- Recognize words that begin with the same sound
- Blend with /a/a, /m/m, /p/p, /s/s

Materials

- Puppet
- Photo Cards: *ant, ax, man, map, moon, mop, mouse, pen, penguin, pie, pizza, pumpkin, seal, soap, sock*
- Word-Building Cards
- pocket chart

Phonemic Awareness

✔ Phoneme Categorization

Model

Display **Photo Cards** for *pie, ant*, and *pizza*. Use the **Puppet**. Repeat the routine with *ant, ax, soap*.

Happy will say three picture names: *pie, ant, pizza*. Repeat the words with Happy. Which picture names begin with the same sound? *Pie* and *pizza* both begin with the /p/ sound. *Ant* does not begin with the /p/ sound. It does not belong.

Guided Practice/Practice

Children identify the picture name that does not belong.

Guide practice with the first set using the routine.

Use these sets of cards: *mouse, mop, seal; pen, moon, map; ax, ant, soap; pumpkin, man, penguin.*

Say the picture names with Happy. Tell me which picture does not belong.

  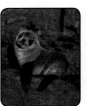

For Tier 2 instruction, see page 485.

Phonics

✔ Review /a/a, /p/p, /s/s, /m/m

Model

Place **Word-Building Card** *s* in the pocket chart. Repeat for *p, m*, and *a*.

This is the letter *s*. The letter *s* stands for /s/. Say /s/.

Hold up the Photo Card for *sock*.

This is a sock. *Sock* begins with /s/. The letter *s* stands for /s/. I will place *sock* under letter *s*.

Hold up the Photo Card for *moon*.

This is the *moon. Moon* begins with /m/. The letter *m* stands for /m/. I will place the *moon* under letter *m*.

Guided Practice/Practice

Children sort the **Photo Cards**.

Guide practice with the first card, using the routine.

Build Fluency: Sound-Spellings

 Display the following **Word-Building Cards**: *a, m, p, s*. Have children
chorally say each sound. Repeat and vary the pace.

Blend with /a/a, /p/p, /m/m, /s/s

Model

Place Word-Building Card *s* in the pocket chart.

This is the letter *s*. The letter *s* stands for the /s/ sound. Say /s/.

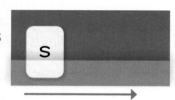

Place Word-Building Card *a* next to *s*. Move your hand from left to right.

This is the letter *a*. The letter *a* stands for the /a/ sound. Listen as I blend the two sounds together: /sssaaa/. Now you blend the sounds with me. (/sssaaa/)

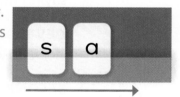

Place Word-Building Card *p* next to *sa*. Move your hand from left to right.

Repeat with *map*.

This is the letter *p*. The letter *p* stands for the /p/ sound. Listen as I blend the three sounds together: /sssaaap/. What is the word? (*sap*)

Guided Practice/Practice

Children blend sounds to form words. Guide practice with the first word, using the routine.

Sam   am   map

Pam   sap

ELL

Reinforce Meaning Review the meanings of the words in the Guided Practice portion of the lesson. For example, point to a map while saying *map*. Point to yourself as you say: *I am [your name]*. Have children complete the sentence frame *I am _____* using their own names.

Objectives

- Read the words *a, I, like, we*
- Predict what might happen next based on the cover and illustrations
- Understand book handling skills
- Reread for fluency

Materials

- Pre-decodable Reader: *I Like, We Like*
- High-Frequency Word Cards: *a, I, like, we*
- pocket chart

Pre-decodable Reader

Read *I Like, We Like*

 REVIEW HIGH-FREQUENCY WORDS Display **High-Frequency Word Cards** for **a**, **I**, **like**, and **we** in the pocket chart. Review the words using the **Read/Spell/Write** routine.

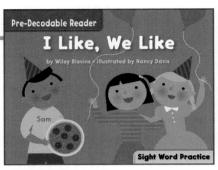

I Like, We Like

MODEL CONCEPTS ABOUT PRINT Demonstrate book handling. Guide children to hold their books right side up and follow along in their books. *Read each word from left to right. Turn to the next page when you reach the last word on the page.*

PREDICT Ask children to describe the cover illustration. Encourage them to ask: *What is the boy holding? What are the girls holding? What kinds of hats do they wear? What might this story be about?*

FIRST READ Point out the rebus and discuss what it stands for. Have children point to each word, sounding out the decodable words and saying the sight words quickly. Children should first chorally read.

DEVELOP COMPREHENSION Ask the following: *Look at page 7. What do you think will happen next?*

 SECOND READ Have partners reread the book together. Circulate, listen in, and provide corrective feedback.

I like a 🍕 pizza .

2

I like a 🎩 hat .

3

I like a 🎮 game .

4

I like a 💬 balloon .

5

I like a 🎁 present .

6

I like a 🤡 clown .

7

We like a 💕 party !

8

Pre-decodable Reader

Writing

Interactive Writing: Sentences

REVIEW

Display and read aloud the lists that children created for the Shared Writing activity.

WRITE

Tell children that today you are going to write sentences about what the children like to do.

- Collaborate with children to write the following sentence frames on the chart:

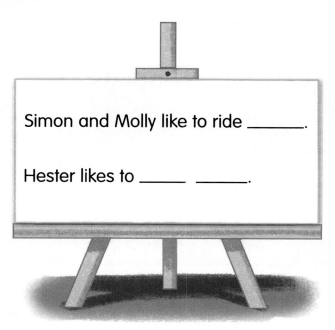

Simon and Molly like to ride _____.

Hester likes to _____ _____.

- Have children suggest a word for the first sentence and two words for the second sentence. (*two-wheelers; make airplanes*) Write the words in the blanks to complete the sentences. Ask children to help by writing the letters they know.

- Read the completed sentences aloud as you track the print. Say that the sentences contain information from the lists children wrote yesterday.

- To extend the lesson, work together to write sentences about a **problem** that Simon, Molly, and Hester might **solve** together.

Write About It

Ask children to draw a picture of themselves and a friend. Help them label it using the high-frequency word *a*.

Objectives

- Continue to plan a first draft by generating ideas for writing
- Use letter knowledge to write letters in a word

Materials

- Shared Writing lists from Day 1

5-Day Writing

Sentences	
DAY 1	Shared: Lists
DAY 2	Interactive: Sentences
DAY 3	Independent: Prewrite and Draft a Sentence
DAY 4	Independent: Revise and Edit a Sentence
DAY 5	Independent: Publish and Present

ELL

Use Personal Experience
Ask children what things are fun to do with one friend and what things are fun to do with two or more friends. Write the number word on a chart and track the print. Tell children to draw a picture showing how they play with one or more friends.

Transitions That Teach

While children line up, have them tell about **problems** they might have getting along with friends.

DAY 3
At a Glance

WHOLE GROUP

Oral Language
- Build Robust Vocabulary
- Oral Vocabulary Cards: "The Turtle and the Sheep"

✓ **Comprehension**
- Read "Helping Hands"
- Text Features: Photographs

✓ **High-Frequency Words**
- Review *a* , *like*

✓ **Phonemic Awareness**
- Phoneme Blending

✓ **Phonics**
- Blend with /s/*s*, /p/*p*, /m/*m*, /a/*a*

Grammar
- Naming Words (Nouns)

Writing
- Independent Writing: Prewrite and Draft a Sentence

SMALL GROUP

- Differentiated Instruction, pages 478–503

Additional Vocabulary

To provide 15–20 minutes of additional vocabulary instruction, see Oral Vocabulary Cards 5-Day Plan. The pre- and posttests for this week can be found in the **Teacher's Resource Book**, pages 216–217.

Oral Language

(Talk About It) ## Build Robust Vocabulary

BUILD BACKGROUND

Introduce the story "The Turtle and the Sheep" using **Oral Vocabulary Card 1** and read the title aloud. *Do you have a friend who has helped you solve a problem? How did you thank your friend or let your friend know you were grateful?* Ask children to tell what they think is going to happen based on the picture.

- Read the story on the back of the cards. Pause at each oral vocabulary word and read the definition. You may wish to check children's understanding using the Identify Story Elements, Use Illustrations, and Discuss prompts.

Oral Vocabulary Cards

Vocabulary Routine

Use the routine below to discuss the meaning of each word.

Define: When somebody helps you, you feel **grateful** . Let's say the word.
Example: Maria was grateful when her sister helped her clean her room.
Ask: What have you been grateful for? How did you show you were grateful?

Define: When you **include** someone in your group, you make the person a part of the group. Say the word with me.
Example: The school play will include students from every classroom.
Ask: How might you include a new student in your group of friends?

Define: A **thoughtful** person thinks about the feelings of other people. Say the word with me.
Example: Dan tries to make me smile when I'm sad. He is a thoughtful friend.
Ask: What is something thoughtful that you have done for a friend?

- Use the routine on Cards 1 and 3 to review the words **problem** and **solve** .

- Review last week's words: *assist, game, honest, pleasant,* and *world.*

Listen for Rhyme

IDENTIFY RHYME

Remind children that rhyming words have the same ending sounds. *Game* and same *rhyme because they both end in /ām/.* Say the following words, guiding children to distinguish between rhyming and non-rhyming words by clapping if the word rhymes with *clap: cap, map, pan, dad, lap.*

Discuss the song. *What is this song about?* (playing a game) *How does the author of the song encourage children to get along?* (The song invites everyone to play. It tells listeners that the game will be easy to play, so they are more likely to join in.)

Join in the Game

Everyone clap like me. Clap, Clap.

It's as easy as can be. Clap, Clap.

Everyone join in the game.

You will find it's always the same.

Everyone tap like me. Tap, Tap.

It's as easy as can be. Tap, Tap.

Everyone join in the game.

You will find it's always the same.

Objectives

- Listen and respond to a folktale
- Use oral vocabulary words *grateful, include, problem, solve,* and *thoughtful*
- Discuss the theme
- Recognize rhyme

Materials

- Oral Vocabulary Cards: "The Turtle and the Sheep"

Digital Learning

Song on **Listening Library Audio CD**

Objectives

- Retell and respond to a nonfiction article
- Use photographs to get information
- Identify ways that people can help in their community
- Recognize and use a map of a community

Materials

- Big Book of Explorations, Vol. 1: "Helping Hands," pp. 29-32
- magazines, catalogs, and newspapers

Content Vocabulary

community a group of people living and working in the same area

office place where people work

firehouse place where firefighters work and keep their equipment

Use a Picture Dictionary
Guide children to look up the content words in a picture dictionary.

Informational Text

Genre

Big Book of Explorations

INFORMATIONAL TEXT: EXPOSITORY Tell children that this nonfiction article is **expository** text. Tell them that in this article they will learn ways that people can be good citizens in their neighborhood. Access children's prior knowledge about neighborhoods by asking them to name some special buildings and places that are near their homes.

READ "HELPING HANDS"

- **Preview and Predict** Display the first page and read the title as you track the print. Point to the children on page 29. *What are the friends doing? What do you think we will learn from this text?*

- **Content Vocabulary** Introduce and discuss the vocabulary words.

- **Text Feature: Photographs** *Photographs tell the reader that the book is about real people, places, or things.* Point to the children. *I look at the photograph to see what information I can learn. I can see friends doing things together to help others.*

CONTENT FOCUS

As you read page 29, introduce a community as a group of people who live, work, and play in the same neighborhood. Discuss how the children are helping the poor of their community. Explain that helping in a community is one way of being a good citizen.

Point to the pictures on pages 30 and 31 and ask the children what they show. Ask them to identify ways that people are helping the community in which they live.

As you read page 32 aloud, point to the picture. Say that the picture shows a map of some possible places and buildings that could be found in a community. Explain that maps tell us where things are located, like an office or a firehouse. As you point to each location, have children identify it as a library, park, and so on.

Use the content vocabulary words as you discuss the selection.

page 29   **pages 30–31**   **page 32**

Retell and Respond

- *What are some important parts of a community? Why are they important?* (Schools, hospitals, stores, and so on; they provide people with the things they need to live, work, and play in the community.)

- *What are some ways that people can help in their community?* (People can keep the places where they live and work clean, follow laws, and help others.)

Connect to Content

Social Studies: Community Collage

- You will need old magazines, catalogs, and newspapers. Discuss how the children's community includes the people and places in the neighborhood where they live.

- Discuss characteristics of the community in which children live. Is it a city with lots of buildings and cars? Or are there farms with lots of cows and sheep? Does it have a hospital and a police station? What kinds of stores does it have?

- Have groups cut out pictures and create collages that tell about the community in which they live.

ELL

Beginning

Gesture and Talk Tell children to look at the photos on pages 29–31. Have them gesture and talk about one of the ways in which people can help the community. Then ask them to tell which action they gestured.

Intermediate

Discuss Complete the beginning activity. Then have children discuss how the action helps the community.

Advanced

Create Captions Complete the Intermediate activity. Then have children orally compose a one-sentence caption for the action they gestured.

Objectives

- Review the high-frequency words *a, like*
- Follow oral directions

Materials

- High-Frequency Word Cards: *a, can, I, like, the, we*
- pocket chart
- Photo Cards: *bike, book, pizza, sandwich*
- Activity Book, pp. 27–28
- Practice Book, pp. 55–56

Activity Book, pages 27–28
Practice Book, pages 55–56

High-Frequency Words

 *a, like*

REVIEW Display the **High-Frequency Word Cards** for **a** and **like**. Review the words using the **Read/Spell/Write** routine.

Repeat the routine for the words **can, I, the, we**.

APPLY Build sentences using High-Frequency Word Cards and **Photo Cards**. Read each sentence aloud, then have children chorally read it as you track the print with your finger. Use the sentence below and the following: *We like pizza. I like a sandwich. We like a bike.*

| I | like | a | 📖 | . |

READ FOR FLUENCY Chorally read the Take-Home Book with children. Then have children reread the book to review high-frequency words and build fluency.

Quick Check

Can children read the words *like* and *a*?

During **Small Group Instruction**

If No → **Approaching Level** Provide additional practice with high-frequency words, page 488.

If Yes → **On Level** Children are ready to read the Take-Home Book.

Beyond Level Children are ready to read the Take-Home Book.

TIME TO MOVE!

Use *like* and *a* to give children instructions to move like different animals. For example: *Bounce like a bunny. Move like a monkey. Slither like a snake.* Have children repeat the phrase as they move.

Phonemic Awareness

Phoneme Blending

Model

Use the **Puppet** to model how to blend sounds to form *sun*.

Happy is going to say the sounds in a word. Listen to Happy: /s/ /u/ /n/. Happy can blend the sounds together: /sssuuunnn/. Say the sounds with Happy: /s/ /u/ /n/. Now blend the sounds to say the word with Happy: *sun*.

Repeat with *mix*.

Guided Practice/Practice

Children blend sounds to form words.

Guide practice with the first word, using the same routine.

Happy is going to say the sounds in a word. Listen to Happy as he says each sound. Then blend the sounds to say the word.

/p/ /i/ /g/   /m/ /o/ /p/   /a/ /m/

/m/ /a/ /p/   /s/ /ō/ /k/   /a/ /n/ /t/

For Tier 2 instruction, see page 488.

Objective

- Blend spoken phonemes to form one-syllable words

Materials

- Puppet

- Review sound-spellings for /s/s, /p/p, /m/m, /a/a
- Identify the common sounds that *s* and *p* represent
- Blend spoken phonemes to form and decode one-syllable words

Materials

- Word-Building Cards
- pocket chart

ELL

Extra Practice Distribute **Word-Building Cards** to reinforce sound-letter relationships. Name classroom and personal objects with /s/s or /p/p. Each time, ask children to show you the letter corresponding to the sounds they hear in the words you say.

Phonics

✔ Review

Model

Display **Word-Building Card** *s*. Say a word. Write the letter *s*.

Repeat for *p, m,* and *a.*

This is the letter *s*. The letter *s* stands for the /s/ sound you hear at the beginning of *sun.* The word *sun* has the /s/ sound at the beginning. The letter *s* stands for the /s/ sound. I will write *s*.

Guided Practice/Practice

Children write the letter that stands for the initial sound. Guide practice with *sock.*

I am going to say some words. Write the letter that stands for the sound at the beginning of the word.

sock   pal   mitt   ant   man   soar

Build Fluency: Sound-Spellings

SPIRAL REVIEW

Display the following Word-Building Cards: *a, m, p, s.* Have children chorally say each sound. Repeat and vary the pace.

✔ Blend with /s/s, /p/p, /m/m, /a/a

Model

Place Word-Building Card *S* in the pocket chart.

This letter is capital *S*. It stands for /s/. Say /sss/.

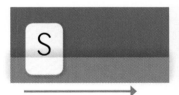

Place Word-Building Card *a* next to *S*. Move your hand from left to right.

This letter is *a*. It stands for /a/. Listen as I blend the two sounds: /sssaaa/. Now you say it. (/sssaaa/)

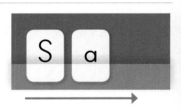

Place Word-Building Card *m* next to *Sa*. Move your hand from left to right.

Repeat with *am.*

This letter is *m*. It stands for /m/. Listen as I blend the three sounds together: /sssaaammm/, *Sam.* Now you say it. (/sssaaammm/, *Sam*)

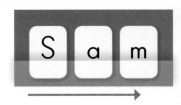

Guided Practice/Practice

Children blend sounds to form words. Guide practice with the first word.

Pam   map   sap

 ## Read Words

APPLY

Write the words and sentences. Guide practice with the first word, using the **Sound-by-Sound Blending Routine**.

Read the sentences with children.

am

Pam

Sam

Pam can.

Sam can.

I am Pam.

I am Sam.

Corrective Feedback

Blending: Sound Error Model the sound that children missed, then have them repeat the sound. For example, for the word *Pam*, say: *My turn.* Tap under the letter *P* in the word *Pam* and say: *Sound? What's the sound?* Then return to the beginning of the word. Say: *Let's start over.* Blend the word with children again.

For Tier 2 instruction, see page 489.

Objective

- Recognize naming words (nouns)

Materials

- Big Book of Explorations, Vol. 1: "Helping Hands"
- Photo Cards: *alligator, ant, bat, bear, bird, camel, cow, deer, dog, dolphin, fish, fly, fox, giraffe, goat, gorilla, hippo, horse, inchworm, kangaroo, kitten, koala, ladybug, moth, mouse, mule, octopus, ostrich, owl, ox, penguin, pig, quail, rabbit, seal, sheep, tiger, turkey, turtle, walrus, whale, wolf, yak*

ELL

Basic and Academic Language Display animal **Photo Cards**. Pair English Language Learners with fluent speakers and have partners complete the sentence frame with the name of a pictured animal and the place it lives. Read the completed sentences together and ask children which noun names an animal and which one names a place.

Grammar

Naming Words (Nouns)

MODEL Use "Helping Hands" in the **Big Book of Explorations** to review nouns. Remind children that they have been learning about naming words, or words that name people, places, animals, and things. Read the first sentence on page 30: *In a community, people help each other.* Ask children to find the naming words in the sentence and repeat the sentence. (*community, people*) Have children tell whether the words name people, things, animals, or places. (people)

- Show children the map on page 32 of the selection. Ask them to tell you naming words on the map, such as *kite, school, library, firehouse,* and *farm.*

- Point out the photographs on page 30 of the book. Say some sentences and have children tell you what the naming words are: *You can clean up at the beach.* (*beach*) *You can plant seeds to grow a tree.* (*seeds, tree*) Have children tell whether the words name people, things, animals, or places. (things)

PRACTICE Display the sentence frame *A _____ lives in a _____.* Read the sentence frame. Pick an animal **Photo Card** and model using the animal on the card to complete the sentence orally, for example: *A fox lives in a forest.*

- Distribute animal Photo Cards to children. Have children identify the animal in the picture and use the animal name to complete the sentence frame.

Writing

Independent Writing: A Sentence

Read the sentences that children created for the Interactive Writing activity.

BRAINSTORM

Tell children that they will begin to write their own sentence about things they like to do with friends. Have children think of examples, such as: *play games, eat lunch.* List ideas and add a small drawing.

PREWRITE

Write the sentence frame *We like to _____ _____.* Read it aloud as you track the print. Point out the high-frequency word *like.*

- Write two words on the blank lines to complete the sentence, such as: We like to *sing songs.* Read aloud as you track the print. Have children chorally repeat. Point out that this is a complete simple sentence.

- Have children choose an activity they like to do to write about.

Tawana
We like to read books.

DRAFT

- Have children write their names on the top of the paper. Then ask them to write the sentence frame *We like to _____ _____.* They can use the sentence you wrote as a model.

- Tell children to draw pictures of things they like to do with friends.

- Guide children to write the words to describe what they drew on the blank lines to complete their sentences. Collect and save children's work to use tomorrow.

Write About It

Ask children to draw a picture of a favorite book or toy. Help them label their drawings.

Objectives

- Write one's own name
- Use complete simple sentences
- Draw pictures
- Use letter knowledge to write letters in a word

Materials

- Interactive Writing sentences from Day 2

5-Day Writing

Sentences	
DAY 1	Shared: Lists
DAY 2	Interactive: Sentences
DAY 3	Independent: Prewrite and Draft a Sentence
DAY 4	Independent: Revise and Edit a Sentence
DAY 5	Independent: Publish and Present

ELL

Use New Language Act out various activities and have children figure out what you are doing. Write the activity on the board and read it. Have children take turns acting out the activities and naming them as they perform.

Transitions That Teach

While getting ready for dismissal, have children list things for which they are **grateful**.

WHOLE GROUP

Oral Language
- Build Robust Vocabulary

✔ **Comprehension**
- Read Aloud: "The Little Red Hen"

Vocabulary
- Number Words
- Story Word: *two-wheeler*

✔ **Phonemic Awareness**
- Phoneme Blending

✔ **Phonics**
- Cumulative Review
- Blend Sounds
- Pre-decodable Reader: *Pam*
- Review High-Frequency Words

Writing
- Independent Writing: Revise and Edit a Sentence

SMALL GROUP

- Differentiated Instruction, pages 478–503

Oral Language

Talk About It

Build Robust Vocabulary

ALONE OR TOGETHER

Discuss times when children worked together with someone else to do an activity and a time they did something on their own.

- *Have you ever worked with others to* **solve** *a* **problem** *or to do a job? How was it easier with friends or family helping? Did you feel* **grateful** *for the help?* Have children ask each other questions.

CREATE A DIAGRAM

Use **Teaching Chart G2** and label it as shown below.

Think Aloud Sometimes I do an activity by myself, such as digging in my garden or painting a picture. Other times I include my friends, such as when building a snow figure.

As children name other activities they can do alone or with friends, add them to the chart. Read all the words as you track the print.

With Friends

build a snow figure
play board games
clean the park
jump rope

Both

read books
play computer games
bake bread
collect seashells

By Myself

paint a picture
do a puzzle
play jacks
work with clay

ELL   ENGLISH LANGUAGE LEARNERS

Beginning	Intermediate	Advanced
Confirm Understanding Give examples of things children do by themselves, such as take a nap and things they do with others, such as play a game. Prompt children to provide additional examples and act them out.	**Enhance Understanding** Talk about things children do by themselves and things they do with friends: *What things do you do with friends? What things do you do by yourself? Do you like doing things with friends or doing things alone? Why?*	**Share Ideas** Have partners name things that they can do alone or with friends and discuss which way they prefer to do them and why. Have children complete the sentence frame, *I prefer to _____ by myself (with friends) because _____.*

Listen for Rhyme

IDENTIFY RHYME

Remind children that words rhyme when they have the same ending sounds. *The word* cap *rhymes with* lap. Tell children *cap* and *lap* end with the sounds: /aaap/, *ap*. Ask: *What other words rhyme with* cap?

FRIENDSHIP RHYME

Tell children that they will recite the rhyme "Out to Play" that they learned earlier in the week. Replay the rhyme and have children join in.

Discuss whether the friends in the rhyme play together or alone. *How might Dad and Sam **include** Pam and Matt when they play? What kinds of activities could the animals do together? What are some things that cat and bat could do to show that they are **thoughtful** friends?*

Remind children that rhyming words sound alike at the end of the word. Say the word pairs: *play/day, hot/both, song/along, Pam/Sam, Dad/Pam*. Model giving a "thumbs up" if the words rhyme. Have children repeat.

Out to Play

Dad and Sam went out to play

On a hot and sunny day.

Pam and Matt both came along.

They played and sang this happy song.

Lamb and ram went out to play

On a hot and sunny day.

Cat and bat both came along.

They played and sang this happy song.

Objectives

- Use oral vocabulary words *grateful, include, problem, solve,* and *thoughtful*
- Contribute to a diagram
- Orally generate rhymes in response to spoken words
- Distinguish orally presented rhyming pairs of words from non-rhyming pairs

Materials

- Graphic Organizer; Teaching Chart G2

Oral Vocabulary

Have children use each word in a sentence about this week's stories.

grateful	include
problem	solve
thoughtful	

Review Work with children to review last week's words. Ask them to list some *pleasant* places to visit. Have children describe why they would want to play a *game* with an *honest* friend. Ask children to list ways they could *assist* someone in another part of the *world*.

assist	game
honest	pleasant
world	

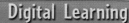

Digital Learning

Rhyme on **Listening Library Audio CD**

Objectives

- Listen and respond to a folktale
- Discuss the big idea of a folktale

Materials

- Read-Aloud Anthology: "The Little Red Hen," pp. 41–44

ELL

Identify Story Words
Explain that a *hen* is a female chicken and a *rooster* is a male chicken. Show children a photo or an illustration of a hen in the Read-Aloud Anthology. Ask them to point to the hen and say the word. Ask children to name the other animal characters in the folktale.

Readers Theater

BUILDING LISTENING AND SPEAKING SKILLS
Distribute copies of "Who Helped the Lion?" Read-Aloud Anthology pages 160–162. Have children practice performing the play throughout the unit. Assign parts and have children present the play or perform it as a dramatic reading at the end of the unit.

Interactive
Read Aloud
Listening Comprehension

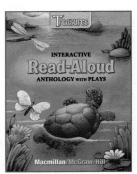

Read Aloud

GENRE: LITERARY TEXT/FOLKTALE
Tell children that "The Little Red Hen" is a **folktale**. Remind them that folktales are very old stories that people have been telling for many years. See the information about folktales found in the **Read-Aloud Anthology**. Read the first sentence aloud. Ask children to explain the words *Once upon a time*. Point out that many fables, folktales, and fairy tales begin with these words. Point out the recurring phrase "Then I will do it myself" throughout this folktale.

CULTURAL PERSPECTIVES
Tell children that "The Little Red Hen" is a folktale from England. Explain that wheat that is used to make bread is grown on farms in many places around the world.

READ "THE LITTLE RED HEN"
- **MODEL ASKING QUESTIONS** Use the Think Alouds provided at point of use in the folktale.

- **MODEL FLUENT READING** Read the folktale aloud with fluent expression. Stop occasionally and ask children to predict what will happen next to the friends.

- **EXPAND VOCABULARY** See page 41 of the Read-Aloud Anthology to teach new words using the **Define/Example/Ask** routine.

Respond to Literature

TALK ABOUT IT Ask children to discuss the theme of the folktale.

- *What did each animal say when Little Red Hen asked for help?*

- *What do you think would have happened if her friends had acted differently?*

- *How does this folktale relate to something in your experience?*

- Provide another version of the folktale. Guide children to compare the two versions.

- Discuss how the dog, the cat, and the mouse view planting wheat differently than the Little Red Hen.

Vocabulary

Number Words

Count on your fingers to review number words *one* through *five*. Then open *Simon and Molly plus Hester* to page 5 and point out the word *two*. Then turn to page 31 and point out the word *three*.

Recite the following poem:

> A rhyme for one: *run.*
>
> A rhyme for two: *shoe.*
>
> A rhyme for three: *knee.*
>
> A rhyme for four: *snore.*
>
> A rhyme for five: *dive.*

■ Then reverse the rhyming words. Chant the revised poem, starting with *A rhyme for run:* one.

NAME NUMBER WORDS Give partners several small items or pictures of items, such as books, pencils, buttons or colored tiles. Ask children to sort their items into sets of one, two, three, four, and five. Then have partners say a sentence about each set, such as: *I have three tiles.*

Story Word: *two-wheeler*

Display page 4 of *Simon and Molly plus Hester* and have a child point out the word *two-wheeler*. Ask children how many wheels the bicycle has. Then display the **Photo Card** for *car*. *How many wheels does a car have? What might we call a car?* Write the word *four-wheeler* on the board.

TIME TO MOVE!

Distribute index cards with number words *one, two, three, four,* and *five* to children. Ask children to move according to the number they have, for example: *All number ones, jump up one time! If you have number two, clap twice!* Have children say the number and movement as they do it, for example: *one jump* or *two claps.*

Objectives

- Use number words
- Identify and sort pictures of objects into conceptual categories
- Review story word *two-wheeler*
- Identify and use words that name actions

Materials

- Read-Aloud Trade Book: *Simon and Molly plus Hester*
- small colored tiles or buttons
- Photo Card: *car*
- index cards with the words *one, two, three, four, five* written on them
- pictures of different classroom objects

ELL

Reinforce Meaning Use index cards with *one, two, three, four,* and *five* written on them. Point to the word *one*, say *one*, and then show one finger. Point to the word *two*, say *two*, and show two fingers. Continue for the remaining numbers. Then have children take turns pointing to a number. Tell all children to repeat after you as you say a number and show that number of fingers.

Objectives

- Blend sounds to form words
- Identify initial sounds in words
- Review sound-spellings for /s/s, /p/p, /m/m, /a/a
- Blend words with /s/s, /p/p, /a/a, /m/m
- Read simple one-syllable words

Materials

- Puppet
- Word-Building Cards
- pocket chart
- Photo Cards: *ant, map, pizza, seal*
- Activity Book, pp. 29–30
- Practice Book, p. 58

Phonemic Awareness

✔ Phoneme Blending

Model

Use the **Puppet** to model how to blend sounds to form *Pam*.

Repeat with *map*.

Happy is going to say the sounds in a word. Listen to Happy: /p/ /a/ /m/. Happy can blend these sounds together: /paaammm/, *Pam*. Say the sounds with Happy: /p/ /a/ /m/. Now blend the sounds to say the word with Happy: *Pam*

Guided Practice/Practice

Children blend sounds to form words.

Guide practice with the first word, using the same routine.

Happy is going to say the sounds in a word. Listen to Happy as he says each sound. Then blend the sounds to say the word.

/m/ /a/ /t/	/s/ /a/ /m/	/p/ /a/ /t/
/p/ /i/ /g/	/m/ /o/ /p/	/s/ /ā/

Phonics

✔ Cumulative Review

a	m

Model

Place **Word-Building Card** *s* in the pocket chart.

This is the letter *s*. The sound for this letter is /s/.

Repeat the routine for *m, p, a*.

Hold up the **Photo Card** for *seal*.

This is a picture of a seal. *Seal* begins with /s/. I will place *seal* under letter *s*.

Repeat for *ant*.

Guided Practice/Practice

Children identify initial sounds to sort the Photo Cards. Guide practice using the routine.

Build Fluency: Sound-Spellings

 Display the following **Word-Building Cards**: *a, m, p, s*. Have children chorally say each sound. Repeat and vary the pace.

 ## Blend with /a/*a*, /m/*m*, /p/*p*, /s/*s*

Model

Place Word-Building Card *m* in the pocket chart.

This letter is *m*. The letter *m* stands for the /m/ sound. Say /m/.

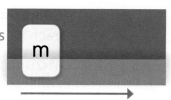

Place Word-Building Card *a* in the pocket chart next to *m*. Move your hand from left to right.

This letter is *a*. The letter *a* stands for the /a/ sound. Listen as I blend the two sounds together: /mmmaaa/. Now blend the sounds with me. (/mmmaaa/)

Place Word-Building Card *p* next to *ma*. Move your hand from left to right.

Repeat the routine with *sap*.

This letter is *p*. The letter *p* stands for the /p/ sound. Listen as I blend the three sounds together: /mmmaaap/, *map*. Now blend the sounds with me. (/mmmaaap/, *map*)

Guided Practice/Practice

Children blend sounds to form words.

Pam   Sam   am
map   sap

For Tier 2 instruction, see page 492.

Corrective Feedback

Blending: Sound Error Model the sound that children missed, then have them repeat the sound. For example, for the word *Pam*, say: *My turn.* Tap under the letter *P* in the word *Pam* and say: *Sound? What's the sound?* Then return to the beginning of the word. Say: *Let's start over.* Blend the word with children again.

Activity Book, pages 29–30
Practice Book, page 58

Objectives

- Read decodable words with /s/s, /p/p
- Read the words *a, I, like*
- Predict what happens next based on cover, title, and illustrations
- Reread for fluency

Materials

- Pre-decodable Reader: *Pam*
- High-Frequency Word Cards: *a, I, like*
- pocket chart

Pre-decodable Reader

Read *Pam*

REVIEW Display the **High-Frequency Word Cards** for **a**, **I**, and **like** in the pocket chart. Use the **Read/Spell/Write** routine to review each word.

Pam

MODEL CONCEPTS ABOUT PRINT *I hold the book so that it is right side up. The cover is on the front and the words are not upside down. The title of this book is* Pam. *Say it with me: The title of this book is* Pam. Now you point to the cover. Turn the page and read from left to right.

PREDICT Ask children to describe the cover illustration. *What season is it? Who is this girl? How do you know? What is she doing?* Have children predict what the story is about.

FIRST READ Have children point to each word and say the high-frequency words quickly. Help them to use syntactic and semantic cues to comprehend decodable text. Children should chorally read the story the first time through.

DEVELOP COMPREHENSION Ask the following: *Who does Pam like?* (Sam) *What game are Pam and Sam playing?* (hide-and-seek)

SECOND READ Have partners reread the book together.

I am Pam.

2

I am Sam.

3

Sam? Sam?

4

Sam!

5

Pam? Pam?

6

Pam!

7

I like Pam.

8

Pre-decodable Reader

Writing

Independent Writing: A Sentence

REVISE AND EDIT

Distribute children's draft sentences. Have them reread their sentence and check for the following:

- Does my sentence tell what my friends and I like to do together?

- Does my sentence make sense?

- Did I draw a picture to show what we like to do?

- Did I write all of the letters in the words that I know?

Circulate and help children as they review, revise, and edit their sentence. Guide children to check their drafts for details and to add additional details. Have children share their sentences with partners. Guide children to revise their sentences based on partner and teacher feedback. Tell them to write their name on the top of their drawing.

- Distribute copies of the Writer's Checklist. Guide children to evaluate their work.

Ty

We like to play ball together.

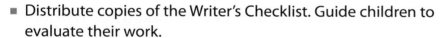

Write About It

Ask children to draw a picture of a friend. Guide them to label their drawings.

Objectives

- Revise sentences and drawings
- Edit sentences and drawings
- Use letter knowledge to write letters in a word
- Write one's own name

Materials

- children's sentences from Day 3
- Writer's Checklist; Teacher's Resource Book, p. 205

5-Day Writing

Sentences	
DAY 1	Shared: Lists
DAY 2	Interactive: Sentences
DAY 3	Independent: Prewrite and Draft a Sentence
DAY 4	Independent: Revise and Edit a Sentence
DAY 5	Independent: Publish and Present

ELL

New Language Have children draw a picture of an activity they do with a friend. Then help children complete the sentence frame We like to _____ together. Have children copy their sentences below their pictures.

Transitions That Teach

While children wait in line, have them talk about ways to **include** others when they play with friends.

Oral Language
- Build Robust Vocabulary

Comprehension ✓
- Strategy: Ask Questions
- Skill: Identify Character
- Read Across Texts

Vocabulary ✓
- Review High-Frequency Words *a, like*
- Review Color Words, Numbers

Phonemic Awareness ✓
- Phoneme Categorization

Phonics ✓
- Read Words
- Dictation

Writing
- Independent Writing: Publish and Present

SMALL GROUP

- Differentiated Instruction, pages 478–503

Review and Assess
Oral Language
Build Robust Vocabulary

REVIEW WORDS

Review this week's oral vocabulary words with children. Explain that all of the words will be used to discuss getting along with a new classmate. Talk about the circumstances that might bring a new child to the class.

Use the following questions to check children's understanding:

- What kinds of **problems** might a child in a new school have?

- How might classmates help a new child **solve** these problems?

- What could children do to **include** a new classmate in school activities?

- Why would it be **thoughtful** to introduce a new classmate to your friends?

- What kinds of things would make a new classmate feel **grateful**? Why?

REVIEW SONGS AND RHYMES ABOUT FRIENDS

Sing the song "Join in the Game" and have children sing along. Have children describe the game and suggest additional ways to play it, such as snap, snap or hop, hop.

Then recite the rhyme "Out to Play" with children. Have them list the friends in the song and identify how they get along. Ask them to name the words that rhyme.

Review and Assess
Comprehension

STRATEGY Ask Questions

REFLECT ON THE STRATEGY Remind children that they have been learning how to ask questions about stories they have read.

Think Aloud Why are lines drawn around Simon when he picks up the paper airplane on page 27? I reread and notice that he wrote *Hester go away* on the paper used to make the plane. The lines show me that he is surprised that Hester is reaching for the plane. He tears it up on page 29. Answering this question helped me learn more about Simon and understand the story better.

SKILL Identify Character

Have children review *Simon and Molly plus Hester* and "The Turtle and the Sheep" and discuss the characters in the stories.

- *How are the characters in* Simon and Molly plus Hester *different from the characters in "The Turtle and the Sheep"?*

- *What did the characters in* Simon and Molly plus Hester *do together? What did Turtle do by himself?*

- *Suppose that Simon met the turtles from "The Turtle and the Sheep." What might he tell them about being a friend?*

Reading Across Texts

Have children compare and contrast *Simon and Molly plus Hester* and "The Turtle and the Sheep." Discuss the **problems** the characters face and how they **solve** them. Record their ideas in a chart.

Simon and Molly plus Hester	The Turtle and the Sheep
story about three children	story about many turtles and sheep
tells about characters who act like real children and do what real children do	tells about animals who act like people and things they do
shows how friends care for and help each other	shows how good friends help and other friends do not

Tell children to dramatize the characters' similarities and differences.

Activity Book, page 31

Getting Along **473**

Objectives

- Review the high-frequency words *a, can, like, the, we*
- Review number words
- Review color words
- Identify and use words that name directions
- Build fluency
- Use the oral vocabulary words *grateful, include, problem, solve,* and *thoughtful*

Materials

- High-Frequency Word Cards: *a, can, like, the, we*
- High-Frequency Word Cards; Teacher's Resource Book, pp. 103–110
- index cards with colors: *red, orange, yellow, green, blue, purple*
- index cards with number words: *one, two, three, four, five*

Fluency

Connected Text Have children reread this week's **Pre-decodable Readers** with a partner. Circulate, listen in, and note those children who need additional instruction and practice reading this week's decodable and sight words.

Pre-Decodable Reader
Pam
by Amy Helfer • illustrated by Nathan Jarvis

Pre-Decodable Reader
I Like, We Like
by Wiley Blevins • illustrated by Nancy Davis

Sight Word Practice

Review and Assess
Vocabulary

 ## High-Frequency Words

Distribute copies of one of the following **High-Frequency Word Cards** to each child: **can**, **we**, **the**, **like**, and **a**. Say: *I am going to read some sentences. When you hear the word that is on your card, hold it up.*

- *In the book, Simon and Hester have a **problem**.*

- *Simon is a good friend.*

- *Can you ride a two-wheeler?*

- *We like toast with cinnamon-sugar.*

- *I know children like Simon, Molly, and Hester.*

Build Fluency: Word Automaticity

Display the High-Frequency Word Cards. Point quickly to each card, at random, and have children read the word as fast as they can.

can	we	the	like	a

Color Words, Numbers

Rapid Naming Display the color cards. Have children chorally name them as quickly as they can. Shuffle the cards and repeat the routine. Ask rhyming questions for colors, such as: *What is a rhyming word for you?* (*blue*)

Guide children in using number words and check their knowledge of personal information. Ask: *What is your phone number? How old are you? When is your birthday?*

TIME TO MOVE!

Play "Simon Says" using color and number commands. *Simon says children wearing blue take two steps forward.* Have children restate the command as they act. For example: *I am wearing blue, so I take two steps forward.* Use *sideways, right and left.*

Review and Assess
Phonemic Awareness

Phoneme Categorization

Objectives
- Review final sounds /m/m, /p/p, /s/s
- Recognize words that end with the same sound

Materials
- Photo Cards: *ant, bus, comb, farm, goat, horse, inchworm, man, mop, nut, rope, soap, sock, soup, top, up*

Guided Practice

Display the **Photo Cards** for *mop, nut*, and *rope*.

I will say three picture names: *mop, nut, rope*. Repeat these words with me. Which picture names end with the same sound? *Mop* and *rope* end with the same sound, /p/. *Nut* does not end with the /p/ sound. It ends with the /t/ sound. It does not belong.

Practice

Children identify the picture name that does not end with the same sound.

Use these sets of cards: *farm, sock, comb; mop, ant, soup; inchworm, farm, goat; man, soap, up; bus, horse, ant; top, soup, farm*

I will show you three pictures. Tell me which picture does not belong.

For Tier 2 instruction, see page 498.

Objectives

- Identify the common sounds that letters represent
- Read simple one-syllable words
- Use letter-sound correspondences to spell one-syllable words

Materials

- Word-Building Cards
- pocket chart
- four index cards with: *We, like, Pam,* period mark
- four index cards with: *Am, I, Pam,* question mark
- Sound Box
- WorkBoard Sound Boxes; Teacher's Resource Book, p. 136
- markers
- Activity Book, p. 32

Activity Book, page 32

Review and Assess
Phonics

Build Fluency: Sound-Spellings

Rapid Naming Display the following **Word-Building Cards**: *a, m, p, s.* Have children chorally say each sound. Repeat and vary the pace.

✔ Read Words

Apply

Distribute the first set of index cards.	Let's read the sentence together.
	We like Pam.
Have children stand in sequence.	
Repeat, using the other set of cards.	Let's read the sentence together.
	Am I Pam?

✔ Dictation

Dictate sounds for children to spell.

Listen as I say a sound. Repeat the sound, then write the letter that stands for the sound.

/s/   /m/   /a/   /p/

Then dictate words for children to spell. Model for children how to use the **Sound Boxes** to segment the sounds in the word. Have them repeat.

Now let's write some words. I will say a word. I want you to repeat the word, then think about how many sounds are in the word. Use your Sound Boxes to count the sounds. Then write one letter for each sound you hear.

am   Sam   Pam   map   sap

Write the letters and words on the board for children to self-correct.

For Tier 2 instruction, see page 498.

Review and Assess
Writing

Independent Writing: Sentences

PUBLISH

Explain to children that you will gather their sentences to make a class book.

- Brainstorm ideas for a title, such as *What We Like to Do Together*.

- Have children work on a cover. Write the title on the cover.

- Make holes along the edges of the cover on each page of the book. Bind the pages together with yarn.

PRESENT

Ask children to take turns reading their illustrated sentences to the class and telling what the pictures show. Have them add descriptions to the pictures, such as: *play ball in the park*. Tell children to speak one at a time.

LISTENING, SPEAKING, AND VIEWING

- Tell children to speak clearly. Tell them that they will get to know each other by being good listeners when a classmate is speaking. Ask children to discuss one another's work.

- Praise children for their hard work and place the finished book in the Reading Workstation for everyone to enjoy. Have children put copies of their work in their Writing Portfolios.

Write About It

Ask children to draw a picture of their favorite place to go with their friends. Help them label their drawing.

Objectives

- Publish and present a piece of writing
- Take turns and speak one at a time

Materials

- children's sentences from Day 4

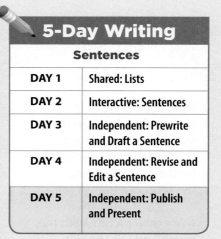

5-Day Writing

	Sentences
DAY 1	Shared: Lists
DAY 2	Interactive: Sentences
DAY 3	Independent: Prewrite and Draft a Sentence
DAY 4	Independent: Revise and Edit a Sentence
DAY 5	Independent: Publish and Present

Transitions That Teach

While lining up, have children name **thoughtful** things that they could do for people in their family.

Approaching Level

Oral Language

Objective Preteach oral vocabulary
Materials • none

THEME WORDS: *problem, solve*

- Discuss the words **problem** and **solve** with children. *A problem is something that causes trouble. When you* solve *a problem, you fix it. It is a* problem *when everyone wants the same toy. We fix, or* solve, *the* problem *by taking turns playing with it.*

- *What* problem *did we have in class today? How did we* solve *the* problem? *What story characters have had* problems? *How did they* solve *their* problems? Have children ask and answer each other's questions about this topic.

- Have children use the following sentence frames to generate oral sentences using the words: *One problem school children have is _____. They can solve that problem by _____.*

Solve a Problem

Have children draw a picture showing how they solved a problem. Help children write a caption for their picture using the sentence frame *I can _____.* Ask them to share their picture with the group and tell about it.

ELL

Partners When pairing children to make up sentences with *a* and *like*, pair English Language Learners with children who are more proficient. Write their sentences, read them together, and point to the words *a* and *like*.

High-Frequency Words

Objective Review high-frequency words *a, like*
Materials • **High-Frequency Word Cards:** *a, can, I, like, the, we*

REVIEW WORDS: *a, like*

- Display the **High-Frequency Word Card** for **like**.

- **Read** Point to and say the word *like*. *This is the word* like. *When you* like *something, you enjoy it or you are pleased with it. I* like *getting along with friends.*

- **Spell** *The word* like *is spelled* l-i-k-e. Have children read and spell *like*.

- **Write** Finally, have children write the word *like*.

- Repeat the **Read/Spell/Write** routine for **a**.

- Have children work with a partner to make up sentences using the words *a* and *like*. Ask them to talk about how they like to solve problems.

HIGH-FREQUENCY WORDS REVIEW

Display the High-Frequency Word Cards for *I, can, we,* and *the,* one card at a time, as children chorally read and spell the word. Mix and repeat. Note words children need to review.

Tier 2

Approaching Level

Phonemic Awareness

Objective Isolate initial /s/ and /p/ sounds

Materials
- **Photo Cards:** *pen, piano, pie, seal, sock, sun*
- **Sound-Spelling Cards:** *Piano, Sun*

PHONEME ISOLATION

Model

- Display the **Photo Card** for *sun. This is the sun. Listen for the beginning sound in* sun: */sssuuunnn/.* Sun *begins with /s/.*

- Display the *Sun* **Sound-Spelling Card**. Point to the articulation picture. *When I say /s/, I place my tongue slightly behind my teeth. I force air over my tongue, past my teeth, and out of my mouth. Repeat for* p. *When I say /p/, a puff of air comes out of my mouth.*

Guided Practice/Practice

- Display the Photo Cards. Have children take turns selecting a picture, naming it, and saying the initial sound of the picture name: *This is a (the) _____. _____ begins with _____.*

Phonics

Objective Recognize words that begin with /s/s and /p/p

Materials
- **Sound-Spelling Cards:** *Piano, Sun* • **Word-Building Cards**
- **Photo Cards:** *pen, penguin, piano, pie, pizza, pumpkin, saw, seal, soap, sock, soup, sun*

PRETEACH: RECOGNIZE /s/s, /p/p

Model

- Display the Photo Card for *sock* and the *Sun* Sound-Spelling Card. *The name of this letter is* s. S *stands for the /s/ sound that you hear at the beginning of* sock. *I will place the* s **Word-Building Card** *on the picture of the sock because* sock *begins with /s/. Listen: /sssoook/,* sock. *Repeat with* saw. *Then repeat procedure for* p.

Guided Practice/Practice

- Display the Photo Cards. Point to the Photo Card for *seal. This is a seal. What sound do you hear at the beginning of* seal? *What letter stands for /s/? I place an* s *on the seal because* seal *begins with /s/. Repeat with remaining Photo Cards for* s *and* p.

- For additional practice, point out objects in the classroom with names that begin with /s/ and /p/.

SOUND-SPELLINGS REVIEW

Tier 2

Display Word-Building Cards *m, a, s,* and *p,* one at a time. Have children chorally say the sound. Repeat and vary the pace.

Corrective Feedback

Mnemonic Display the *Sun* and *Piano* Sound-Spelling Cards. *This is the* Sun *Sound-Spelling Card. The sound is /s/. The /s/ sound is spelled with the letter* s. *Say /s/ with me: /s/. This is the sound at the beginning of* sun. *What is the letter? What is the sound? What word begins with /s/?* Sun *is the word we can use to remember the sound for* s, */s/. Repeat with* Pp *and the* Piano *Sound-Spelling Card.*

ELL

Sound-Letter Relationships Provide additional practice in pronouncing the /s/ and /p/ sounds and naming the letters *s* and *p,* as children point to them.

On Level

High-Frequency Words

Objective Review high-frequency words *a*, *like*, *the*, and *we*
Materials • **High-Frequency Word Cards:** *a*, *like*, *the*, *we*

REVIEW: *a, like, the, we*

- Display the **High-Frequency Word Cards** for **a**, **like**, **the**, **we**.

- **Read** Point to and say the word *like*. *This is the word* like. *When you* like *something, you enjoy it or you are pleased with it. I like learning new things.*

- **Spell** Like *is spelled* l-i-k-e. Have children read and spell *like*.

- **Write** Finally, have children write the word *like*.

- Repeat with *a*, *we*, and *the*. Then have partners make up sentences using the words *a*, *we*, and *the*.

Phonemic Awareness/Phonics

Objective Review recognizing and blending /s/s and /p/p
Materials • **Word-Building Cards** • pocket chart • Puppet

PHONEME CATEGORIZATION

Model

- Hold up the **Puppet**. *Listen for the words Happy says that begin with the same sound:* sand, soap, bus, sink. *I heard the /s/ sound at the beginning of* sand, soap, sink. *I heard /s/ at the end of* bus. Bus *does not belong. It ends with /s/.*

Practice

- Say the following groups of words. Have children identify the word in each group that does not begin with the /s/ sound. Say: *soft, moon, silly, sell*. Repeat with *grapes, soon, six, seed*.

- Then have children identify the word that does not begin with /p/. Say: *pay, pie, peach, milk* and then *top, puff, pole, penny*.

REVIEW /s/s, /p/p

Model

- Display **Word-Building Card** *s*. *The name of this letter is* s. S *stands for the /s/ sound we hear at the beginning of* sun. *What is the sound? I'll hold up the* s *card and say /s/ because* sun *begins with /s/.* Repeat with *p* and *piano*.

Practice

- Say: *pack, soft, seem, point, song, pull, sour, pond,* and *such*. Children hold up their small Word-Building Cards and say /s/ for words that begin with *s* and /p/ for words that begin with *p*. Guide practice with the first two words.

Puppet

Beyond Level

High-Frequency Words/Vocabulary

Objective   Review high-frequency words
Materials   • none

ACCELERATE

- Write *good* and *down* on the board.
- **Read** Point to and say the word *good*. *This is the word* good. *Someone who is good at something does it well.*
- **Spell** Good *is spelled* g-o-o-d. Have children read and spell *good*.
- **Write** Finally, have children write the word *good*.
- Repeat the routine with *down*.
- Have children work with a partner to make up oral sentences using the words *good* and *down*.

EXPAND ORAL VOCABULARY

- **Antonyms** Review the meaning of the oral vocabulary word *problem* with children. Then explain that an *antonym* is a word that means the opposite of another word.
- Say: *An* antonym *for the word* problem *is* solution. *A* solution *is an answer to a* problem. *When you have a* problem, *you want to figure out how to make it better. Your answer is the* solution.
- Have children take turns using the new word *solution* in a sentence. Then tell children that they will work with a partner to discuss problems they have had and the solutions they found.

Phonics

Objectives   Review /s/s and /p/p; introduce short /o/o; blend and read words
Materials   • **Sound-Spelling Cards:** *Octopus, Piano, Sun*
• **Word-Building Cards**   • **Sound-Spelling WorkBoards**

ENRICH

- *What word do the sounds* /sssaaannnd/ *make?*
- Display the *Sun* **Sound-Spelling Card**. Say that the /s/ sound is spelled with the letter *s*. *Sock begins with* /s/. *What other words begin with* /s/? Repeat with /p/p, the *Piano* Sound-Spelling Card and word *piano*; *Octopus* Sound-Spelling Card and word *October*.
- Display **Word-Building Cards** *a, b, c, ck, d, f, g, h, i, j, k, l, m, n, p, qu, r, s, t, v, w, x, y, z,* pointing to each letter. Say the letter name and sound. Have children repeat and write the letter on their **WorkBoards**.

Rhyme

Have children write a rhyme using the sentence frame *We like _____.* Ask children to illustrate their rhyme and share it with the group.

Corrective Feedback

Association Error If children cannot discern medial short /o/o, review the letter-sound relationship. Write *o* on the board and say /ooo/. Have children repeat. Then write *box* on the board and blend the word with children: /b/ /o/ /ks/, /boooks/, *box*. Repeat with *fox* and *lox*. Contrast the words with *fix* and *fax*.

Sound-Spelling WorkBoard

ELL ENGLISH LANGUAGE LEARNERS

Oral Language Warm-Up

Content Objective Learn theme vocabulary
Language Objective Repeat and sing the song to demonstrate understanding
Materials • **Listening Library Audio CD**

BUILD BACKGROUND KNOWLEDGE

All Language Levels

- Continue developing vocabulary around the unit theme "Friends" using the song "Join in the Game." Display a picture of several friends, such as a picture from *Simon and Molly plus Hester*. Teach the word *everyone* as you point to all of the friends in the picture. Have children repeat the word three times.

- Play "Join in the Game" on the **Listening Library Audio CD**. Act out each line as you sing the song.

- Then teach children the song and hand motions. Emphasize the key words *everyone* and *join*.

- Play the song several times until children begin to correctly repeat the song and perform the hand motions.

- Ask children to tell about things they do together with friends. Build on their responses to model speaking in complete sentences. For example: *You go to school with your friends.*

Academic Language

Language Objective Use academic language in classroom conversations

All Language Levels

- This week's academic words are **boldfaced** throughout the lesson. Define the word in context and provide a clear example from the selection. Then ask children to generate an example or a word with a similar meaning.

Academic Language Used in Whole Group Instruction

Oral Vocabulary Words	Vocabulary and Grammar Concepts	Strategy and Skill Words
grateful	color words	ask
include	naming words	questions
problem		identify
solve		character
thoughtful		naming words

Cognates

Help children identify similarities and differences in pronunciation and spelling between English words and Spanish cognates:

problem   *problema*

ELL ENGLISH LANGUAGE LEARNERS

Vocabulary

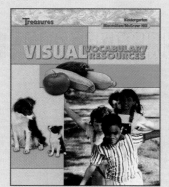

Visual Vocabulary Resources

Language Objective Demonstrate understanding and use of key words by describing how friends solve problems

Materials • **Visual Vocabulary Resources**

✓ PRETEACH KEY VOCABULARY

All Language Levels

Use the **Visual Vocabulary Resources** to preteach the weekly oral vocabulary words *grateful, include, problem, solve,* and *thoughtful.* Focus on one or two words per day. Use the following routine that appears in detail on the cards.

- Define the word in English and provide the example given.
- Define the word in Spanish, if appropriate, and indicate if the word is a cognate.
- Display the picture and explain how it illustrates or demonstrates the word. Engage children in structured partner-talk about the image, using the key word.
- Ask children to chorally say the word three times.
- Point out any known sound-spellings or focus on a key aspect of phonemic awareness related to the word.

PRETEACH FUNCTION WORDS AND PHRASES

All Language Levels

Use the Visual Vocabulary Resources to preteach the function words and phrases *by myself* and *in a group.* Focus on one phrase per day. Use the detailed routine on the cards.

- Define the phrase in English and, if appropriate, in Spanish. Point out if the phrase is a cognate.
- Refer to the picture and engage children in talk about the phrase. For example, children will partner-talk using sentence frames, or they will listen to sentences and replace a word or phrase with the new function word or phrase.
- Ask children to chorally repeat the phrase three times.

TEACH BASIC WORDS

Beginning/Intermediate

Use the Visual Vocabulary Resources to teach the basic words *fold, rip, color, write, paint (verb),* and *crumple.* Teach these "things you can do to paper" words using the routine provided on the card.

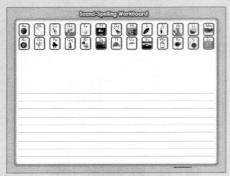

Sound-Spelling WorkBoard

ELL

Partners When pairing children to make up sentences with *like* and *a*, pair English Language Learners with children who are more proficient. Write their sentences, read them together, and point out the words *like* and *a*.

Pre-decodable Reader

Approaching Level

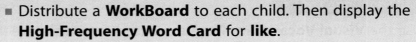
High-Frequency Words

Objective	Reteach high-frequency words *a*, *like*
Materials	• **High-Frequency Word Cards:** *a*, can, *like*, the, we
	• **Sound-Spelling WorkBoards**

RETEACH WORDS: *a*, *like*

Tier 2

- Distribute a **WorkBoard** to each child. Then display the **High-Frequency Word Card** for **like**.

- Use the **Read/Spell/Write** routine to reteach the word. Point to and say the word. *This is the word* like. *When you like something, you enjoy it or you are pleased with it. I like reading new books.* Like *is spelled* l-i-k-e. Have children read and spell *like*. Then have them write the word on their WorkBoards.

- Repeat for the word **a**.

- Have children work with a partner to make up sentences using the words *like* and *a*. Ask them to talk about things they like at school.

CUMULATIVE REVIEW

Display the High-Frequency Word Cards *I*, *can*, *we*, and *the*, one card at a time, as children chorally read and spell the word. Mix and repeat. Note words children need to review.

Pre-decodable Reader

Objective	Preteach Pre-decodable Reader *I Like, We Like*
Materials	• **Pre-decodable Reader:** *I Like, We Like*

PRETEACH: *I Like, We Like*

- Have children point to the cover of the book and read the title. Then tell children to open to the title page and point out the title. *Let's read the title together.* Have children use the illustration on the cover to predict what the book will be about.

- Page through the book. Ask children what they see in each picture. Point out each rebus. Ask children to find the words *I*, *like*, *a*, and *we*.

- Read the book chorally with children. Have children point to each word or rebus as they read it. Provide corrective feedback as needed.

- Ask children to use *I*, *like*, *a*, and *we* to talk about things from the book that they like, too. *I like a pizza. We like a game.*

- After reading, ask children to recall things they read about.

Approaching Level

Phonemic Awareness

Objective Blend and categorize sounds
Materials • **Puppet**

Puppet

✔ PHONEME BLENDING

Tier 2

Model

■ *Listen as Happy says the sounds in a word. First he'll say each sound: /s/ /u/ /n/.* Then he will blend the sounds together and say the word: /s/ /u/ /n/, /sssuuunnn/, sun. *The word is* sun. *Repeat for* piano.

Practice

■ Repeat with the following words. Guide practice with the first word using the same routine.

/p/ /e/ /n/   /s/ /o/ /k/   /p/ u/ /p/   /s/ /a/ /p/   /p/ /i/ /t/

✔ PHONEME CATEGORIZATION

Model

■ *Listen as Happy says three words:* sat, ant, sip. Sat *and* sip *begin with /s/. Listen: /sssaaat/, sat; /sssiiip/, sip. Ant doesn't belong.*

Practice

■ *Listen as Happy says three words:* pan, pear, mop. *Which word doesn't belong? Repeat with* soap, park, pink.

Phonics

Objective Reinforce letter-sound correspondence for /s/s and /p/p
Materials • **Sound-Spelling Cards:** *Piano, Sun*
• **Word-Building Cards** • **Sound-Spelling WorkBoards**

✔ RETEACH

Model

■ Display the *Sun* **Sound-Spelling Card**. *The letter* s *stands for the /s/ sound as in* sun. *What is this letter? What sound does it stand for?* Repeat with the *Piano* Sound-Spelling Card.

Guided Practice/Practice

■ Distribute **WorkBoards**. Have children write *s* on their WorkBoard when they hear a word with /s/. Have them write *p* when they hear a word with /p/. Say several initial *s* or *p* words.

CUMULATIVE REVIEW

Display **Word-Building Cards** *m, a, s, p,* one at a time. Have children chorally say the sound. Repeat and vary the pace.

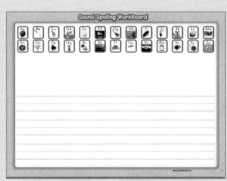
Sound-Spelling WorkBoard

Corrective Feedback

If children cannot discern the initial /s/, review the word *sun.* Have children stop at the first sound and repeat /s/, /s/, /s/ before saying *sun.*

On Level

Pre-decodable Reader

Objective Reread *I Like, We Like* to develop fluency

Materials • **Pre-decodable Reader:** *I Like, We Like*

REREAD FOR FLUENCY

- Ask children to look back at the illustrations in *I Like, We Like*. Have them use their own words to retell what the book is about.

- Have children reread a page or two of *I Like, We Like*. Model reading a page to show children how to read with expression. Point out how you use your voice to say the words as the person in the picture would say them: *When I read, "I like a pizza," I emphasize* pizza *by saying it stronger than the other words. I use my voice to show that the boy in the picture really likes pizza.*

- Provide time to listen as children read their page(s). Have them identify high-frequency words. Comment on their accuracy. Provide corrective feedback by modeling proper fluency.

- Use the same routine for **Pre-decodable Reader** *Pam* on Day 4.

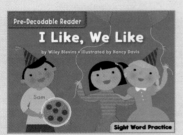

Pre-Decodable Reader

I Like, We Like
by Wiley Blevins • illustrated by Nancy Davis

Sam

Sight Word Practice

Pre-decodable Reader

Beyond Level

Pre-decodable Reader

Objective Reread *I Like, We Like* and *Pam* to reinforce fluency

Materials • **Pre-decodable Readers:** *I Like, We Like; Pam*

REREAD FOR FLUENCY

- Ask children to review the illustrations in *I Like, We Like* and *Pam* and retell events from each. Have children reread the books. Comment on their accuracy and provide corrective feedback.

INNOVATE

- Have children write their own story by changing some of the rebuses in *I Like, We Like*. Have each child copy the words *I like a* and add a new rebus. Put all the pages together to form a book.

- Ask children to write a new ending for the story *Pam*. Suggest that children have the characters do something else or they may introduce a new character. Have them draw the new ending. Then help them add sentences to their papers. Ask children to share their stories with the group.

ELL ENGLISH LANGUAGE LEARNERS

Access to Core Content

Content Objective Develop listening comprehension
Language Objective Discuss text using key words and sentence frames
Materials • **ELL Resource Book,** pp. 50–57

PRETEACH BIG BOOK/TRADE BOOK

All Language Levels

Use the Interactive Question-Response Guide on **ELL Resource Book** pages 50–57 to introduce children to *Simon and Molly plus Hester*. Preteach half of the selection on Day 1 and half on Day 2.

- Use the prompts provided in the guide to develop meaning and vocabulary. Use the partner-talk and whole-class responses to engage children and increase student talk.

- When completed, revisit the selection and prompt children to talk about the illustrations. Provide sentence starters as needed and build on children's responses to develop language.

ELL Resource Book

Trade Book

Beginning	Intermediate	Advanced
Use Visuals During the Interactive Reading, select several pictures. Describe them and have children summarize what you said.	**Summarize** During the Interactive Reading, select a few lines of text. After you read them and explain them, have children summarize the text.	**Expand** During the Interactive Reading, select a larger portion of text. After you read it and explain it, have children summarize the text.

Approaching Level

High-Frequency Words

Objective   Recognize high-frequency words *a*, *like*, *the*, *we*

Materials
- **High-Frequency Word Cards:** *a*, *can*, *like*, *the*, *we*
- **Word-Building Cards**

✓ REVIEW WORDS: *a, like, the, we*

- Display the **High-Frequency Word Card** for **like**. Say the word and have children repeat it. Point to each letter and have children name it.

- Distribute small **Word-Building Cards** *l*, *i*, *k*, and *e*. Model putting the letters together to form *like*. Have children form *like*.

- Repeat the above routines with the words **a**, **we**, and **the**.

- Ask a question with the words *like* and *a*: *Do you like getting a present?* Have children use *like* and *a* to answer the question. Continue with the words *we* and *the*.

CUMULATIVE REVIEW

Display the High-Frequency Word Cards for *I*, *can*, *we*, and *the*, one card at a time, as children chorally read and spell the word. Mix and repeat. Note words children need to review.

Phonemic Awareness

Objective   Blend sounds to form words

Materials
- **Photo Cards:** *pen, pie, sock, sun* • **Sound Boxes** • markers
- **WorkBoard Sound Boxes; Teacher's Resource Book,** p. 136

✓ PHONEME BLENDING

Tier 2

Model

- Use the **Sound Boxes**. Display the **Photo Card** for *sun*. *I will say the sounds in* sun. *I'll put a marker in a different box for each sound. Listen to the sounds: /s/ /u/ /n/. There are three sounds. I'll point to the box for each sound as I blend the sounds together: /sssuuunnn/,* sun. *Blend the sounds with me: /sssuuunnn/,* sun. *What's the word?*

- Repeat the routine with *pen*, *sock*, and *pie*.

Guided Practice/Practice

- Distribute Sound Boxes and markers. *I will say the sounds in a word. Listen to the sounds: /p/ /a/ /m/. There are three sounds. Let's all put a marker in a box for each sound we hear: /p/ /a/ /m/. Now let's point to the box for each sound as we blend the sounds together: /paaammm/,* Pam. *What's the word?*

- Repeat the routine with *Sam*, *pat*, *bus*, *map*, *am*, and *sap*.

Approaching Level

Phonics

Objectives Reinforce and blend with /s/s and /p/p; build fluency
Materials • **Word-Building Cards** • pocket chart

✔ REVIEW SKILLS

Tier 2

Model

- Place **Word-Building Card** P in the pocket chart. *The name of this letter is* P. *The letter* P *stands for the /p/ sound. Say /p/. What is the letter? What is the sound?*

- Place *a* next to P. Follow the above routine for *a*. Move your hand from left to right below the letters. *Listen as I blend the two sounds together: /paaa/,* Pa.

- Place *m* next to *a*. Follow the above routine for *m*. *Listen as I blend the three sounds together: /paaammm/,* Pam. *What's the word? Let's blend the word together: /p/ /a/ /m/, /paaammm/,* Pam.

Guided Practice/Practice

- Give small Word-Building Cards *S*, *a*, and *m* to children. Have them say the sound for the letter and blend the sounds to say the word *Sam*. Repeat with *map*, *am*, and *sap*.

Build Fluency

- Write *Pam*, *Sam*, *map*, *am*, and *sap* on the board. Have children blend the sounds in the words as quickly as they can.

Pre-decodable Reader

Objective Preteach Pre-decodable Reader *Pam*
Materials • **Pre-decodable Reader:** *Pam*

PRETEACH *Pam*

- Display the cover of the book and read the title. Have children open to the title page and point out the title. *Now let's read the title together.* Have children blend the sounds as you track the print. Have children look at the picture and say what Pam is doing and what they think will happen in the story.

- Page through the book. Ask children to describe each picture. Have them point to the high-frequency words *I* and *like*.

- Read the book chorally with children. Have them point to each word as they read it. Provide corrective feedback.

- Have children use the words *Pam* and *Sam* to talk about the pictures. *This is Pam. This is Sam. Pam looks for Sam. Sam looks for Pam. Sam likes Pam.*

- After reading, ask children to recall things they read about.

Pre-decodable Reader

ON YOUR OWN

Pam or Sam?

Have children draw a picture of their favorite character from the story *Pam*. Have them write the name of the character below the picture. Ask children to display their picture and tell why they like the character.

ELL

Sound-Letter Relationships Provide additional practice in pronouncing and blending the /s/ and /p/ sounds and naming the letters *s* and *p* as children point to them.

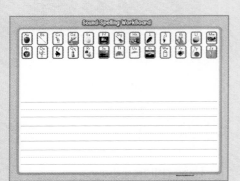

Sound-Spelling WorkBoard

Corrective Feedback

Association Error
If children cannot discern medial short /o/*o*, review the letter-sound relationship. Write *o* on the board and say /ooo/. Have children repeat. Then write *box* on the board and blend the word with children: /b/ /o/ /ks/, /boooks/, *box*. Repeat with *fox* and *lox*. Contrast the words with *fix* and *fax*.

On Level

Phonics

Objective Review recognizing and blending /s/*s* and /p/*p*
Materials • **Word-Building Cards** • pocket chart

✔ CONSOLIDATE LEARNING

- Display **Word-Building Card** *s*. Say: *The name of this letter is* s. S *stands for the /s/ sound we hear at the beginning of* sun. Repeat with *p* and *piano*.

- Say: *pick, sift, sing, paint, song, push, sour, pen,* and *sun*. Children hold up their small Word-Building Cards and say /s/ for words that begin with *s* and /p/ for words that begin with *p*. Guide practice with the first two words.

- **Blend Words** Place Word-Building Cards *S, a,* and *m* in the pocket chart. Point to each letter for children to identify. Move your hand from left to right below the letters as you blend the word. *Now listen as I blend the sounds together: /sssaaammm/,* Sam. *What's the word?*

- Have children use small Word-Building Cards to build *am* with you. Have them blend the word they build: /a/ /m/, /aaammm/, *am*. Repeat with *Pam, sap,* and *map*.

Beyond Level

Phonics

Objectives Review /s/*s* and /p/*p*; introduce short /o/*o*; blend and read words
Materials • **Word-Building Cards** • **Sound-Spelling WorkBoards**

✔ ACCELERATE

- Display the **Word-Building Cards** for *o* and *x*. Point to each letter for children to identify. *I can blend the sounds for these letters to read the word. Listen: /o/ /ks/, /oooks/,* ox. *The word is* ox. *Now it is your turn.* Guide children to repeat.

- Help children read simple words with short *o,* such as *on* and *ox*. For children who are ready, extend the lesson by adding a consonant to each word, such as *box, fox, Don,* and *Ron*. Write the letters in the **WorkBoard** boxes and guide children in blending the sounds to read the words.

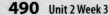

ELL ENGLISH LANGUAGE LEARNERS

Access to Core Content

Content Objective Develop listening comprehension
Language Objective Discuss text using key words and sentence frames
Materials • **ELL Resource Book,** pp. 58–59

PRETEACH BIG BOOK OF EXPLORATIONS

> **All Language Levels**

Use the Interactive Question-Response Guide on **ELL Resource Book** pages 58–59 to preview the **Big Book of Explorations** selection "Helping Hands." Preteach half of the selection on Day 3 and half on Day 4.

Grammar

Content Objective Identify nouns
Language Objective Speak in complete sentences, using sentence frames
Materials • **Listening Library Audio CD** • **Photo Cards**

NAMING WORDS (NOUNS)

> **All Language Levels**

Out to Play
Dad and Sam went out to play,
On a hot and sunny day.
Pam and Matt both came along,
They played and sang this happy song.
Lamb and ram went out to play,
On a hot and sunny day.
Cat and bat both came along,
They played and sang this happy song.

- Review nouns. Remind children that nouns can name people, places, and things. Give examples of each. Point to a child and name him or her. Have children repeat and name another child. Point to the desk and name it. Have children repeat and name another thing.

- Play "Out to Play" from the **Listening Library Audio CD.** Tell children to listen for naming words that name people or animals.

- Point out the naming words that name people or animals: *Dad, Sam, Pam, Matt, lamb, ram, cat,* and *bat.* Say each word and have children tell if it is a person or animal.

PEER DISCUSSION STARTERS

> **All Language Levels**

- Distribute Photo Cards of things friends like, such as *bike, sandwich, dog, kitten,* and *balloon.*

- Pair children and have them complete the sentence frame *I like a _____.* Ask them to expand by providing as many details as they can. For example: *It is _____.* Circulate, listen in, and take note of each child's language use and proficiency.

Big Book of Explorations

Puppet

Approaching Level

Phonemic Awareness

Objective	Blend sounds to form words with /s/ and /p/
Materials	• **Photo Cards:** *map, pen, pie, seal, soap, sock, soup, top*
	• **Puppet** • pocket chart

PHONEME BLENDING

Tier 2

Model

■ Display the **Photo Card** for *map* in the pocket chart. Hold up the **Puppet.** *Listen as Happy says the sounds in a word. First, he'll say each sound: /m/ /a/ p/. Then, he will blend these three sounds together to say the word: /m/ /a/ /p/, /mmmaaap/,* map. *The word is* map. *What is the word?*

Guided Practice/Practice

■ Display the Photo Cards. Have children name each card with you.

■ Point to the Photo Card for *pen. Happy will say the sounds in this word: /p/ /e/ /n/. Now you say the sounds with Happy: /p/ /e/ /n/. Let's blend the sounds with Happy: /p/ /e/ /n/, /peeennn/,* pen. *What's the word?*

■ Repeat the routine with the remaining Photo Cards.

Phonics

Objective	Blend with /s/s and /p/p
Materials	• **Word-Building Cards** • pocket chart

REVIEW SKILLS

Tier 2

Model

■ Place **Word-Building Cards** *a* and *m* in the pocket chart. *The name of this letter is* a. *The letter* a *stands for the /a/ sound. Say /a/. The name of this letter is* m. *The letter stands for the /m/ sound. Say /m/.*

■ *Listen as I blend the two sounds together to say the word: /a/ /m/, /aaammm/,* am. *What's the word?*

■ Place Word-Building Card *S* in front of *am. The name of this letter is* s. *The letter* s *stands for the /s/ sound. Now blend this word with me: /s/ /a/ /m/, /sssaaammm/,* Sam. *What's the word?*

Guided Practice/Practice

■ Distribute small Word-Building Cards *a* and *m.* Have children form *am.* Have them take turns touching each letter and saying the letter sound. Then ask them to blend the sounds and say the word. Repeat with *Sam, Pam, map,* and *sap.*

Approaching Level

Leveled Reader Lesson 1

Objective Read *We Like Painting* to apply skills and strategies

Materials • **Leveled Reader:** *We Like Painting*

Leveled Reader

BEFORE READING

- **Preview** Read the title and the names of the author and illustrator. *Who do you see on the cover? What are they doing?* Have children turn to the title page and point out that it also has the names of the author and illustrator. *What is this child doing? What do you think the book will be about?* Tell children to name unfamiliar items and identify the rebuses.

- **Model Concepts About Print** Use pages 4–5 to demonstrate book handling. *This is the top of the page. This is the bottom. I read the left page first and then the right. I read words from left to right.* Demonstrate the direction with your fingers.

- **Review High-Frequency Words** Write **a**, **I**, **like**, and **we** on chart paper. Have children find each word in the title or on the book pages and point to the word as they read it.

- **Set a Purpose for Reading** *Let's find out what each child likes to paint.*

DURING READING

- Have children turn to page 2 and begin whisper-reading the first two pages.

- Remind children to look for the high-frequency words and to use the rebus pictures and illustrations.

- Monitor children's reading and provide help as needed. Stop during the reading and ask open-ended questions to facilitate discussion, such as: *What animals do the children paint? What does the author show us about the fun of painting?* Build on children's responses to develop deeper understanding of the text.

AFTER READING

- Ask children to point out words they had trouble reading and to share strategies they used to figure them out.

- Have children turn to a partner and ask each other questions about the story. Tell children to respond in complete sentences.

- **Retell** Ask children to retell the story. Help them make a personal connection. *When have you painted? What was it like? How did you do it? What animals do you like to paint?*

ON YOUR OWN

Be an Artist

Have children paint or draw a picture of their favorite animal. Have them label their picture with the sentence *I like a _____.* Help children write animal names.

I like a cat.

Leveled Reader

ELL

Retell Use the Interactive Question-Response Guide Technique to help English Language Learners understand *Hats*. As you read, make meaning clear by pointing to pictures, demonstrating word meaning, paraphrasing text, and asking children questions.

ON YOUR OWN

A Hat of Your Own

Have children write a rebus sentence to tell what kind of hat they like. Have them use the following sentence frame and add a picture of the hat to complete the sentence: *I like a _____.*

On Level

Leveled Reader Lesson 1

Objective Read *Hats* to apply skills and strategies
Materials • **Leveled Reader:** *Hats*

BEFORE READING

- **Preview** Read the title and the names of the author and illustrator. *What kind of animal is on the cover? What is she doing?* Tell children to turn to the title page. Point out that it also has the title and names of the author and illustrator. Have children look at the cover and illustrations and predict what the book will be about.

- **Model Concepts About Print** Demonstrate book handling for children. Guide them as they follow along on pages 2–3. *First, I read the words on the left page. Then, I read the words on the right page. When I read the words, I start on the left and read from left to right.* Indicate the direction with your finger.

- **Review High-Frequency Words** Write **a**, **I**, **like**, **we** and read the words aloud. Have children point to the words in the book.

- **Page Through the Book** Name unfamiliar items and identify the rebus pictures.

- **Set a Purpose for Reading** *Let's find out what kinds of hats the animals like.*

DURING READING

- Remind children to use the rebuses and the illustrations to help them read about the animals and their hats. Tell them to look for high-frequency words as they read.

- Show children how to self-correct if a word doesn't sound right or doesn't make sense in the sentence. *On page 2, I look at the rebus picture, and I think, "We like hat." Then I look at the illustration, and I notice there are a lot of hats in the store window. The rebus picture also shows two hats. So the word is* hats, *not* hat. *"We like hats." That makes sense, and it matches the story picture.*

AFTER READING

- Ask children to identify words they had trouble reading and to share strategies they used. Reinforce good behaviors.

- Have children retell the story and share personal responses. *What kinds of hats do you like? Would you rather wear a pink, blue, purple, or green hat? Why?*

- Have children turn to a partner and ask each other questions about the story. Tell children to respond in complete sentences.

Beyond Level

Leveled Reader Lesson 1

Objective Read *Ice Skating Fun!* to apply skills and strategies
Materials • **Leveled Reader:** *Ice Skating Fun!*

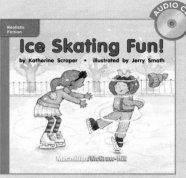

Leveled Reader

BEFORE READING

- **Preview** Read the title and the names of the author and illustrator. Tell children to look at the cover illustration to help them predict what the story will be about. For example, encourage children to ask: *What are the children on the cover doing? Which season is it? How can you tell?* Page through the book with children and pause to name unfamiliar items.

- **Introduce Story Words** Point to the word *plop* on page 5. Read the sentence. Have children use the picture to explain what *plop* means. Repeat with *spin* on page 7.

- **Set a Purpose for Reading** *Let's find out what the girl and her friend do.*

DURING READING

- Remind children that when they come to an unfamiliar word, they can look for familiar chunks in the word, break the word into syllables and sound out each part, or think about what the word might mean. If the word does not sound right or make sense in the sentence, children can self-correct.

- Monitor children's reading and provide help as needed.

AFTER READING

- Ask children to point out words they had trouble reading and to share the strategies they used to figure them out.

- Have children turn to a partner and ask each other questions about the story. Tell children to respond in complete sentences.

- Have children retell the story and share personal responses.

- **Synthesize** *Does Kate's friend learn to skate right away? What do you predict Kate will do if her friend falls down again?*

- Have children work in pairs to discuss times they have tried to do something new. Have them focus on what they did to accomplish the new skill, such as practice often or try very hard.

- **Model** As a group, list words that describe children's experiences. Model using these words to create new lyrics for a familiar melody. For example, to the tune of "Row, Row, Row Your Boat," sing: *Try, try, try your best/Every chance you get./It might be hard, but don't give up/You will do it yet.*

More Fun!

Have children choose something they have fun doing and write about it. Ask them to write a title at the top of the page and draw a picture showing the activity. Then have them write a sentence about the picture.

Dancing Fun!

I can slide.

Leveled Reader

Vocabulary

Preteach Vocabulary Use the routine in the **Visual Vocabulary Resources**, pages 311–312, to preteach the ELL Vocabulary listed on the inside front cover of the Leveled Reader.

ELL ENGLISH LANGUAGE LEARNERS

Leveled Reader

Content Objective Read to apply skills and strategies

Language Objective Retell information using complete sentences

Materials • **Leveled Reader:** *Hats*

BEFORE READING

All Language Levels

- **Preview** Read the title *Hats*. Ask: *What's the title? Say it again.* Repeat with the author's name. Point to the cover illustration and say: *I see hippo trying on lots of hats.* Point to the hippo and hats as you name them. *This hat is purple. This hat is red. Now turn to a partner and tell more about this picture.*

- **Page Through the Book** Use simple language to tell about the photo on each page. Immediately follow up with questions, such as: *Is this a red hat? What animal is this?*

- **Review Skills** Use the inside front cover to review the phonics skill and high-frequency words.

- **Set a Purpose** Say: *Let's read to find out which hat the hippo will buy.*

DURING READING

All Language Levels

- Have children whisper-read each page, or use the differentiated suggestions below. Circulate, listen in, and provide corrective feedback, such as modeling how to accurately pronounce words.

- **Retell** Stop after every two pages and ask children to state what they have learned so far. Reinforce language by restating children's comments when they have difficulty using story-specific words. Provide differentiated sentence frames to support children's responses and engage children in partner-talk where appropriate.

Beginning	Intermediate	Advanced
Echo-Read Have children echo-read after you.	**Choral-Read** Have children choral-read with you.	**Choral-Read** Have children choral-read.
Check Comprehension Point to pictures and ask questions such as: *Do you see the red hat? Point to the hat. Is this a hippo?*	**Check Comprehension** Ask questions/prompts such as: *Where is the hippo? Which hat is the hippo wearing?*	**Check Comprehension** Ask: *What did the hippo do? Why did the hippo try on so many hats? Why is the hippo having fun?*

ELL ENGLISH LANGUAGE LEARNERS

AFTER READING

All Language Levels

Book Talk Children will work with peers of varying language abilities to discuss their books for this week. Display the four **Leveled Readers** read this week: *Ice Skating Fun!* (Beyond Level), *Hats* (On Level), *We Like Painting* (Approaching Level), and *Hats* (English Language Learners).

Ask the questions and provide the prompts below. Call on children who read each book to answer the questions or respond to the prompt. If appropriate, ask children to find the pages in the book that illustrate their answers.

> • **What are the friends in your book doing?**
> • **Name some of the different things they like.**
> • **What did you learn about the friends in this book?**
> • **How are these friends like your friends? How are they different?**
> • **What do you like to do that you read about in the book? Why do you like to do this?**

Develop Listening and Speaking Skills Tell children to remember the following:

■ Share information in cooperative learning interactions. Remind children to work with their partners to retell the story and complete any activities. Ask: *What happened next in the story?*

■ Employ self-corrective techniques and monitor their own and other children's language production. Children should ask themselves: *What parts of this passage were confusing to me? Can my classmates help me clarify a word or sentence that I don't understand?*

■ Use high-frequency English words to describe people, places, and objects.

■ Narrate, describe, and explain with specificity and detail. Ask: *Where did the story take place? Can you describe the setting? What else did you notice?*

■ Express opinions, ideas, and feelings on a variety of social and academic topics. Ask: *What do you think about the characters in the story?*

Puppet

ELL

Sound-Letter Relationships Provide additional practice in pronouncing the /m/, /s/, /p/ sounds and naming the corresponding letters as children point to them.

Approaching Level

Phonemic Awareness

Objective Categorize words with final /m/, /s/, /p/
Materials
• **Puppet** • pocket chart
• **Photo Cards:** *ant, bus, corn, dime, game, gem, jar, lock, nut, octopus, rope, sheep, top, up, walrus, wheel*

 PHONEME CATEGORIZATION

Tier 2

Model

■ Display the **Photo Cards** for *dime, nut,* and *game. Listen as Happy says the names of these pictures:* dime, nut, game. *Listen for the ending sound in each word:* /d/, /ī/, /m/, dime; /n/, /u/, /t/, nut; /g/, /ā/, /m/, game. Dime *and* game *end with the* /m/ *sound.* Nut *does not end with* /m/. Nut *does not belong. Repeat for final* /s/ *using the words* bus, octopus, jar.

Guided Practice/Practice

■ Display the Photo Cards for *ant, rope, top* in a pocket chart. Have children name each photo with you. Repeat the names, emphasizing the final sound. Ask children which word does not belong. Repeat using the words *dime, gem, lock; sheep, corn, up; wheel, bus, walrus.*

Phonics

Objectives Identify initial /m/m, /s/s, /p/p; build fluency
Materials
• **Photo Cards:** *man, map, moon, mop, mouse, pen, penguin, piano, pie, pizza, pumpkin, saw, seal, soap, sock, soup, sun* • pocket chart
• **Word-Building Cards** • **Sound-Spelling WorkBoards**

 BUILD FLUENCY: LETTER-SOUND CORRESPONDENCE

Tier 2

Model

■ Display **Word-Building Cards** *m, s,* and *p* in the pocket chart. Place the **Photo Cards** facedown. Pick a card, name the picture, and say the beginning sound. Then place it in the pocket chart under the corresponding letter.

Guided Practice/Practice

■ Have each child pick a Photo Card, say the picture name, identify the beginning sound, and place it in the pocket chart under the corresponding letter. Guide practice with the first card.

Build Fluency

■ Display the Word-Building Cards for *m, s, p.* Have children name the letter as quickly as they can. Then ask them to write the letters *m, s,* and *p* on their **WorkBoards** several times as they say /m/, /s/, and /p/.

Approaching Level

Leveled Reader Library

Leveled Reader Lesson 2

Objective Reread *We Like Painting* to reinforce fluency and identifying character

Materials • **Leveled Reader:** *We Like Painting*

FOCUS ON FLUENCY

- Tell children that you will read one page of the book and they should read that page right after you. They should follow along in their books and try to read at the same speed and with the same expression that you use.

SKILL IDENTIFY CHARACTER

- *Who are the characters in this story? How are the characters alike? How are they different? What are they doing? How do they feel about their work? Where are they? Look at page 8. What might the characters say to each other?*

REREAD BOOKS

- Distribute copies of previously read **Leveled Readers**. Tell children that rereading the books will help them develop their reading skills.

- Circulate and listen in as children read. Stop them periodically and ask them how they are figuring out words or checking their understanding of the story.

High-Frequency Words

Objective Review high-frequency words *a*, *like*, *the*, and *we*

Materials • **High-Frequency Word Cards:** *a, like, the, we*

BUILD WORD AUTOMATICITY: *a, like, the, we*

- Distribute copies of the word **like**. Say the word and have children repeat it. Have children name the letters in the word. Repeat with the words **a**, **we**, and **the**.

- **Build Fluency** Use the High-Frequency Word Cards to review previously taught words. Repeat, guiding children to read more rapidly.

Leveled Reader

Meet Grade-Level Expectations

As an alternative to this day's lesson, guide children through a reading of the On Level Practice Reader. See page 494. Because both books contain the same vocabulary, phonics, and comprehension skills, the scaffolding you provided will help most children gain access to this more challenging text.

ON YOUR OWN

Pick a Favorite

Ask children to choose their favorite animal painting from *We Like Painting*. Have each child write a rebus sentence to name the picture: *I like a [picture of animal]*. Make a class chart that shows children's choices. Use the chart to determine the favorite animal picture.

I like a ____ .

Use Illustrations

Ask children to draw a picture of a new animal wearing a hat. Children can use the illustrations in the Leveled Reader as a model. Have them complete a rebus sentence to tell what the animal would say: *I like a _____.* Ask children to display and read their work.

Leveled Reader

On Level

Leveled Reader Lesson 2

Objective   Reread to apply skills and strategies to retell a story
Materials   • Leveled Reader: *Hats*

BEFORE READING

- Ask children to look through *Hats* and recall what the book is about. Reinforce vocabulary by repeating children's sentences using more sophisticated language. For example: *Yes, the characters in this story like different types of hats.*

DURING READING

- Have children join you in a choral-reading of the story. Model reading with expression. *When I read page 4, I emphasize the type of hat the animal likes by saying the word* pink *a little stronger than the other words. I use the same strong voice when I read* blue *and* purple *on pages 5 and 6. I do this to emphasize which hat each animal likes to wear.* Ask children to use the same kind of expression when they read.

- Assign each child a page. Have children practice by whisper-reading. *Follow along as other children read, and be ready to come in when it is your turn. Remember, speak one at a time and use lots of expression.*

AFTER READING

- Have children retell the selection in their own words. *What questions did you ask yourself to help you understand the story?*

- *Who are the characters in this story? How are they alike? Which character likes a pink hat? Which one likes a blue hat? Who likes a purple hat? What color hat does the giraffe like? What are the reasons that each animal in the story likes a different hat?*

Beyond Level

Leveled Reader Library

Leveled Reader Lesson 2

Objective Reread to apply skills and strategies to retell a story

Materials • **Leveled Reader:** *Ice Skating Fun!*

BEFORE READING

- Ask children to look back at *Ice Skating Fun!* and recall what happens in the story. *Describe your favorite character in the book. Why do you like that character?*

DURING READING

- Assign each child a page of the book to read aloud. Have children practice by whisper-reading. *Follow along as each child reads, and be ready to come in when it is your turn. Remember, use lots of expression.*

AFTER READING

- Explain that by asking questions as you read, you can better understand what is happening in a story. Model the strategy: *Kate's friend is learning to skate. As I begin to read, I see that Kate's friend is wobbly on his skates. I ask myself, what will happen next? Will Kate's friend fall, or will he stay up on the ice? I continue reading to find the answer. Plop! He falls!*

- *What questions did you ask as you read?* Have children share some of the questions they asked when reading. Have them tell how they found the answers.

Expand Vocabulary

Objectives Learn and apply the meaning of the new words *spin* and *plop*; brainstorm other words related to skating

Materials • **Leveled Reader:** *Ice Skating Fun!*

ENRICH: *spin, plop*

Gifted & Talented

- Write the words *spin* and *plop* on cards. Display *spin* and read aloud the sentence *Kate can spin.* Have children point to *spin* in the **Leveled Reader**. *Why is it easy to fall if you spin on ice?*

- Ask children to use the picture to determine what it means to *spin*. (turn around quickly) Have children demonstrate a spin. Ask them to use *spin* in sentences. Then repeat with *plop*.

- Brainstorm with children the names of other words that relate to ice skating, such as *skate, ice, glide,* and *twirl*. Record the words in a word list titled "Ice Skating Words."

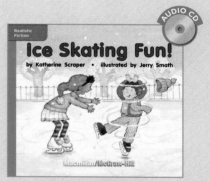

ELL   ENGLISH LANGUAGE LEARNERS

Fluency

Content Objectives Reread Pre-decodable Readers to develop fluency; develop speaking skills

Language Objective Tell a partner what a selection is about

Materials • **Pre-decodable Readers:** *I Like, We Like; Pam*

REREAD FOR FLUENCY

Beginning

- Review the high-frequency words **like**, **a**, **we**, **can**, and **the** using the **Read/Spell/Write** routine.

Intermediate/Advanced

- Use each word in a sentence that illustrates its use, such as: *Do you like the book?* Hold up a book and have children answer yes or no. *We can read a book.* Have the whole group act out reading a book.

All Language Levels

- Guide children through a choral-reading of *I Like, We Like* and *Pam*. Model how to read dialogue with appropriate expression. For example, read the words *I like pizza* in the book *I Like, We Like* by emphasizing the word *pizza* to show how the boy might sound. Have children chorally repeat the sentence with appropriate expression.

DEVELOP SPEAKING/LISTENING SKILLS

All Language Levels

- Have children reread *I Like, We Like* and *Pam* to a partner. Remind them to listen carefully and follow along in their book as their partner is reading. Work with children to read with accuracy and appropriate expression.

- Ask children to tell their partner about the pictures on each page. Then have the other partner describe the pictures. Circulate, listen in, and provide additional language as needed.

Beginning	Intermediate	Advanced
Confirm Understanding Point to the pictures for partners to identify. Ask: *What do you see?* Restate the correct answer in a complete sentence.	**Share Preferences** Ask partners to tell you which is their favorite picture in the book. Prompt them to explain why it is their favorite picture.	**Compare and Contrast** Have partners compare two different pictures and describe them. Prompt them to explain how they are alike and different.

ELL ENGLISH LANGUAGE LEARNERS

High-Frequency Words

Content Objective Spell high-frequency words correctly

Language Objective Write in complete sentences, using sentence frames

Materials • **Sound-Spelling WorkBoards** • **Sound-Spelling Cards** • **Photo Cards**

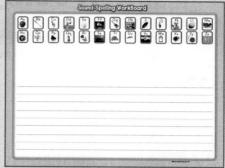

Sound-Spelling WorkBoard

Beginning/Intermediate

- Write the high-frequency words **like** and **a** on the board. Have children copy the words on their **WorkBoards**. Then help them say, then write, a sentence for the words. Provide the sentence starter *I like a* _____.

Advanced

- Children should first orally state their sentence. Correct as needed. Then they can draw a picture to complete the sentence. For children who are ready, help them spell words using their growing knowledge of English sound-spelling relationships. Model how to segment the word children are trying to spell and attach a spelling to each sound. Use the **Sound-Spelling Cards** to reinforce the spellings for each English sound.

Writing

All Language Levels

- Dictate the following sounds and ask children to write the letters: /s/, /p/. Have them write each letter five times as they say /s/ and /p/. Demonstrate correct letter formation, as needed.

- Then display a set of **Photo Cards**. Select at least five cards whose picture names begin with /s/ (seal, six, sun, star, sock) and five whose picture names begin with /p/ (pen, pie, pizza, pumpkin, penny).

- Say the name of each card, stretching the initial sound to emphasize it. You may also need to reinforce the meaning of each word and model correct mouth formation when forming the sound. Use the articulation pictures and prompts on the back of the small Sound-Spelling Cards for support. Tell children that you want them to write the first letter in each picture's name on their WorkBoards.

Phonemic Awareness/ Phonics

For English Language Learners who need more practice with this week's phonemic awareness and phonics skills, see the Approaching Level lessons. Focus on minimal contrasts, articulation, and those sounds that do not transfer from the child's first language to English. For a complete listing of transfer sounds, see pages T10–T31.

End-of-Week Assessment

Weekly Assessment

Use your Quick Check observations and the assessment opportunities identified below to evaluate children's progress in key skill areas.

Skills	Quick Check Observations	Pencil and Paper Assessment
PHONEMIC AWARENESS/ PHONICS /s/s, /p/p **s p**	439	Activity Book, pp. 24, 29–30, 32 Practice Book, pp. 47, 57
HIGH-FREQUENCY WORDS *like, a* **like a**	460	Activity Book, pp. 27–28 Practice Book, pp. 55–56
COMPREHENSION Identify Character	450	Activity Book, pp. 25, 31 Practice Book, p. 54

Quick Check Rubric

Skills	1	2	3
PHONEMIC AWARENESS/ PHONICS	Does not connect the /s/, /p/ sounds with the letters *Ss, Pp* and has difficulty blending the CVC words *Sam, Pam, map,* and *sap*.	Usually connects the /s/, /p/ sounds with the letters *Ss, Pp* and blends the CVC words *Sam, Pam, map,* and *sap* with only occasional support.	Consistently connects the /s/, /p/ sounds with the letters *Ss, Pp* and blends the CVC words *Sam, Pam, map,* and *sap*.
HIGH-FREQUENCY WORDS	Does not identify the high-frequency words.	Usually recognizes the high-frequency words with accuracy, but not speed.	Consistently recognizes the high-frequency words with speed and accuracy.
COMPREHENSION	Does not identify character using the pictures and text.	Usually identifies characters using the pictures and text.	Consistently identifies characters using the pictures and text.

DIBELS LINK

PROGRESS MONITORING
Use your DIBELS results to inform instruction.
IF...
Initial Sound Fluency (ISF)   0–7

THEN...
Evaluate for Intervention

TPRI LINK

PROGRESS MONITORING
Use your TPRI scores to inform instruction.
IF...
Phonemic Awareness   Still Developing
Graphophonemic Knowledge   Still Developing
Listening Comprehension   Still Developing

THEN...
Evaluate for Intervention

Diagnose		Prescribe
Review the assessment answers with children. Have them correct their errors. Then provide additional instruction as needed.		
PHONEMIC AWARENESS/ PHONICS /s/s, /p/p	**IF...** **Quick Check Rubric:** Children consistently score 1 or **Pencil and Paper Assessment:** Children get 0–2 items correct	**THEN...** Reteach Phonemic Awareness and Phonics Skills using the **Phonemic Awareness** and **Phonics Intervention Teacher's Editions**. *SPIRAL REVIEW* Use the Build Fluency lesson in upcoming weeks to provide children practice reading words with /p/p.
HIGH-FREQUENCY WORDS like, a	**Quick Check Rubric:** Children consistently score 1 or **Pencil and Paper Assessment:** Children get 0–2 items correct	Reteach High-Frequency Words using the **Phonics Intervention Teacher's Edition**. *SPIRAL REVIEW* Use the High-Frequency Words lesson in upcoming weeks to provide children practice reading the word a.
COMPREHENSION Skill: Identify Character	**Quick Check Rubric:** Children consistently score 1 or **Pencil and Paper Assessment:** Children get 0–2 items correct	Reteach Comprehension Skill using the **Comprehension Intervention Teacher's Edition**.

Response to Intervention

To place children in Tier 2 or Tier 3 Intervention use the *Diagnostic Assessment*.

- Phonemic Awareness
- Phonics
- Vocabulary
- Comprehension
- Fluency

Use this page to record lessons that work well or need to be adapted for future reference.

Lessons that work well

Lessons that need adjustments

Use this page to record lessons that work well or need to be adapted for future reference.

Lessons that work well.

Lessons that need adjustments.

Unit 2 Computer Literacy

Objectives

- Learn about the Internet
- Learn about appropriate multimedia resources
- Use the mouse and keyboard to enter information

Materials

- www.macmillanmh.com

Vocabulary

arrow keys the buttons that move the cursor up, down, left, or right inside a document

cursor the little arrow that moves when the mouse moves

drag to hold down the mouse button while moving the mouse

click to press and then let go of the mouse button

space bar a long, horizontal key on the keyboard used to put spaces in a document

electronic reference information that is stored on a CD-ROM or on the Internet, such as an encyclopedia or dictionary

Computer Literacy
Focus on Keyboard and Internet Skills and Media Literacy
www.macmillanmh.com

Remind children not to bang on the keyboard, monitor, or mouse.

Computer Literacy
Using the Mouse and Keyboard

ACCESS PRIOR KNOWLEDGE

Discuss with children and encourage them to answer in complete sentences:

- *What part of the computer looks like a mouse?*

- *What are some of the things we can do on a computer with a mouse?*

EXPLAIN

- Remind children that the keyboard and mouse are used to enter information into the computer.

- Talk with children about how to move around a computer using the mouse.

- Tell children about the **arrow keys** on a keyboard. Explain how we use the arrow keys to move around.

MODEL

- Show children how the **cursor** moves across the computer screen when they move the mouse. Teach them how to **drag** an object on the screen.

- Tell children they will mainly use the left button on the mouse. Show them the difference between a left **click** and a right click.

- Point out the keyboard to children. Show them the arrow keys and **space bar**. Model how to use the space bar.

Technology Makes a Difference

Explain that:

▶ **Electronic references**, such as a CD-ROM or the Internet, can be used to find information. Discuss the differences between print and electronic references.

▶ Interactive books and multimedia dictionaries and encyclopedias are all examples of electronic references.

▶ Not all information found on a computer is appropriate for children. Always get permission from an adult before using a computer.

Media Literacy

In the News: Headlines

ACCESS PRIOR KNOWLEDGE

Discuss with children:

- *How is a newspaper headline like the title of a book?*

- *In your opinion, what makes a good title or headline?*

- *Why are headlines an important part of a newspaper article?*

EXPLAIN

Introduce the lesson vocabulary by discussing each word and its definition with children.

- A **headline** is the text at the top of a **newspaper** article, indicating what the article below it will be about.

- Headlines are usually written in text that is **bold** and larger than the article text. Headlines on the **front page** of a newspaper are often written in all capital letters.

- Many people decide whether or not they will read a newspaper **article** based on how interesting the headline of the article is.

MODEL

- Collect a variety of news articles that will be of interest to children from local or national newspapers or from online news sources.

- Read the articles aloud to children. Ask children to state the main idea of the article and then to volunteer a headline reflecting the article's main idea.

- Compare the children's headlines with the original headlines of the articles. Ask: *Do our headlines match the actual headlines? Do they express the same ideas as the newspaper headlines? Are our headlines an improvement on the actual headlines?* Remind children that headlines should reflect the main idea of the article.

- With children, make a list of events that have taken place in your classroom in the last week. Have children brainstorm a headline for each event. Remind children that their headlines should be interesting and exciting so that people will want to learn more about the event.

Objectives

- **Identify newspaper headlines**
- **Consider the main ideas of news stories**
- **Write headlines that reflect the main idea of a news story**

Materials

- a variety of newspaper articles

Media Literacy Activities
Lessons that help children identify and explore the use of headlines in news media

Theme Project Wrap-Up
Research/Organizing and Presenting Ideas

After children complete their projects, they can have a Friendship Day to present what they have learned.

 Step 3 Review and Evaluate

How do I share what I have learned?

These checklists and the Scoring Rubric will help you and children assess their projects.

Teacher's Checklist

Assess the Research Process

Plan the Project
- ✔ Participated in identifying qualities of friendship.
- ✔ Identified appropriate research tools to answer questions.
- ✔ Used multiple sources to gather information.

Do the Project
- ✔ Identified informational genre.
- ✔ Gathered evidence from text sources.
- ✔ Chose an appropriate form to present information.

Assess the Presentation

Speaking
- ✔ Compared ideas from informational texts.
- ✔ Spoke clearly and audibly.
- ✔ Demonstrated correct sentence structure and verb tense.

Representing
- ✔ Summarized and shared findings visually and orally.
- ✔ Used pictures and photos appropriate for the topic.
- ✔ Used visuals in conjunction with writing to document research.

Assess the Listener

Listening
- ✔ Listened attentively.
- ✔ Waited until speaker finished before asking clarifying questions.

Children's Checklist

Research Process
- ✔ Where did you find the best project ideas?
- ✔ Did you ask questions if you did not understand something?

Presenting

Speaking
- ✔ Did you stand still while you spoke?
- ✔ Did you speak in a clear voice and use complete sentences?

Representing
- ✔ How did you decide what visuals to use?
- ✔ Did your visuals and writing help the audience understand your research?

SCORING RUBRIC FOR THEME PROJECT

4 Excellent	3 Good	2 Fair	1 Unsatisfactory
The child	The child	The child	The child
• presents the main idea with supporting details; • may make sophisticated observations; • presents accurate, well-produced visuals that enhance the topic.	• clearly fulfills all the steps of the project; • provides adequate details; • makes several relevant observations.	• attempts to present some of the required steps; • demonstrates some difficulty with research; • may make somewhat unclear observations.	• does not appear to grasp the task in its entirety; • has great difficulty with organizational skills; • presents unnecessary or inaccurate information.

Home-School Connection

Have family members attend Friendship Day. This is an excellent opportunity for home and community involvement.

Big Question Wrap-Up

Review the Big Question for this unit with the children. Discuss what they learned about friends. Help them respond to the following questions: *What activities can friends do together? What activities do you do with your friends? What do you think makes a good friend?* Remind children to take turns when speaking.

Administer the Test

Unit 2 TEST

TESTED SKILLS AND STRATEGIES

COMPREHENSION STRATEGIES AND SKILLS

- Strategy: Ask questions
- Skills: Identify character, compare and contrast

HIGH-FREQUENCY WORDS

- *like, a*

PHONEMIC AWARENESS

- Phoneme isolation (initial /s/, /p/)
- Phoneme blending

PHONICS

- *s, p*

CONCEPT WORDS

- Color words

Use Multiple Assessments for Instructional Planning

To create instructional profiles for your children, look for patterns in the results from any of the following assessments.

Running Records

Use the instructional reading level determined by the Running Record calculations for regrouping decisions.

Benchmark Assessments

Administer tests three times a year as an additional measure of both children's progress and the effectiveness of the instructional program.

Analyze the Data

Use information from a variety of informal and formal assessments, as well as your own judgment, to assist in your instructional planning. Children who consistently score at the lowest end of each range should be evaluated for Intervention. Use the **Diagnostic Assessment** for guidelines in the **Intervention Teacher's Editions**.

Diagnose		Prescribe
ASSESSMENTS	**IF...**	**THEN...**
UNIT TEST	0–15 Correct	Reteach skills using the **Intervention Teacher's Editions**.

For users of DIBELS

Use the results from the DIBELS Progress Monitoring tests to confirm instructional decisions.

DIBELS LINK

PROGRESS MONITORING

Use your DIBELS results to inform instruction.

IF...

Initial **S**ound **F**luency (**ISF**)	0–7
Phoneme **S**egmentation **F**luency (**PSF**)	Start midyear

THEN...
Evaluate for Intervention

For users of TPRI

Use the scores from the TPRI as a progress monitoring tool to confirm instructional decisions.

TPRI LINK

PROGRESS MONITORING

Use your TPRI scores to inform instruction.

IF...

Phonemic Awareness	Still Developing
Graphophonemic Knowledge	Still Developing
Listening Comprehension	Still Developing

THEN...
Evaluate for Intervention

Response to Intervention

To place children in Tier 2 or Tier 3 Intervention use the *Diagnostic Assessment*.

- Phonemic Awareness
- Phonics
- Vocabulary
- Comprehension
- Fluency

Additional Resources

Contents

Instructional Routines

Professional Development

- Read the routine prior to using *Treasures*. Use the Routine QuickNotes as a reminder of key routine steps throughout Unit 1, or as needed.

- View the online classroom video clip through **TeacherWorks Plus**. Watch master teachers use these routines.

1. **Phonological Awareness/ Phonemic Awareness**
   Rhyme
   Oddity Tasks
   Sound Categorization
   Oral Blending
   Oral Segmentation
   Manipulation

2. **Phonics**
   Blending
   Introducing Sound-Spelling Cards
   Letter Recognition
   Building Words
   Building Fluency
   Reading Decodables
   Multisyllabic Words Routine

3. **Fluency**
   Strategies

4. **Vocabulary**
   Define/Example/Ask Routine
   Strategies

5. **High-Frequency Words**
   Read/Spell/Write Routine
   Reading Pre-decodables

6. **Spelling**
   Dictation

7. **Comprehension**
   Strategies
   Skills
   Reading Big Books
   Reading Student Book

8. **Writing**
   Conferences
   Revision Assignments
   Writing Process
   Using Rubrics
   Using Anchor Papers
   Writers' Express Sequence

9. **Research Process**
   Big Question Board

10. **Classroom Management**
    Workstation Flip Charts
    Contracts
    Centers
    Small Groups

11. **Listening/Speaking/Viewing**

12. **Assessment**

Additional Readings

By the Authors and Illustrators

For additional information on authors, illustrators, and selection content, go to www.macmillanmh.com.

Grejniec, Michael. *Good Morning, Good Night.* North-South, 1997. A girl and a boy go about their day and through their experiences show the reader a range of opposites, such as far/close and low/high, through magnified watercolor compositions.

Related to the Theme

Use these and other classroom or library resources to provide additional read alouds to build academic language.

Aliki. *We Are Best Friends.* HarperTrophy, 1982. When Robert's best friend moves away, he is very unhappy, but he learns that he can make new friends and still have old friends.

Carle, Eric. *Do You Want to Be My Friend?* HarperFestival, 1995. A little mouse goes from animal to animal and asks a horse, a peacock, and an alligator, "Do you want to be my friend?"

Hobbie, Holly. *Toot and Puddle.* Little, Brown, 1997. Two friends live happily together but are clearly different in their ideas for adventure.

Howe, James. *Horace and Morris but Mostly Dolores.* Simon & Schuster, 2001. Three mice friends learn that the best clubs include everyone.

Rohmann, Eric. *My Friend Rabbit.* Roaring Brook Press, 2002. Mouse and Rabbit are very good friends, but somehow trouble follows Rabbit wherever he goes.

Waddell, Martin. *Hi, Harry.* Candlewick Press, 2003. A tortoise needs to find someone to play with at his own speed.

Ford, Miela. *Sunflower.* **Greenwillow, 1995.** This is a story about spring and a young girl as she plants, waters, and watches her sunflower grow.	**Jahn-Clough, Lisa.** *My Friend and I.* **Houghton Mifflin, 2003.** Two young friends, a boy and a girl, have a dispute over a toy and discover that friendship is about sharing and forgiveness.

Carlson, Nancy. *My Best Friend Moved Away.* **Viking, 2001.** When her best friend moves away, a young girl wonders how she will ever have fun with anyone again.	**Cousins, Lucy.** *Maisy Cleans Up.* **Candlewick Press, 2002.** Maisy the mouse and her friend Charley clean her house together, and as a reward they treat themselves to cupcakes.
Cohen, Miriam. *Will I Have a Friend?* **Aladdin, 1989.** It's the first day of school, and Jim wonders if he'll find a new friend.	**Elliott, Laura Malone.** *Hunter's Best Friend at School.* **HarperCollins, 2002.** Hunter, the raccoon, learns a valuable lesson about friendship.
Fisher, Valorie. *My Big Brother.* **Atheneum, 2002.** Photographs and simple text depict what a big brother looks like through the eyes of his baby sibling.	**Heide, Florence Parry.** *That's What Friends Are For.* **Candlewick Press, 2003.** Opossum has to inform his animal friends that a good friend is supposed to help, not just give advice.
Fox, Mem. *Hunwick's Egg.* **Harcourt, 2004.** Hunwick, a bandicoot, makes a new friend when he finds a beautiful egg and gives it a home.	**Howe, James.** *Horace and Morris but Mostly Dolores.* **Atheneum, 1999.** When three close friends find that they all can't join the same club, they each realize that they miss playing together.
Hutchins, Pat. *Titch and Daisy.* **Greenwillow, 1996.** Titch hides in one place after another because he can't find his friend Daisy at the party, until he discovers Daisy hiding because she can't find him.	**Lionni, Leo.** *Little Blue and Little Yellow.* **HarperTrophy, 1995.** Little Blue and Little Yellow have a great time together, but one day they can't find each other. When they finally meet up, they hug each other so hard that they become green.
Pak, Soyung. *Sumi's First Day of School Ever.* **Viking, 2003.** It's a strange and lonely day when Sumi, a young girl from Korea, begins school, until she makes a new friend.	**Minarik, Else Holmelund.** *Little Bear's Friend.* **HarperTrophy, 1984.** One summer Little Bear makes friends with a young girl, Emily, and her doll, Lucy.

Theme Bibliography

Selection Honors, Prizes, and Awards

What Do You Like?
by *Michael Grejniec*

Parents' Choice Silver Honor (1995)

Friends All Around
by *Miela Ford*

Author: *Miela Ford*, winner of the Please Touch Book Award (1992) from the Philadelphia Please Touch Museum for *Children for Bear Play* and (1996) for *Follow the Leader*

Simon and Molly plus Hester
by *Lisa Jahn-Clough*

Author: *Lisa Jahn-Clough*, winner of the Parents' Choice Honor Book (2000) for *Missing Molly; Child Magazine* Best Kids' Books (1999) for *My Friend and I*

Resources

Audio Bookshelf
44 Ocean View Drive
Middletown, RI 02842
800-234-1713
www.audiobookshelf.com

Discovery Communications
4540 Preslyn Drive
Raleigh, NC 27616
888-892-3484

Dorling Kindersley
375 Hudson Street
New York, NY 10014
Tel: 800-631-8571
Fax: 201-256-0000
http://us.dk.com

Great Plains National Instructional Television Library
GPN Educational Media
1407 Fleet Street
Baltimore, MD 21231
800-228-4630
http://shopgpn.com

Innovative Educators
P.O. Box 520
Montezuma, GA 31063
888-252-KIDS
Fax: 888-536-8553
www.innovative-educators.com

Library Video Co.
P.O. Box 580
Wynnewood, PA 19096
800-843-3620
www.libraryvideo.com

Listening Library
400 Hahn Road
Westminster, MD 21157
800-243-4504

Live Oak Media
P.O. Box 652
Pine Plains, NY 12567
800-788-1121
www.liveoakmedia.com

Macmillan/McGraw-Hill
220 East Danieldale Road
DeSoto, TX 75115-9960
Tel: 800-442-9685
Fax: 972-228-1982
www.macmillanmh.com

MCA Video
MCA Records/Universal Studios
100 Universal City Plaza
Universal City, CA 91608
818-777-1000

Microsoft Corp.
One Microsoft Way
Redmond, WA 98052
800-426-9000
www.microsoft.com

National Geographic Society
1145 17th Street N.W.
Washington, DC 20036
800-647-5463
www.nationalgeographic.com

Recorded Books
270 Skipjack Road
Prince Frederick, MD 20678
800-636-3399
www.recordedbooks.com

Sunburst Communications
Sunburst Technology
1550 Executive Drive
Elgin, IL 60123
888-492-8817
www.sunburst.com

SVE & Churchill Media
6465 North Avondale Avenue
Chicago, IL 60631
800-253-2788

Tom Snyder Productions
100 Talcott Avenue
Watertown, MA 02472
800-342-0236
www.tomsnyder.com

Weston Woods
143 Main Street
Norwalk, CT 06851
800-243-5020
www.teacher.scholastic.com/products/
westonwoods/

Web Sites

Go to www.macmillanmh.com.
Use the zip code finder to locate other resources in your area.

The Academy of Natural Sciences
http://www.ansp.org/

Acadia National Park
http://www.nps.gov/acad

Agriculture in the Classroom
http://www.agclassroom.org/

Arches National Park
http://www.nps.gov/arch

Asian American History Resources Online - CET
http://www.cetel.org/res.html

Association of Zoos and Aquariums
http://www.aza.org/

Bronx Zoo
http://www.bronxzoo.com/

Cincinnati Zoo
http://www.cincinnatizoo.org/

Colonial Williamsburg
http://www.history.org/

Denali National Park and Preserve
http://www.nps.gov/dena

Ellis Island
http://www.ellisisland.org/

Glacier National Park
http://www.nps.gov/glac

Grand Canyon National Park
http://www.nps.gov/grca

Grand Teton National Park
http://www.nps.gov/grte

High Museum of Art, Atlanta
http://www.high.org/

International Civil Rights Center and Museum
http://www.sitinmovement.org/

Japanese American National Museum
http://www.janm.org/

K12Station – Library of K–12 Education Links
http://www.k12station.com/k12link_library.html

Kids.gov
http://www.kids.gov/

KidsHealth in the Classroom
http://classroom.kidshealth.org/

Meteorology
http://www.wxdude.com/

The Metropolitan Museum of Art, New York
http://www.metmuseum.org/

Minneapolis Institute of Arts
http://www.artsmia.org/

Minnesota Zoo
http://www.mnzoo.com/

MoMA | The Museum of Modern Art
http://www.moma.org/

Monterey Bay Aquarium
www.montereybayaquarium.org

Mount Rushmore National Memorial
http://www.nps.gov/moru

Museum of Fine Arts, Boston
http://www.mfa.org/

Museum of Science, Boston
http://www.mos.org/

Museum of Science and Industry, Chicago
http://www.msichicago.org/

NASA
http://www.nasa.gov/

NASA Kids' Club
http://www.nasa.gov/audience/forkids/kidsclub/flash/index.html

National Air and Space Museum
http://www.nasm.si.edu/

National Civil Rights Museum
http://www.civilrightsmuseum.org/home.htm

National Museum of African American History and Culture
http://nmaahc.si.edu/

National Museum of American History
http://americanhistory.si.edu/

National Museum of the American Indian
http://www.nmai.si.edu/

National Museum of Women in the Arts
http://www.nmwa.org/

National Music Museum
http://www.usd.edu/smm/

National Park Service
http://www.nps.gov/

National Weather Service Education Resources
http://www.nws.noaa.gov/om/edures.shtml

National Women's History Museum
http://www.nwhm.org/

National Zoo
http://nationalzoo.si.edu/

Native American Facts for Kids: Resources on American Indians for Children and Teachers
http://www.native-languages.org/kids.htm

New England Aquarium
http://www.neaq.org/index.php

New York Aquarium
http://www.nyaquarium.com/

Newseum
http://www.newseum.org/

Omaha's Henry Doorly Zoo
http://www.omahazoo.com/

Philadelphia Museum of Art
http://www.philamuseum.org/

Philadelphia Zoo
http://www2.philadelphiazoo.org/

Plimoth Plantation
http://www.plimoth.org/

Redwood National and State Parks
http://www.nps.gov/redw

Rocky Mountain National Park
http://www.nps.gov/romo

Saint Louis Art Museum
http://www.slam.org/

San Diego Zoo
http://www.sandiegozoo.com/

San Francisco Museum of Modern Art
http://www.sfmoma.org/

Shedd Aquarium
http://www.sheddaquarium.org/

Smithsonian Education
http://www.smithsonianeducation.org/

Smithsonian: Science and Technology
http://www.si.edu/Encyclopedia_SI/science_and_technology/

Space Center Houston
http://www.spacecenter.org/

Tennessee Aquarium
http://www.tennis.org/

United States Holocaust Memorial Museum
http://www.ushmm.org/

University of California Museum of Paleontology
http://www.ucmp.berkeley.edu/

The White House Historical Association
http://www.whitehousehistory.org/

Yellowstone National Park
http://www.nps.gov/yell

Yosemite National Park
http://www.nps.gov/yose

Zion National Park
http://www.nps.gov/zion

Web Sites

Web Sites   T7

High-Frequency Words	UNIT/WEEK
I	Start Smart Week 1
can	Start Smart Week 2
we	Unit 1 Week 1
the	Unit 1 Week 2
like	Unit 2 Week 1
a	Unit 2 Week 2
see	Unit 3 Week 1
go	Unit 3 Week 2
to	Unit 4 Week 1
have	Unit 4 Week 2
is	Unit 5 Week 1
play	Unit 5 Week 2
are	Unit 6 Week 1
for	Unit 6 Week 2
you	Unit 6 Week 2
this	Unit 7 Week 1
do	Unit 7 Week 1
and	Unit 7 Week 2
what	Unit 7 Week 2
little	Unit 8 Week 1
said	Unit 8 Week 1
here	Unit 8 Week 2
was	Unit 8 Week 2
she	Unit 9 Week 1
he	Unit 9 Week 1
has	Unit 9 Week 2
look	Unit 9 Week 2
with	Unit 10 Week 1
my	Unit 10 Week 1
me	Unit 10 Week 2
where	Unit 10 Week 2

Oral Vocabulary

Week		Theme Words	Oral Vocabulary Card Words	
1	**What Do You Like?**	friend favorite	partner hobby compete	favorite friend
2	**Friends All Around**	game world	pleasant assist honest	world game
3	**Simon and Molly plus Hester**	problem solve	grateful include thoughtful	problem solve

Language Transfers:

The Interaction Between English and Students' Primary Languages

Dr. Jana Echevarria
California State University, Long Beach

Dr. Donald Bear
University of Nevada, Reno

It is important for teachers to understand why English Language Learners (ELLs) use alternative pronunciations for some English words. Many English sounds do not exist or transfer to other languages, so English Language Learners may lack the auditory acuity to "hear" these English sounds and have difficulty pronouncing them. These students are not accustomed to positioning their mouth in a way the sound requires. The charts that appear on the following pages show that there is variation among languages, with some languages having more sounds in common and thus greater transfer to English than others.

For example, an English speaker may be able to pronounce the /r/ in the Spanish word *pero* ("but"), but not the /rr/ trill in *perro* ("dog"). The English speaker may also lack the auditory acuity to detect and the ability to replicate the tonal sounds of some Chinese words. Similarly, a Vietnamese speaker may have difficulty pronouncing /th/ in words such as *thin* or *thanks*.

Further, English Language Learners make grammatical errors due to interference from their native languages. In Spanish, the adjective follows the noun, so often English Language Learners say "the girl pretty" instead of "the pretty girl." While English changes the verb form with a change of subject (*I walk. She walks.*), some Asian languages keep the verb form constant across subjects. Adding /s/ to the third person may be difficult for some English Language Learners. Students may know the grammatical rule, but applying it consistently may be difficult, especially in spoken English.

When working with English Language Learners, you should also be aware of sociocultural factors that affect pronunciation. Students may retain an accent because it marks their social identity. Speakers of other languages may feel at a social distance from members of the dominant English-speaking culture.

English Language Learners improve their pronunciation in a nonthreatening atmosphere in which participation is encouraged. Opportunities to interact with native English speakers provide easy access to language models and give English Language Learners practice using English. However, students should not be forced to participate. Pressure to perform—or to perform in a certain way—can inhibit participation. In any classroom, teacher sensitivity to pronunciation differences contributes to a more productive learning environment.

Phonics, word recognition, and spelling are influenced by what students know about the sounds, word structure, and spelling in their primary languages. For example, beginning readers who speak Spanish and are familiar with its spelling will often spell short *o* with an *a*, a letter that in Spanish makes the short *o* sound. Similarly, English Language Learners who are unaccustomed to English consonant digraphs and blends (e.g., /ch/ and *s*-blends) spell /ch/ as *sh* because /sh/ is the sound they know that is closest to /ch/. Students learn about the way pronunciation influences their reading and spelling, beginning with large contrasts among sounds, then they study the finer discriminations. As vocabulary advances, the meaning of words leads students to the sound contrasts. For example, *shoe* and *chew* may sound alike initially, but meaning indicates otherwise. Students' reading and discussions of what they read advances their word knowledge as well as their knowledge in all language and literacy systems, including phonics, pronunciation, grammar, and vocabulary.

Phonics Transfers:
Sound Transfers

This chart indicates areas where a positive transfer of sounds and symbols occurs for English Language Learners from their native languages into English. This symbol (✔) identifies a positive transfer. "Approximate" indicates that the sound is similar.

Sound Transfers	Spanish	Cantonese	Vietnamese	Hmong	Korean	Khmer
Consonants						
/b/ as in bat	✔	approximate	approximate	approximate	approximate	✔
/k/ as in cake, kitten, peck	✔	✔	✔	✔	✔	✔
/d/ as in dog	✔	approximate	approximate	✔	approximate	✔
/f/ as in farm	✔	✔	✔	✔		
/g/ as in girl	✔	approximate	✔	approximate	approximate	
/h/ as in ham	✔	✔	✔	✔	✔	approximate
/j/ as in jet, page, ledge		approximate	approximate		approximate	
/l/ as in lion	✔	✔	✔	✔	✔	
/m/ as in mat	✔	✔	✔	✔	✔	✔
/n/ as in night	✔	✔	✔	✔	✔	✔
/p/ as in pen	✔	✔	✔	approximate	✔	✔
/kw/ as in queen	✔	approximate	✔		✔	✔
/r/ as in rope	approximate					✔
/s/ as in sink, city	✔	✔	✔	✔	✔	approximate
/t/ as in ton	✔	✔	approximate	approximate	✔	✔
/v/ as in vine	✔		✔	✔		
/w/ as in wind	✔	✔			✔	✔
/ks/ as in six	✔				✔	✔
/y/ as in yak	✔	✔		✔	✔	✔
/z/ as in zebra			✔			
Digraphs						
/ch/ as in cheek, patch	✔	approximate		✔	✔	✔
/sh/ as in shadow			✔	✔	✔	
/hw/ as in whistle					✔	✔
/th/ as in path	approximate		approximate			
/TH/ as in that	approximate					
/ng/ as in sting	✔	✔	✔	✔	✔	approximate

Sound Transfers	Spanish	Cantonese	Vietnamese	Hmong	Korean	Khmer
Short Vowels						
/a/ as in cat	approximate		approximate	✔	✔	
/e/ as in net	✔	approximate	approximate		✔	
/i/ as in kid	approximate	approximate			✔	
/o/ as in spot	approximate	approximate	approximate	approximate	approximate	✔
/u/ as in cup	approximate	approximate	✔		✔	✔
Long Vowels						
/ā/ as in lake, nail, bay	✔	approximate	approximate	approximate	✔	✔
/ē/ as in bee, meat, cranky	✔	approximate	✔	✔	✔	✔
/ī/ as in kite, tie, light, dry	✔	approximate	✔	✔	✔	✔
/ō/ as in home, road, row	✔	approximate	approximate		✔	
/ū/ as in dune, fruit, blue	✔	approximate	✔	✔	✔	✔
/yü/ as in mule, cue	✔	approximate			✔	
r-Controlled Vowels						
/är/ as in far	approximate	approximate				
/ôr/ as in corn	approximate	approximate				
/ûr/ as in stern, bird, suburb	approximate	approximate				
/âr/ as in air, bear						
/îr/ as in deer, ear						
Variant Vowels						
/oi/ as in boil, toy	✔	approximate	approximate		✔	✔
/ou/ as in loud, down	✔	approximate	✔	approximate	✔	✔
/ô/ as in law	approximate	✔	✔	approximate	approximate	✔
/ô/ as in laundry	approximate	approximate	✔	approximate	approximate	✔
/ôl/ as in salt, call	approximate	approximate			approximate	✔
/ü/ as in moon, drew	✔	approximate	approximate	✔	✔	✔
/u̇/ as in look		approximate	approximate		approximate	✔
/ə/ as in askew			approximate		✔	

Phonics Transfers:
Sound-Symbol Match

Sound-Symbol Match	Spanish	Cantonese	Vietnamese	Hmong	Korean	Khmer
Consonants						
/b/ as in bat	✔		✔			
/k/ as in cake	✔		✔			
/k/ as in kitten	✔		✔	✔		
/k/ as in peck						
/d/ as in dog	✔		✔	✔		
/f/ as in farm	✔			✔		
/g/ as in girl	✔		✔			
/h/ as in ham			✔	✔		
/j/ as in jet, page, ledge						
/l/ as in lion	✔		✔	✔		
/m/ as in mat	✔		✔	✔		
/n/ as in night	✔		✔	✔		
/p/ as in pen	✔		✔	✔		
/kw/ as in queen			✔			
/r/ as in rope	approximate					
/s/ as in sink, city	✔		✔			
/t/ as in ton	✔		✔	✔		
/v/ as in vine	✔		✔	✔		
/w/ as in wind	✔					
/ks/ as in six	✔					
/y/ as in yak	✔			✔		
/z/ as in zebra						
Digraphs						
/ch/ as in cheek, patch	✔					
/sh/ as in shadow						
/hw/ as in whistle						
/th/ as in path			✔			
/TH/ as in that						
/ng/ as in sting	✔		✔			
Short Vowels						
/a/ as in cat			✔	✔		
/e/ as in net	✔		✔			
/i/ as in kid						
/o/ as in spot			✔	✔		
/u/ as in cup						

Sound-Symbol Match	Spanish	Cantonese	Vietnamese	Hmong	Korean	Khmer
Long Vowels						
/ā/ as in lake						
/ā/ as in nail						
/ā/ as in bay						
/ē/ as in bee						
/ē/ as in meat						
/ē/ as in cranky						
/ī/ as in kite, tie, light, dry						
/ō/ as in home, road, row						
/ū/ as in dune			✔	✔		
/ū/ as in fruit, blue						
/yü/ as in mule, cue						
***r*-Controlled Vowels**						
/är/ as in far	✔					
/ôr/ as in corn	✔					
/ûr/ as in stern	✔					
/ûr/ as in bird, suburb						
/âr/ as in air, bear						
/îr/ as in deer, ear						
Variant Vowels						
/oi/ as in boil	✔		✔			
/oi/ as in toy	✔					
/ou/ as in loud						
/ou/ as in down						
/ô/ as in law						
/ô/ as in laundry						
/ôl/ as in salt	✔					
/ôl/ as in call						
/ü/ as in moon, drew						
/ú/ as in look						
/ə/ as in askew						

How to Use the Phonics Transfer Charts

To read and speak fluently in English, English Language Learners need to master a wide range of phonemic awareness, phonics, and word study skills. The Phonics Transfer Charts are designed to help you anticipate and understand possible student errors in pronouncing or perceiving English sounds.

1. Highlight Transferrable Skills If the phonics skill transfers from the student's primary language to English, state that during the lesson. In most lessons an English Language Learner feature will indicate which sounds do and do not transfer in specific languages.

2. Preteach Non-Transferrable Skills Prior to teaching a phonics lesson, check the chart to determine if the sound and/or spelling transfers from the student's primary language into English. If it does not, preteach the sound and spelling during Small Group time. Focus on articulation, using the backs of the small **Sound-Spelling Cards**, and the minimal contrast activities provided.

3. Provide Additional Practice and Time If the skill does NOT transfer from the student's primary language into English, the student will require more time and practice mastering the sound and spellings. Continue to review the phonics skill during Small Group time in upcoming weeks until the student has mastered it. Use the additional resources, such as the extra decodable stories in the **Teacher's Resource Book**, to provide oral and silent reading practice.

Teaching Supports for Students Transitioning from Spanish to English

The **Sound-Spelling Cards** have been created to assist you in working with English Language Learners. For example:

1. The dotted border on many of the cards indicates that the sound transfers from Spanish to English. On these cards, the same image is used in both English and Spanish (e.g., *camel/camello*). Therefore, students learning the sound in Spanish can easily transfer that knowledge to English.

2. Students whose primary language is not English will need additional articulation support to pronounce and perceive non-transferrable English sounds. Use the articulation photos on the backs of the Sound-Spelling Cards and the student-friendly descriptions of how to form these sounds during phonics lessons.

Sound-Spelling Cards

Transfer Skill Support

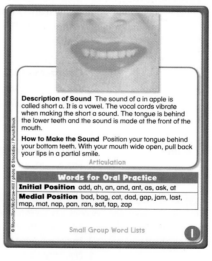

Description of Sound The sound of a in apple is called short a. It is a vowel. The vocal cords vibrate when making the short a sound. The tongue is behind the lower teeth and the sound is made at the front of the mouth.

How to Make the Sound Position your tongue behind your bottom teeth. With your mouth wide open, pull back your lips in a partial smile.

Articulation

Words for Oral Practice	
Initial Position add, ah, an, and, ant, as, ask, at	
Medial Position bad, bag, cat, dad, gap, jam, last, map, mat, nap, pan, ran, sat, tap, zap	

Small Group Word Lists

Articulation Support

Grammar Transfers:
Grammatical Form

This chart can be used to address common mistakes that some English Language Learners make when they transfer grammatical forms from their native languages into English.

Grammatical Form	Transfer Mistakes in English	Native Language	Cause of Difficulty
Nouns			
Plural Marker -s	**Forgets plural marker -s** *I have 3 sister.*	Cantonese, Haitian Creole, Hmong, Korean, Vietnamese, Khmer	Native language does not use a plural marker.
Countable and Uncountable Nouns	**Confuses countable and uncountable nouns** *the homeworks* or *the informations*	Haitian Creole, Spanish	Countable and uncountable nouns are different in English and native language.
Possessives	**Uses prepositions to describe possessives** *the book of my brother* as opposed to *my brother's book*	Haitian Creole, Hmong, Spanish, Vietnamese	Possession is often described using a prepositional phrase.
	Avoids using 's *dog my father* as opposed to *my father's dog*	Haitian Creole, Vietnamese, Khmer	A noun follows the object in the native language.
Articles			
	Consistently omits articles *He has book. They want dog not cat.*	Cantonese, Haitian Creole, Hmong, Korean, Vietnamese, Khmer	There is no article in the native language or no difference between *the* and *a*.
	Overuses articles *The English is difficult. The soccer is popular in the Europe.*	Haitian Creole, Hmong, Spanish	Some languages use articles that are omitted in English.
a/an	**Mistakes one for *a/an*** *She is one nurse.*	Haitian Creole, Hmong, Vietnamese	The native language either does not use articles or uses articles differently.
Pronouns			
Gender-Specific Pronouns	**Uses pronouns with the inappropriate gender** *He is my sister.*	Cantonese, Haitian Creole, Hmong, Korean, Spanish, Khmer	The third person pronoun in the native language is gender free, or the personal pronoun is omitted.
	Uses inappropriate gender, particularly with neutral nouns *The day is sunny. She is beautiful.*	Spanish	Nouns have feminine or masculine gender in the native language, and the gender may be carried over into English.

Grammatical Form	Transfer Mistakes in English	Native Language	Cause of Difficulty
Pronouns			
Object Pronouns	**Confuses subject and object pronouns** *Her talks to me.*	Cantonese, Hmong, Khmer	The same pronoun form is used for subject and object in the native language.
	Omits object pronouns *That girl is very rude, so nobody likes.*	Korean, Vietnamese	The native language does not use direct objects.
Pronoun and Number Agreement	**Uses the wrong number for pronouns** *I saw many red birds. It was pretty.*	Cantonese, Korean	The native language does not require number agreement.
Subject Pronouns	**Omits subject pronouns** *Mom isn't home. Is at work.*	Korean, Spanish	Subject pronouns may be dropped because in the native language the verb ending gives information about the number and/or gender.
Pronouns in Clauses	**Omits pronouns in clauses** *If don't do homework, they will not learn.*	Cantonese, Vietnamese	The native language does not need a subject in the subordinate clause.
Pronouns and Nouns	**Overuses pronouns with nouns** *This school, it very good.*	Hmong, Vietnamese	This is popular in speech in some languages. The speaker mentions a topic, then makes a comment about it.
	Avoids pronouns and repeats nouns *Carla visits her sister every Sunday, and Carla makes a meal.*	Korean, Vietnamese	In the native language, the speaker repeats nouns and does not use pronouns.
Pronoun *one*	**Omits the pronoun *one*** *I saw two dogs, and I like the small.*	Spanish	Adjectives can stand alone in the native language, but English requires a noun or *one*.
Possessive Forms	**Confuses possessive forms** *The book is my.*	Cantonese, Hmong, Vietnamese	Cantonese and Hmong speakers tend to omit the final *n* sound, which may create confusion between *my* and *mine*.

Grammar Transfers:
Grammatical Form

Grammatical Form	Transfer Mistakes in English	Native Language	Cause of Difficulty
Verbs			
Present Tense	**Omits -s in present tense, third person agreement** *He like pizza.*	Cantonese, Haitian Creole, Hmong, Korean, Vietnamese, Khmer	Subject-verb agreement is not used in the native language.
Irregular Verbs	**Has problems with irregular subject-verb agreement** *Tom and Sue has a new car.*	Cantonese, Hmong, Korean, Khmer	Verbs' forms do not change to show the number of the subject in the native language.
Inflectional Endings	**Omits tense markers** *I study English yesterday.*	Cantonese, Haitian Creole, Hmong, Korean, Vietnamese, Khmer	The native language does not use inflectional endings to change verb tense.
Present and Future Tenses	**Incorrectly uses the present tense for the future tense** *I go next week.*	Cantonese, Korean	The native language may use the present tense to imply the future tense.
Negative Statements	**Omits helping verbs in negative statements** *Sue no coming to school.*	Cantonese, Korean, Spanish	The native language does not use helping verbs in negative statements.
Present-Perfect Tense	**Avoids the present-perfect tense** *Marcos live here for three months.*	Haitian Creole, Vietnamese	The native language does not use the present-perfect verb form.
Past-Continuous Tense	**Uses the past-continuous tense for recurring action in the past** *When I was young, I was talking a lot.*	Korean, Spanish	In the native language, the past-continuous tense is used but in English the expression *used to* or the simple past tense is used.
Main Verb	**Omits the main verb** *Talk in class not good.*	Cantonese	Cantonese does not require an infinitive marker when using a verb as a noun. Speakers may confuse the infinitive for the main verb.
Main Verbs in Clauses	**Uses two or more main verbs in one clause without any connectors** *I took a book went studied at the library.*	Hmong	In Hmong, verbs can be used consecutively without conjunctions or punctuation.
Linking Verbs	**Omits the linking verb** *He hungry.*	Cantonese, Haitian Creole, Hmong, Vietnamese, Khmer	In some languages, *be* is implied in the adjective form. In other languages, the concept is expressed with a verb.
Helping Verb in Passive Voice	**Omits the helping verb in the passive voice** *The homework done.*	Cantonese, Vietnamese	In Cantonese and Vietnamese, the passive voice does not require a helping verb.

Grammatical Form	Transfer Mistakes in English	Native Language	Cause of Difficulty
Verbs			
Passive Voice	**Avoids the passive voice** *They speak English here.* *One speaks English here.* *English is spoken here.*	Haitian Creole	The passive voice does not exist in the native language.
Transitive Verbs	**Confuses transitive and intransitive verbs** *The child broke.* *The child broke the plate.*	Cantonese, Korean, Spanish	Verbs that require a direct object differ between English and the native language.
Phrasal Verbs	**Confuses related phrasal verbs** *I ate at the apple.* *I ate up the apple.*	Korean, Spanish	Phrasal verbs are not used in the native language, and there is often confusion over their meaning.
Have* and *be	**Uses *have* instead of *be*** *I have thirst.* *He has right.*	Spanish	Spanish and English have different uses for *have* and *be*.
Adjectives			
Word Order	**Places adjectives after nouns** *I saw a car red.*	Haitian Creole, Hmong, Spanish, Vietnamese, Khmer	Nouns often precede adjectives in the native language.
	Consistently places adjectives after nouns *This is a lesson new.*	Cantonese, Korean	Adjectives always follow nouns in the native language.
-*er* and -*est* Endings	**Avoids -*er* and -*est* endings** *I am more old than you.*	Hmong, Korean, Spanish, Khmer	The native language shows comparative and superlative forms with separate words.
-*ing* and -*ed* Endings	**Confuses -*ing* and -*ed* forms** *Math is bored.*	Cantonese, Korean, Spanish, Khmer	Adjectives in the native language do not have active and passive meanings.
Adverbs			
Adjectives and Adverbs	**Uses an adjective where an adverb is needed** *Talk quiet.*	Haitian Creole, Hmong, Khmer	Adjectives and adverb forms are interchangeable in the native language.
Word Order	**Places adverbs before verbs** *He quickly ran.* *He ran quickly.*	Cantonese, Korean	Adverbs usually come before verbs in the native language, and this tendency is carried over into English.
Prepositions			
	Omits prepositions *I like come school.*	Cantonese	Cantonese does not use prepositions the way that English does.

How to Use the Grammar Transfer Charts

The grammar of many languages differs widely from English. For example, a student's primary language may use a different word order than English, may not use parts of speech in the same way, or may use different verb tenses. The Grammar Transfer Charts are designed to help you anticipate and understand possible student errors in speaking and writing standard English. With all grammar exercises, the emphasis is on oral communication, both as a speaker and listener.

1. **Highlight Transferrable Skills** If the grammar skill transfers from the student's primary language to English, state that during the lesson. In many lessons an English Language Learner feature will indicate which skills do and do not transfer.

2. **Preteach Non-Transferrable Skills** Prior to teaching a grammar lesson, check the chart to determine if the skill transfers from the student's primary language into English. If it does not, preteach the skill during Small Group time. Provide sentence frames and ample structured opportunities to use the skill in spoken English. Students need to talk, talk, and talk some more to master these skills.

3. **Provide Additional Practice and Time** If the skill does NOT transfer from the student's primary language into English, the student will require more time and practice mastering it. Continue to review the skill during Small Group time. Use the additional resources, such as the grammar lessons in the **Intervention Kit** (K–3) or review lessons, in upcoming weeks.

4. **Use Contrastive Analysis** Tell students when a skill does not transfer and include contrastive analysis work to make the student aware of how to correct their speaking and writing for standard English. For example, when a student uses an incorrect grammatical form, write the student sentence on a **WorkBoard**. Then write the correct English form underneath. Explain the difference between the student's primary language and English. Have the student correct several other sentences using this skill, such as sentences in their Writer's Notebooks.

5. **Increase Writing and Speaking Opportunities** Increase the amount of structured writing and speaking opportunities for students needing work on specific grammatical forms. Sentence starters and paragraph frames, such as those found in the lessons, are ideal for both written and oral exercises.

6. **Focus on Meaning** Always focus on the meanings of sentences in all exercises. As they improve and fine-tune their English speaking and writing skills, work with students on basic comprehension of spoken and written English.

To help students move to the next level of language acquisition and master English grammatical forms, recast their responses during classroom discussions or provide additional language for them to use as they respond further. Provide leveled-language sentence frames orally or in writing for students to use as they respond to questions and prompts. Below are samples.

English Language Learner Response Chart

Beginning (will respond by pointing or saying one word answers)	**Sample Frames** (simple, short sentences) *I see a _____.* *This is a _____.* *I like the _____.*
Early Intermediate (will respond with phrases or simple sentences)	**Sample Frames** (simple sentences with adjectives and adverbs added, and compound subjects or predicates) *I see a _____ _____.* *The _____ animal is _____.* *There are _____ and _____.*
Intermediate (will respond with simple sentences and limited academic language)	**Sample Frames** (harder sentences with simple phrases in consistent patterns; some academic language included) *The animal's prey is _____ because _____.* *The main idea is _____ because _____.* *He roamed the park so that _____.*
Early Advanced (will begin to use more sophisticated sentences and some academic language)	**Sample Frames** (complex sentences with increased academic language, beginning phrases and clauses, and multiple-meaning words) *When the violent storm hit, _____.* *As a result of the revolution, the army_____.* *Since most endangered animals are _____, they _____.*
Advanced (will have mastered some more complex sentence structures and is increasing the amount of academic language used)	Use the questions and prompts provided in the lessons for the whole group. Provide additional support learning and using academic language. These words are boldfaced throughout the lessons and sentence starters are often provided.

Cognates

Cognates are words in two languages that look alike and have the same or similar meaning (e.g., *school/escuela*, *telephone/teléfono*) and can be helpful resources for English Language Learners. This list identifies some Spanish cognates for the academic language used during the lessons.

Students must also be aware of false cognates—words that look similar in two languages, but have different meanings, such as *soap* in English and *sopa* (meaning *soup*) in Spanish.

accent	*acento*	**context**	*contexto*
action	*acción*	**contrast**	*contrastar*
action verb	*verbo de acción*	**definition**	*definición*
adjective	*adjetivo*	**demonstrative**	*demostrativo*
adverb	*adverbio*	**denotation**	*denotación*
alphabetical order	*orden alfabético*	**description**	*descripción*
analogy	*analogía*	**dialogue**	*diálogo*
analyze	*analizar*	**dictionary**	*diccionario*
antecedent	*antecedente*	**direct**	*directo*
antonym	*antónimo*	**effect**	*efecto*
apostrophe	*apóstrofe*	**evaluate**	*evaluar*
article	*artículo*	**event**	*evento*
author	*autor*	**example**	*ejemplo*
cause	*causa*	**exclamation**	*exclamación*
classify	*clasificar*	**family**	*familia*
combine	*combinar*	**fantasy**	*fantasía*
compare	*comparar*	**figurative**	*figurativo*
complex	*complejo*	**fragment**	*fragmento*
comprehension	*comprensión*	**future**	*futuro*
conclusion	*conclusión*	**generalization**	*generalización*
confirm	*confirmar*	**generalize**	*generalizar*
conjunction	*conjunción*	**glossary**	*glosario*
connotation	*connotación*	**Greek**	*Griego*
consonant	*consonante*	**homophone**	*homófono*

idea	*idea*	**prefix**	*prefijo*
identify	*identificar*	**preposition**	*preposición*
illustration	*ilustración*	**prepositional**	*preposicional*
indirect	*indirecto*	**present**	*presente*
introduction	*introducción*	**problem**	*problema*
irregular	*irregular*	**pronunciation**	*pronunciación*
language	*lenguaje*	**punctuation**	*puntuación*
Latin	*Latín*	**reality**	*realidad*
myth	*mito*	**relationship**	*relación*
negative	*negativo*	**sequence**	*secuencia*
object	*objeto*	**singular**	*singular*
opinion	*opinión*	**solution**	*solución*
order	*orden*	**structure**	*estructura*
origin	*orígen*	**subject**	*sujeto*
paragraph	*párrafo*	**suffix**	*sufijo*
part	*parte*	**syllable**	*sílaba*
perspective	*perspectiva*	**synonym**	*sinónimo*
persuasion	*persuación*	**technique**	*técnica*
phrase	*frase*	**text**	*texto*
plural	*plural*	**theme**	*tema*
possessive adjective	*adjetivo posesivo*	**verb**	*verbo*
predicate	*predicado*	**visualize**	*visualizar*
prediction	*predicción*	**vowel**	*vocal*

English Language Learners

The **English Language Learners** in your classroom have a variety of backgrounds. An increasing proportion of English Language Learners are born in the United States. Some of these students are just starting school in the primary grades; others are long-term English Language Learners, with underdeveloped academic skills. Some students come from their native countries with a strong educational foundation. The academic skills of these newly arrived students are well developed and parallel the skills of their native English-speaking peers. Other English Learners immigrate to the United States with little academic experience.

These English Learners are not "blank slates." Their oral language proficiency and literacy in their first languages can be used to facilitate literacy development in English. Systematic, explicit, and appropriately scaffolded instruction and sufficient time help English Learners attain English proficiency and meet high standards in core academic subjects.

Beginning

This level of language proficiency is often referred to as the "silent" stage, in which students' receptive skills are engaged. It is important that teachers and peers respect a language learner's initial silence or allow the student to respond in his or her native language. It is often difficult for teachers to identify the level of cognitive development at this stage, due to the limited proficiency in the second language. It is important to realize that these beginning students have a wide range of abilities in their first language. They are able to transfer knowledge and skills from their first language as they develop English and learn grade-level content. Beginning students include those with limited formal schooling: young students just starting school, as well as older students. Other beginning students have had schooling in their native language and are academically parallel to nativeEnglish-speaking peers.

The Beginning Student...

- recognizes English phonemes that correspond to phonemes produced in primary language;
- is able to apply transferable grammar concepts and skills from the primary language;
- initially demonstrates more receptive than productive English skills;
- produces English vocabulary to communicate basic needs in social and academic settings;
- responds by pointing to, nodding, gesturing, acting out, and manipulating objects/pictures;
- speaks in one-or two-word responses as language develops;
- draws pictures and writes letters and sounds being learned.

Early Intermediate

At this level, students are considered more advanced beginning English Learners. They are developing early production skills, but their receptive skills are much more advanced than their speaking ability. At this stage it is critical that the students continue to listen to model speakers.

The Early Intermediate Student...

- recognizes English phonemes that correspond to phonemes produced in primary language;
- is able to apply transferable grammar concepts and skills from the primary language;
- understands more spoken English than the beginning student;
- speaks in one- or two-word utterances;
- may respond with phrases or sentences;
- produces English vocabulary words and phrases to communicate basic needs in social and academic settings;
- begins to ask questions, role-play, and retell;
- begins to use routine expressions;
- demonstrates an internalization of English grammar and usage by recognizing and correcting some errors when speaking and reading aloud;
- increases correct usage of written and oral language conventions.

Intermediate

Students at this level begin to tailor their English language skills to meet communication and learning demands with increasing accuracy. They possess vocabulary and knowledge of grammatical structures that allow them to more fully participate in classroom activities and discussions. They are generally more comfortable producing both spoken and written language.

The Intermediate Student...

- pronounces most English phonemes correctly while reading aloud;
- can identify more details of information that has been presented orally or in writing;
- uses more complex vocabulary and sentences to communicate needs and express ideas;
- uses specific vocabulary learned, including academic language;
- participates more fully in discussions with peers and adults;
- reads and comprehends a wider range of reading materials;
- writes brief narratives and expository texts;
- demonstrates an internalization of English grammar and usage by recognizing and correcting errors when speaking and reading aloud.

English Language Learners

Early Advanced

Students at this language proficiency level possess vocabulary and grammar structures that approach those of an English-proficient speaker. These students demonstrate consistent general comprehension of grade-level content that is presented.

The Early Advanced Student...

- applies knowledge of common English morphemes in oral and silent reading;
- understands increasingly more nonliteral social and academic language;
- responds using extensive vocabulary;
- participates in and initiates more extended social conversations with peers and adults;
- communicates orally and in writing with fewer grammatical errors;
- reads with good comprehension a wide range of narrative and expository texts;
- writes using more standard forms of English on various content-area topics;
- becomes more creative and analytical when writing.

Advanced

The student at this language proficiency level communicates effectively with peers and adults in both social and academic situations. Students can understand grade-level text but still need some English language development support, such as preteaching concepts and skills. While the English language proficiency of these students is advanced, some linguistic support for accessing content is still necessary.

The Advanced Student...

- understands increasingly more nonliteral social and academic language;
- responds using extensive vocabulary;
- communicates orally and in writing with infrequent errors;
- creates more complex narratives and expository writing in all content areas.

English Language Learner Profiles
Facilitating Language Growth

Beginning

Student's Behaviors	Teacher's Behaviors	Questioning Techniques
■ Points to or provides other nonverbal responses ■ Actively listens ■ Responds to commands ■ Understands more than he or she can produce	■ Gestures ■ Focuses on conveying meanings and vocabulary development ■ Does not force students to speak ■ Shows visuals and real objects ■ Writes words for students to see ■ Pairs students with more proficient learners ■ Provides speaking and writing frames and models	■ Point to the _____. ■ Find the _____. ■ Put the _____ next to the _____. ■ Do you have the _____? ■ Is this the _____? ■ Who wants the _____?

Early Intermediate

Student's Behaviors	Teacher's Behaviors	Questioning Techniques
■ Speaks in one- or two-word utterances ■ Uses short phrases and simple sentences ■ Listens with greater understanding	■ Asks questions that can be answered by yes/no ■ Asks either/or questions ■ Asks higher-order questions with one-word answers ■ Models correct responses ■ Ensures supportive, low-anxiety environment ■ Does not overtly call attention to grammar errors ■ Asks short "wh" questions	■ Yes/no (Did you like the story?) ■ Either/or (Is this a pencil or a crayon?) ■ One-word responses (Why did the dog hide?) ■ General questions that encourage lists of words (What did you see in the book bag?) ■ Two-word responses (Where did I put the pen?)

Intermediate

Student's Behaviors	Teacher's Behaviors	Questioning Techniques
■ Demonstrates comprehension in a variety of ways ■ Speaks in short phrases or sentences ■ Begins to use language more freely	■ Provides frequent comprehension checks ■ Asks open-ended questions that stimulate language production	■ Why? ■ How? ■ How is this like that? ■ Tell me about _____. ■ Talk about _____. ■ Describe _____. ■ What is in your book bag?

Early Advanced

Student's Behaviors	Teacher's Behaviors	Questioning Techniques
■ Participates in reading and writing activities to acquire information ■ Demonstrates increased levels of accuracy and correctness and is able to express thoughts and feelings ■ Produces language with varied grammatical structures and academic language ■ May experience difficulties in abstract, cognitively demanding subjects	■ Fosters conceptual development and expanded literacy through content ■ Continues to make lessons comprehensible and interactive ■ Teaches thinking and study skills ■ Continues to be alert to individual differences in language and culture	■ What would you recommend/why? ■ How do you think this story will end? ■ What is this story about? ■ What is your favorite part of the story? ■ Describe/compare _____. How are these similar/different? ■ What would happen if _____? ■ Why do you think that? Yes, tell me more about _____.

Fostering Classroom Discussions

Strategies for English Language Learners

One of the most effective ways in which to increase the oral language proficiency of your English Language Learners is to give students many opportunities to do a lot of talking in the classroom. Providing the opportunities and welcoming all levels of participation will motivate students to take part in the class discussions. You can employ a few basic teaching strategies that will encourage the participation of all language proficiency levels of English Language Learners in whole class and small group discussions.

☑ WAIT/DIFFERENT RESPONSES

- Be sure to give students enough time to answer the question.

- Let students know that they can respond in different ways depending on their levels of proficiency. Students can
    - answer in their native language;
    - ask a more proficient ELL speaker to repeat the answer in English;
    - answer with nonverbal cues (pointing to related objects, drawing, or acting out).

> **Teacher:** Where is Charlotte?
>
> **ELL Response:** (Student points to the web in the corner of the barn.)
>
> **Teacher:** Yes. Charlotte is sitting in her web. Let's all point to Charlotte.

☑ REPEAT

- Give positive confirmation to the answers that each English Language Learner offers. If the response is correct, repeat what the student has said in a clear, loud voice and at a slower pace. This validation will motivate other ELLs to participate.

> **Teacher:** How would you describe the faces of the bobcats?
>
> **ELL Response:** They look scared.
>
> **Teacher:** That's right, Silvia. They are scared. Everyone show me your scared face.

☑ REVISE FOR FORM

- Repeating an answer allows you to model the proper form for a response. You can model how to answer in full sentences and use academic language.

- When you repeat the answer, correct any grammar or pronunciation errors.

> **Teacher:** Who are the main characters in the story *Zathura*?
>
> **ELL Response:** Danny and Walter is.
>
> **Teacher:** Yes. Danny and Walter <u>are</u> the main characters. Remember to use the verb <u>are</u> when you are telling about more than one person. Let's repeat the sentence.
>
> **All:** Danny and Walter <u>are</u> the main characters.

☑ REVISE FOR MEANING

- Repeating an answer offers an opportunity to clarify the meaning of a response.

> **Teacher:** Where did the golden feather come from?
>
> **ELL Response:** The bird.
>
> **Teacher:** That's right. The golden feather came from the Firebird.

☑ ELABORATE

- If students give a one-word answer or a nonverbal cue, elaborate on the answer to model fluent speaking and grammatical patterns.

- Provide more examples or repeat the answer using proper academic language.

> **Teacher:** Why is the girls' mother standing with her hands on her hips?
>
> **ELL Response:** She is mad.
>
> **Teacher:** Can you tell me more? Why is she mad?
>
> **ELL Response:** Because the girls are late.
>
> **Teacher:** Ok. What do you think the girls will do?
>
> **ELL Response:** They will promise not to be late again.
>
> **Teacher:** Anyone else have an idea?

☑ ELICIT

- Prompt students to give a more comprehensive response by asking additional questions or guiding them to get to an answer.

> **Teacher:** Listen as I read the caption under the photograph. What information does the caption tell us?
>
> **ELL Response:** It tells about the butterfly.
>
> **Teacher:** What did you find out about the butterfly?
>
> **ELL Response:** It drinks nectar.
>
> **Teacher:** Yes. The butterfly drinks nectar from the flower.

Making the Most of Classroom Conversations

Use all the speaking and listening opportunities in your classroom to observe students' oral language proficiency.

- Response to oral presentations
- Responding to text aloud
- Following directions
- Group projects
- Small Group work
- Informal, social peer discussions
- One-on-one conferences

The **English Language Learner Resource Book** provides Speaking and Listening Checklists to help you monitor students' oral language proficiency growth.

Support for Students with Dyslexia

Characteristics of Dyslexia

A student with dyslexia is a student who continually struggles with reading and spelling but displays an ability to learn when there are no print materials involved. Even though the student receives the same classroom instruction as most other students, he continues to have difficulties with reading and spelling.

Students identified with dyslexia often have difficulties in the following areas

- reading words in isolation
- decoding nonsense words accurately
- oral reading (slow and inaccurate)
- learning to spell

The difficulties in these areas are usually the result of student's struggles with:

- phonological awareness: segmenting, blending, and manipulating words
- naming letters and pronouncing their sounds.
- phonological memory
- rapid naming of the letters of the alphabet or familiar objects

Effective Instruction

To address the needs of a student with dyslexia, instruction should be delivered in small groups. The instruction should be explicit, intensive, employ multisensory methods, as needed, and be individualized. It should include instruction on:

- phonemic awareness that has students detect, segment, blend and manipulate sounds
- phonics, emphasizing the sound/symbol relationships for decoding and encoding words
- morphology, semantics and syntax
- fluency with patterns of language
- strategies for decoding, encoding, word recognition, fluency and comprehension

Resources:
The International Dyslexia Association Website: www.interdys.org
The Dyslexia Handbook: Procedures Concerning Dyslexia and Related Disorders (Revised 2007) Texas Education Agency, Austin, TX, Publication Number: GE8721001

Treasures Reading and Language Arts Program

Treasures is a scientifically-based core program that offers sequential, explicit, and effective instruction in phonological awareness, phonics, morphology, fluency, vocabulary, and reading comprehension. Students are given many opportunities to practice and review these skills to help prevent reading difficulties before they begin.

 **INTERVENTION**

Weekly Small Group Lessons
Intervention Teacher's Editions

Tier 2 Instruction is provided in weekly small group lessons in the *Treasures* **Teacher's Editions**. These lessons provide targeted instruction in priority skills taught in the week. *Tier 2 Intervention* **Teacher's Editions** provide additional instruction for struggling students in the areas of phonemic awareness, phonics, vocabulary, fluency, and comprehension, grammar and writing.

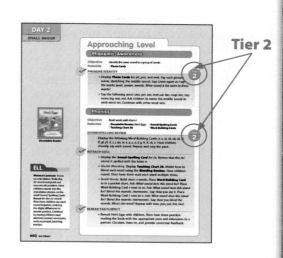

Tier 2

 **INTERVENTION**

Reading Triumphs
Intervention Program

Reading Triumphs provides intensive instruction. Explicit, sequential lessons delivered through clear instructional routines for all the key components of reading are embedded in the program. The "no assumption instruction" allows for both teacher and student success.

Index

A

C

D

E

F

G

Genre

Key 1 = Unit 1

H

J

L

M

Main idea and details, identifying. *See* **Comprehension strategies: main idea and details, identifying.**

Math, **8**:1977

Media Literacy, **1**:257, **2**:509, **3**:769, **4**:1029, **5**:1289, **6**:1549, **7**:1809, **9**:2329, **10**:2589

Mental images, creating. *See* **Comprehension skills: mental images, creating.**

Monitor Comprehension: reread. *See* **Comprehension skills: monitor comprehension: reread.**

Music, **1**:S63, S81, S87

See also **Songs, rhymes, chants.**

N

National tests correlation charts. *See* **Assessment: unit assessment.**

O

On Level Options

comprehension, **1**:74, 80, 158, 164, 242, 248, **2**:326, 332, 410, 416, 494, 500, **3**:586, 592, 670, 676, 754, 760, **4**:846, 930, 1014, **5**:1106, 1190, 1274, **6**:1366, 1450, 1534, **7**:1626, 1710, 1794, **8**:1886, 1970, 2054, **9**:2146, 2230, 2314, **10**:2406, 2490, 2574

Decodable Reader, rereading the, **1**:74, 80, 158, 164, 242, 248, **2**:326, 332, 410, 416, 494, 500, **3**:586, 592, 670, 676, 754, 760, **4**:842, 926, 1010, **5**:1102, 1186, 1270, **6**:1362, 1446, 1530, **7**:1622, 1706, 1790, **8**:1966, 2050, **9**:2142, 2226, 2310, **10**:2402, 2486, 2570

high-frequency words, **1**:60, 74, 144, 158, 228, 242, **2**:312, 326, 396, 410, 480, 494, **3**:572, 586, 656, 670, 740, 754, **4**:832, 846, 916, 930, 1000, 1014, **5**:1092, 1106, 1176, 1190, 1260, 1274,

6:1352, 1366, 1436, 1450, 1520, 1534, **7**:1612, 1626, 1696, 1710, 1780, 1794, **8**:1872, 1886, 1956, 1970, 2040, 2054, **9**:2132, 2146, 2216, 2230, 2300, 2314, **10**:2392, 2406, 2476, 2490, 2560, 2574

Leveled Reader Lessons, **1**:74, 80, 158, 164, 242, 248, **2**:326, 332, 410, 416, 494, 500, **3**:586, 592, 670, 676, 754, 760, **4**:846, 852, 930, 936, 1014, 1020, **5**:1106, 1112, 1190, 1196, 1274, 1280, **6**:1366, 1372, 1450, 1456, 1534, 1540, **7**:1626, 1632, 1710, 1716, 1794, 1800, **8**:1886, 1892, 1970, 1976, 2054, 2060, **9**:2146, 2152, 2230, 2236, 2314, 2320, **10**:2406, 2412, 2490, 2496, 2574, 2580

phonemic awareness and phonics, **1**:60, 144, 228, **2**:312, 396, 480, **3**:572, 656, 740, **4**:832, 916, 1000, **5**:1092, 1176, 1260, **6**:1352, 1436, 1520, **7**:1612, 1696, 1780, **8**:1872, 1956, 2040, **9**:2132, 2216, 2300, **10**:2392, 2476, 2560

Pre-decodable Reader, rereading the, **1**:66, 150, 234, **2**:318, 402, 486, **3**:578, 662, 746

Online instruction. *See* **Digital learning.**

Oral grammar. *See* **Grammar.**

Oral language, **1**:S7, S11, S21, S25, S31, S35, S39, S49, S53, S59, S63, S67, S77, S81, S87, 14, 22, 34, 44, 52, 58, 62, 98, 106, 118, 128, 136, 142, 146, 182, 190, 202, 212, 220, 226, 230, **2**:266, 274, 286, 296, 304, 310, 314, 350, 358, 370, 380, 388, 394, 398, 434, 442, 454, 464, 472, 478, 482, **3**:526, 534, 546, 556, 564, 570, 574, 610, 618, 630, 640, 648, 654, 658, 694, 702, 714, 724, 732, 738, 742, **4**:786, 794, 806, 816, 824, 830, 834, 836, 870, 878, 890, 900, 908, 914, 918, 920, 954, 962, 974, 984, 992, 998, 1002, 1004, **5**:1046, 1054, 1066, 1076, 1084, 1090, 1094, 1096, 1130, 1138, 1150, 1160, 1168, 1174, 1178, 1180, 1214, 1222, 1234, 1244, 1252, 1258, 1262, 1264, **6**:1306, 1314, 1336, 1344, 1350, 1354, 1356, 1390, 1398, 1420, 1428, 1434, 1438, 1440, 1474, 1482, 1504, 1512, 1518, 1522, 1524, **7**:1566, 1574, 1596, 1604, 1610, 1614, 1616, 1650, 1658, 1680, 1688, 1694, 1698, 1700, 1734, 1742, 1764, 1772, 1778, 1782, 1784, **8**:1826, 1834,

1864, 1870, 1874, 1876, 1910, 1918, 1930, 1940, 1948, 1954, 1958, 1960, 1994, 2002, 2014, 2024, 2032, 2038, 2042, 2044, **9**:2086, 2094, 2124, 2130, 2134, 2136, 2170, 2178, 2208, 2214, 2218, 2220, 2254, 2262, 2274, 2284, 2292, 2298, 2302, 2304, **10**:2346, 2354, 2376, 2384, 2390, 2394, 2396, 2430, 2438, 2450, 2460, 2468, 2474, 2478, 2480, 2522, 2544, 2552, 2558, 2562, 2564

See also **Vocabulary development: oral vocabulary.**

Oral Vocabulary. *See* **Vocabulary development: oral vocabulary.**

Oral Vocabulary Cards, **1**:34, 118, 202, **2**:286, 370, 454, **3**:546, 630, 714, **4**:806, 890, 898, 974, 982, **5**:1066, 1150, 1234, 1242, **7**:1594, 1762, **8**:1854, 1930, 1938, 2014, **9**:2274, 2282, **10**:2450, 2458, 2542

P

Paired selections. *See* **Big Book of Explorations.**

Peer discussion starters. *See* **English Language Learners: grammar.**

Penmanship, **1**:19, 103, 187, **2**:271, 355, 439, **3**:531, 615, 699, **4**:791, 875, 959, **5**:1051, 1135, 1219, **6**:1311, 1395, 1417, 1479, **7**:1571, 1655, 1677, 1739, **8**:1831, 1915, 1999, **9**:2091, 2113, 2175, 2197, 2259, **10**:2351, 2373, 2435, 2457

directionality (left-to-right, top-to-bottom), **1**:19, 103, 187, **2**:271, 355, 439, **3**:531, 615, 699, **4**:791, 875, 959, **5**:1051, 1135, 1219, **6**:1311, 1395, 1417, 1479, **7**:1571, 1655, 1677, 1739, **8**:1831, 1915, 1999, **9**:2091, 2113, 2175, 2197, 2259, **10**:2351, 2373, 2435, 2457

uppercase and lowercase letters, **1**:19, 103, 187, **2**:271, 355, 439, **3**:531, 615, 699, **4**:791, 875, 959, **5**:1051, 1135, 1219, **6**:1311, 1395, 1417, 1479, **7**:1571, 1655, 1677, 1739, **8**:1831, 1915, 1999, **9**:2091, 2113, 2175, 2197, 2259, **10**:2351, 2373, 2435, 2457

Personal response. *See* **Literary response; Talk/Sing About It.**

Key 1 = Unit 1

R

S

W

Key 1 = Unit 1

"Friends All Around" by Miela Ford. Copyright © 2007 by Miela Ford. Published by The McGraw-Hill Companies, Inc.

"Join in the Game" adaptation from "Come on and Join into the Game" from EYE WINKER, TOM TINKER, CHIN CHOPPER adapted and arranged by Tom Glazer. Copyright © 1973 by Tom Glazer. Reprinted by permission of Songs Music, Inc. Scarborough, NY.

"Making Friends" from NATHANIEL TALKING by Eloise Greenfield. Copyright © 1988 by Eloise Greenfield. Reprinted by permission of Nancy Galt Agency.

"Sam, Sam" from SING A SONG OF POETRY by Gay Su Pinnell and Irene C. Fountas. Copyright © 2004 by Gay Su Pinnell and Irene C. Fountas. Reprinted by permission of FirstHand, an imprint of Heinemann, a division of Reed Elsevier Inc. (Original Title: Billy, Billy).

"Simon and Molly plus Hester" by Lisa Jahn-Clough. Copyright © 2001 by Lisa Jahn-Clough. Published by arrangement with Houghton Mifflin Company.

"The Fight" from A POEM A DAY by Helen H. Moore. Copyright © 1997 by Helen H. Moore. Reprinted by permission of Scholastic, Inc.

"What Do You Like?" by Michael Grejniec. Copyright © 1992 by Michael Grejniec. Published by arrangement with North-South Books Inc.

Book Covers

DO YOU WANT TO BE MY FRIEND? Reprinted by permission of HarperCollins Publishers.

HORACE AND MORRIS BUT MOSTLY DOLORES. Reprinted by permission of Simon & Schuster Children's Publishing Division.

LITTLE BEAR'S FRIEND. Reprinted by permission of HarperCollins Publishers.

LITTLE BLUE AND LITTLE YELLOW. Reprinted by permission of Astor Book.

MAISY CLEANS UP. Reprinted by permission of Candlewick Press.

MY BIG BROTHER. Reprinted by permission of Simon & Schuster Children's Publishing Division.

TITCH AND DAISY. Reprinted by permission of HarperCollins Publishers.

WE ARE BEST FRIENDS. Reprinted by permission of HarperCollins Publishers.

WILL I HAVE A FRIEND? Reprinted by permission of Simon & Schuster Books for Young Readers.

Photography Credits

All Photographs are by Ken Cavanagh or Ken Karp for Macmillan/McGraw-Hill (MMH) except as noted below:

xiii: Veer. 261: Brad Perks Lightscapes/ Alamy. 268: Anne Hoppe. 345: Medioimages/PunchStock. 352: Anne Hoppe. 429: Rich Reid/ National Geographic/AGE Fotostock. 436: Anne Hoppe. 513: Pixtal/PunchStock.

Use this page to record lessons that work well or need to be adapted for future reference.

Lessons that work well.

Lessons that need adjustments.

Use this page to record lessons that work well or need to be adapted for future reference.

Lessons that work well.

Lessons that need adjustments.

Teacher Notes

Use this page to record lessons that work well or need to be adapted for future reference.

Lessons that work well.

Lessons that need adjustments.